Francis Bacon Retrieved:
Lost Words / New Writing

FRANCIS BACON
STUDIES V

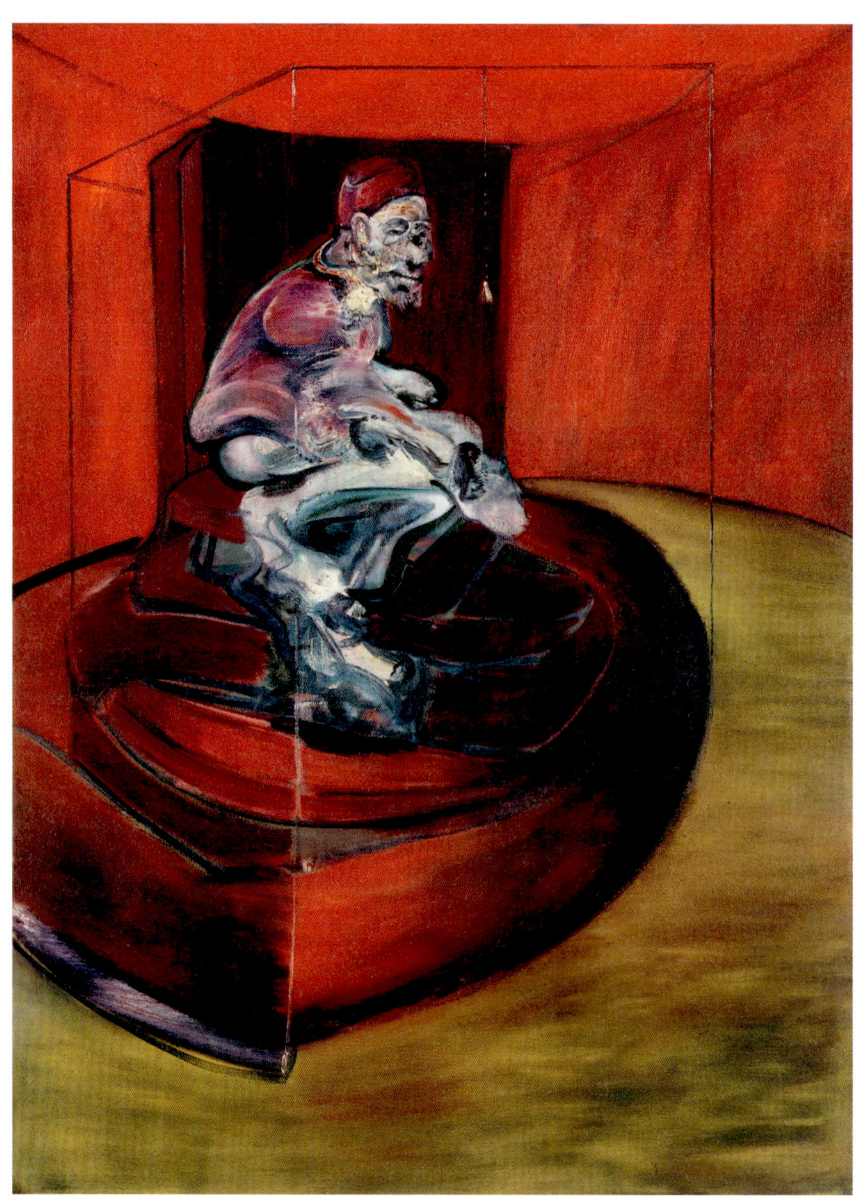

1. *Study from Innocent X,* 1962

Francis Bacon Retrieved:
Lost Words / New Writing

Maria Balaska

Amanda J. Harrison

Martin Harrison

Darian Leader

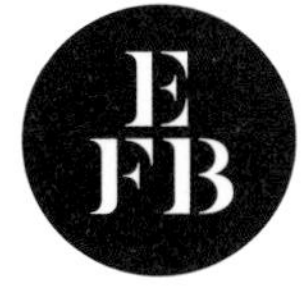

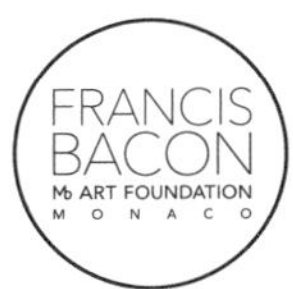

The Estate of Francis Bacon Publishing,
supported by Francis Bacon MB Art Foundation Monaco,
in association with Thames & Hudson

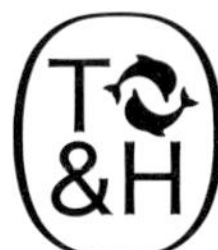

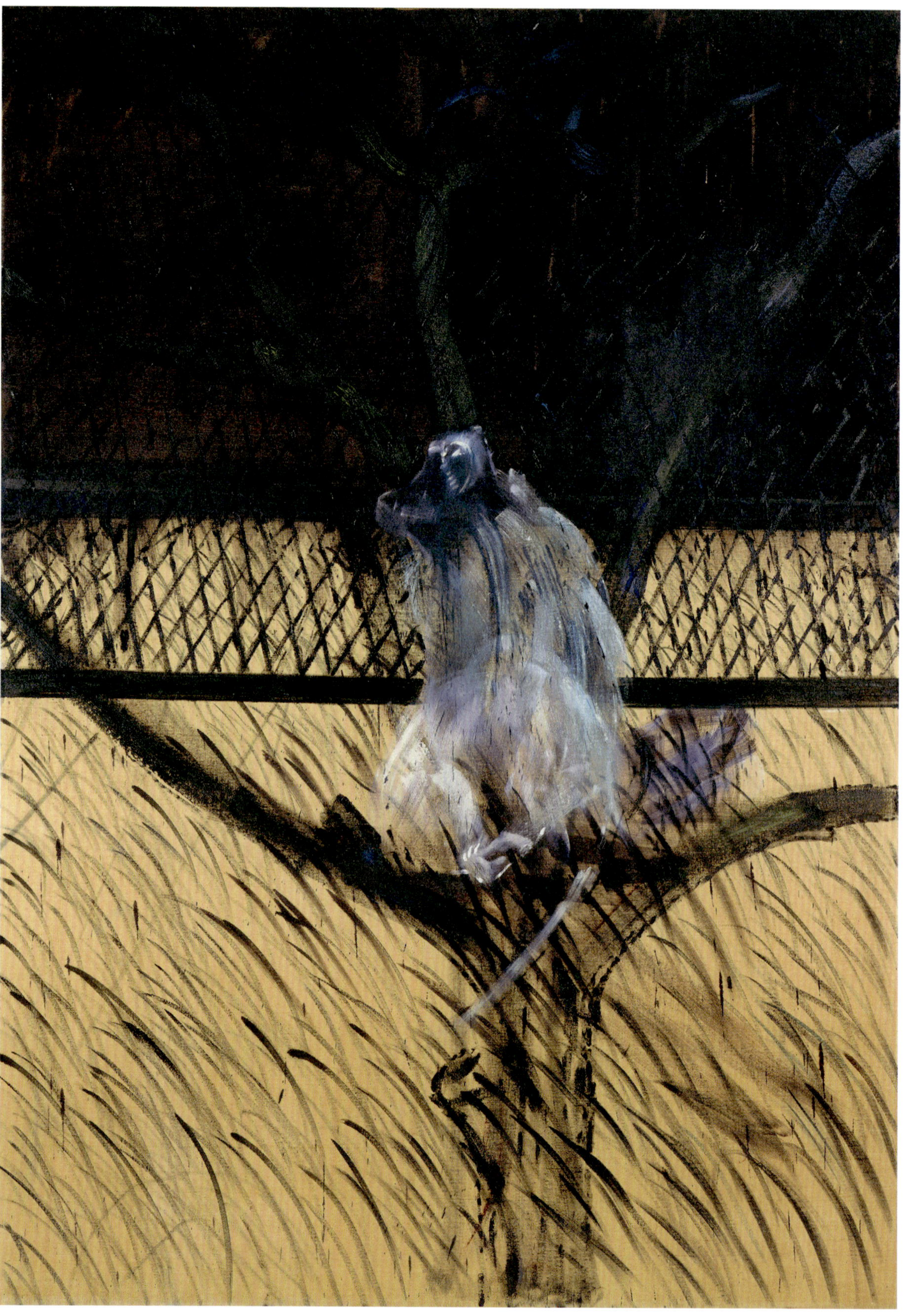

2. *Study of a Baboon*, 1953

Contents

Contributors

Maria Balaska was a lecturer and Research Fellow in Philosophy at the University of Hertfordshire and at Åbo Akademi University. Her most recent books are *Wittgenstein and Lacan at the Limit* (2019) and *Anxiety and Wonder: On Being Human* (2024).

Amanda J. Harrison is a poet and occasional art historian. Her essay, 'A sudden blow' was published in *Francis Bacon: Monaco et la culture française* (2016) and 'Bacon and the Occult' in *Francis Bacon Studies IV* (2021).

Martin Harrison was the editor of *Francis Bacon: Catalogue Raisonné* (2016). He is editor of the Francis Bacon Studies series and Head of Publishing for the Estate of Francis Bacon Publishing.

Darian Leader, the eminent Lacanian psychoanalyst and author, has published many books, including *Stealing the Mona Lisa* (2002). He also presented the BBC 2 TV documentary about Bacon, *In the Name of the Father?* (1996), and contributed essays to *Francis Bacon Studies I* and *II*.

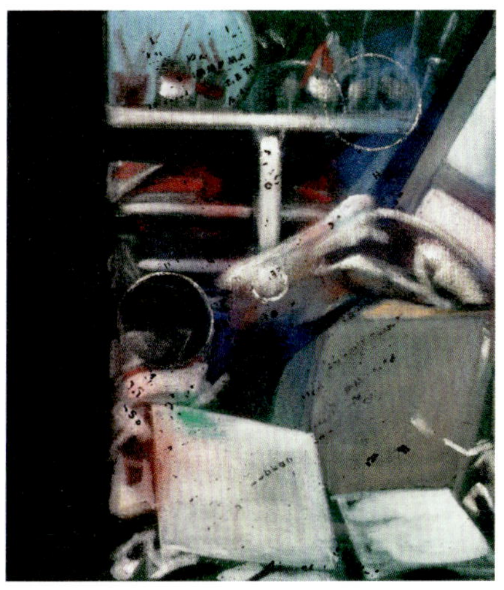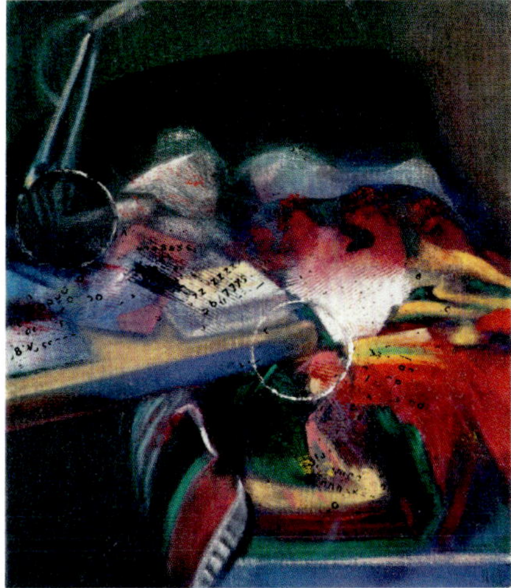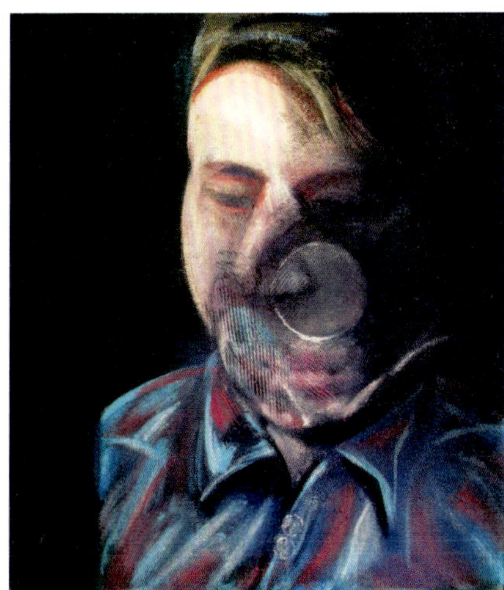

3. *Triptych*, 1977

When Bacon characterised two of his large triptychs of George Dyer as his 'most descriptive' paintings, [p. 95] he may have been overlooking this small and overtly autobiographical triptych. Furthermore, the left and centre panels, painted from colour photographs of his studio and living quarters, were, with the arguable exceptions of *Skull of a Gorilla*, 1957, and *Side of Beef*, 1978, the only still-lifes in his oeuvre.

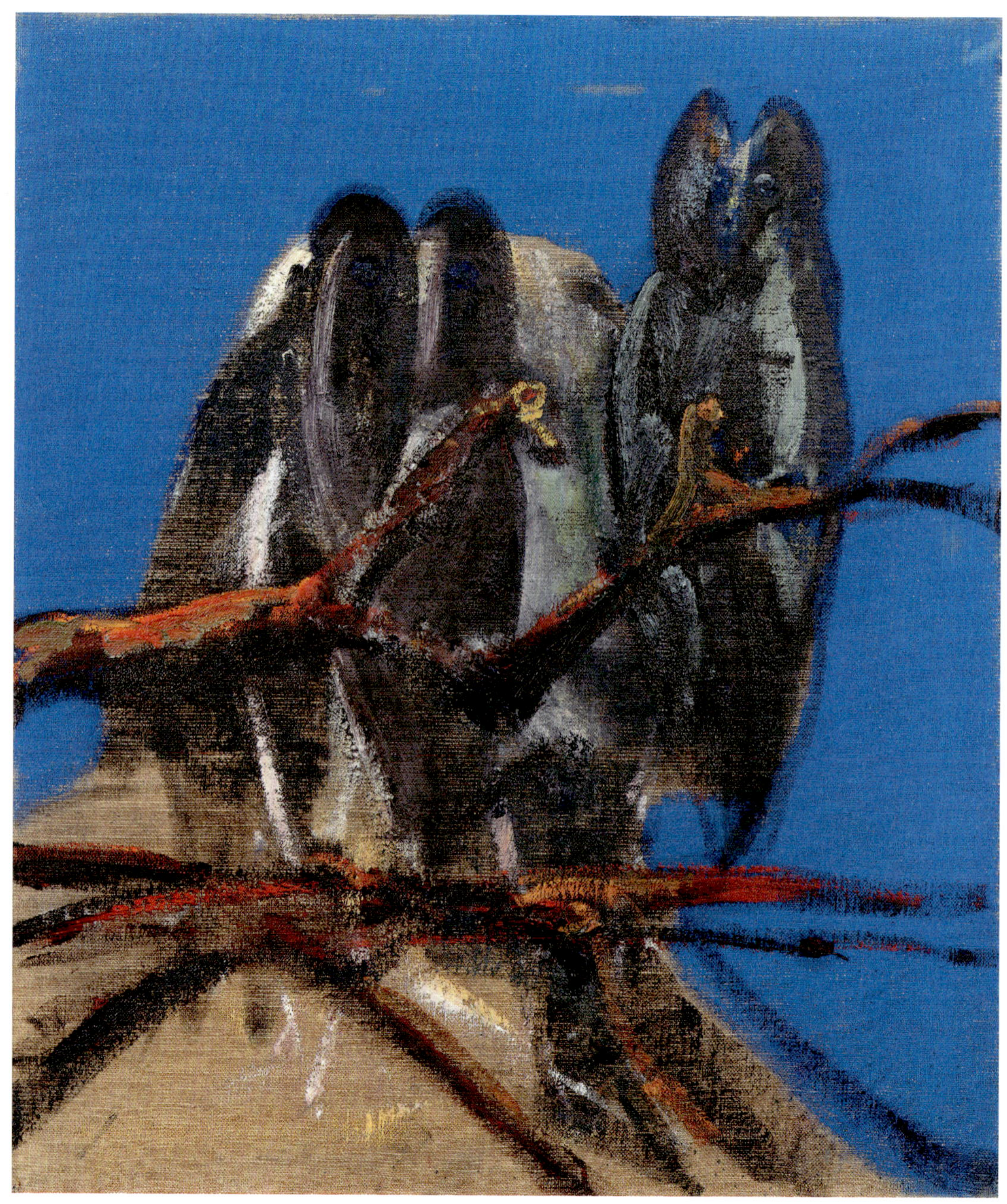

4. *Owls*, 1956

Introduction

Martin Harrison

The guiding principle of the Francis Bacon Studies series has been to disseminate new information and original thinking about the artist. Although *Francis Bacon Retrieved: Lost Words / New Writing,* the fifth in the series, came together in an organic and somewhat piecemeal fashion, I believe it fulfils this aim. Yet it is undeniably an eclectic mix, in that there is no over-arching theme, and the 'Afterwords' section introduces further different topics.

Amanda Harrison explores Bacon's non-human imagery from several different perspectives, and her discursive approach sheds significant light on several aspects of Bacon's imagery that have only recently begun to be investigated. Maria Balaska considers Bacon's essence by reading his aims and methodology through the philosophy of Martin Heidegger; in doing so she has found many illuminating parallels. Darian Leader's engaging essay yields fascinating insights into the minds and motivations of art forgers. His contribution is even more timely than we could have anticipated, for at the time this is being written a London club is exhibiting the work of Cristiano Lovatelli Ravarino, notwithstanding the legal case against him in Italy is nearing its conclusion and is scheduled to be announced by the time this book appears. My selection of what I consider the most interesting passages of Bacon's interviews with David Sylvester that have remained unpublished would not have been possible without the transcriptions made by Sophie Pretorius.

The 'Afterwords' were added shortly before the book went to press in order to present some exciting recent discoveries. The commonplace notion that paintings reveal far more when viewed directly than in reproduction is especially true in Bacon's case. Amanda Harrison's interpretation of *Triptych May-June 1973* was inspired by its inclusion in the National Portrait Gallery's exhibition, *Francis Bacon: Human Presence* (October 2024 – January 2025), and the close observation of crucial details that this facilitated. Similarly, the X-radiography of *Man in a Cap*, c. 1945, proved to be of far greater significance than we dared hope. Finally, *Study for Portrait*, 1969, had been intended as the cover of this volume since its inception; at the eleventh hour the fortuitous emergence of Bacon's 'model' enabled us to expand on Bacon's biography in the 1960s.

Martin Harrison, January 2025

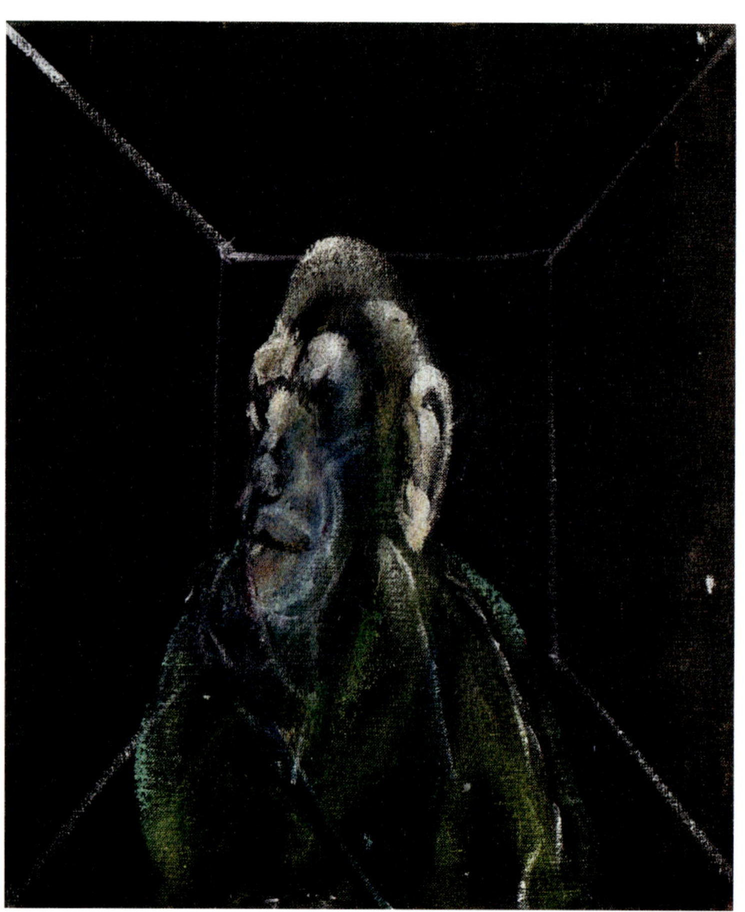

5. *Monkey*, 1953

Man and simian merged. Final proof that fossilised remains of 'Piltdown Man' were, as long suspected, a forgery, was published in 1953. Coincidentally, it appeared on the same day that *Monkey* was sold by Erica Brausen. Proposed as 'The Missing Link', it was found that a human skull had been given a fossilised orangutan's jaw fitted with chimpanzee teeth.

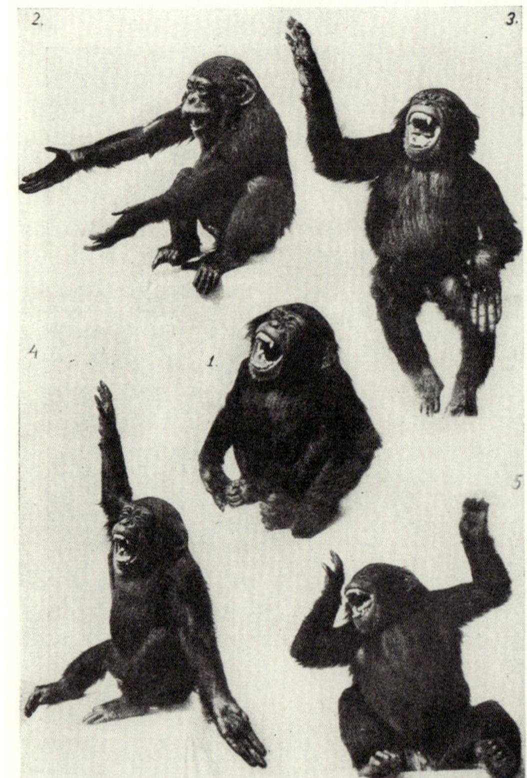

Plate 7. POSTURES AND GESTURES OF THE YOUNG CHIMPANZEE WHEN CRYING OR IN A TEMPER TAN-TRUM.

From Kohts, 1935; courtesy of the Darwinian Museum, Moscow.

6. Page from Robert and Ada Yerkes, *The Great Apes: A Study of Anthropoid Life*, 1945, a copy of which was in Bacon's collection.

'Attitudes of Apes': Exploring Bacon's Creatures

Amanda J. Harrison

Introduction

Francis Bacon was essentially a painter of the human body. However, this essay will concentrate on a significant but still under-researched aspect of his iconography – his animal-related imagery.[1] Bacon marshalled his visual resources to express his emotional and psycho-physiological response to his experience of life – his feelings, fears, desires and what he called his drives. In this endeavour, his images of animals expressed his 'psyche' as revealingly as did those of humans.[2] He interpreted specific thoughts or sensations as extra-morphological beings, depicting his obsessions such as the sex-drive, fear, dismay, dread, or guilt, in the form of creatures, whether natural or imagined.

Bacon spoke of images dropping into his mind like slides;[3] that may be how he perceived their origins, but the impression of spontaneity is belied by what we now know about the extent to which he planned his paintings. He wrote notes to remind himself to recall these mental 'slides' before starting work on a canvas. He had seen the images or their components in various forms *before* he painted them. He amassed a vast collection of cuttings, magazines and an extensive library of books. He went to the theatre, he watched films, read books, listened to the radio. While none of this is exceptional, what is unique to Bacon is the transmutations he wrought on the stimuli he had absorbed, to create some of the most singular paintings of his era.

The forms Bacon painted leak from one category to another. Shadows become flesh, or fall in the wrong place. Reflections appear on screens that are not in the space depicted. Faces emanate from, or are superimposed on, another person's head. His techniques of blurring and smudging incite pareidolia.[4] Bacon's paintings reflect his personality in striving to balance his contradictions and conflicts: turbulence and instability coexist with resignation and the starkly factual. These aspects of his artistic agenda were all manifested with special force in his non-human imagery.

Bacon's interest in animals situates him within a long historical tradition. Cultures from antiquity to the present have imagined or developed symbolic characters to stand for abstract yet real elements in human experience. Fearsome monsters and therianthropic beings have been modelled on amalgamations of animals and human characteristics: werewolves, Beowulf's foes Grendel and his mother, dragons, devils, harpies, gorgons – the list is long. They embody fears more than desires – there are far fewer benign or benevolent types, such as angels and unicorns. Then there are creatures representing or generated by the gods, whose imagery was employed by some of Bacon's contemporaries in a sustained fashion: Michael Ayrton's Minotaurs come to mind, or Sidney Nolan's multiple variations of Leda and the Swan. Besides these theriomorphic figures, Bacon's iconography was also informed by Egyptian archaeology and Greek and Roman mythology through his reading of Aeschylus's dramas, and by works of art ranging from cave paintings through the Renaissance and including those of his contemporaries. And, crucially, Bacon was also inspired by literature that embraced Nietzsche, Freud, Jung, Shakespeare and a wide range of nineteenth- and twentieth-century poetry.

Although a professed atheist, Bacon certainly felt there was more to being human than the solely corporeal; he commented, 'When I look at you across the table, I don't only see you but I see a whole *emanation* which has to do with personality and *everything else*.'[5] [my itals.] This was said in a conversation about perceived violence in his paintings, which he attributed to his act of revealing the inner person: '... perhaps I have from time to time been able to clear away one or two of the veils or screens.'[6] To represent the 'everything else' and 'emanations' behind the screens he painted animals, living shadows, and entities derived from mythology. Mostly these are separated from his figures' bodies, but in a few instances are entangled with, or emerge from them.

Bacon conflated simian features and movements with his human figures' poses to demonstrate humans' fundamental nature.[7] He also employed animal imagery or his own versions of mythological beings to communicate his emotions and accompanying physiological reactions. He depicted dogs and simians concurrently and equally frequently, but apes and monkeys assumed a stronger, wider cultural significance than dogs. Bacon's dogs may be compared with his Furies as iconographical indicators of dread or feelings of persecution, whereas simians relate to the question of what it is to be human.

Simians

Bacon's view of monkeys or apes aligned closely with the accepted position that they acted as ciphers for human behaviour. The 'simian' holds both an ambivalence and a fascination: clever yet uncivilised, trained or wild, the human-like gestures and features of monkeys and apes have mainly been appropriated to stress their inferiority to Man. Mimics of human behaviour, victims of Man's disregard and cruelty, or kept as exotic pets, their significance in art and literature is multivalent. Bacon used his apes and monkeys as metaphors and symbols of all of these, while maintaining an emphasis on their physicality. Their implications for his iconography are reflected in his lists of ideas for paintings (at least forty-three of Bacon's paintings are of animals, excluding hybrids):

> Aug 18th 1958
>
> Concentrate entirely on studies of Human figure and on heads. Situate
> figure(s?) in attitudes of apes background brilliant colour – netting – brick
> – tiles – and corrugated iron. Keep figures nude.
> 8/ Figure staring into mirror as of apes
> 11/ Study of Baby in a tall chair with owls or monkey?'[8]

Known in Europe for at least two millennia, apes and monkeys were subjects in stories such as the Fables of Aesop, originating in Greece during the fourth century BC, and are mentioned in the Old Testament.[9] Bacon's admiration for Egyptian Art is well documented and he owned many books on the subject.[10] The Egyptians' gods were depicted with human bodies and animal heads: E.A. Wallis

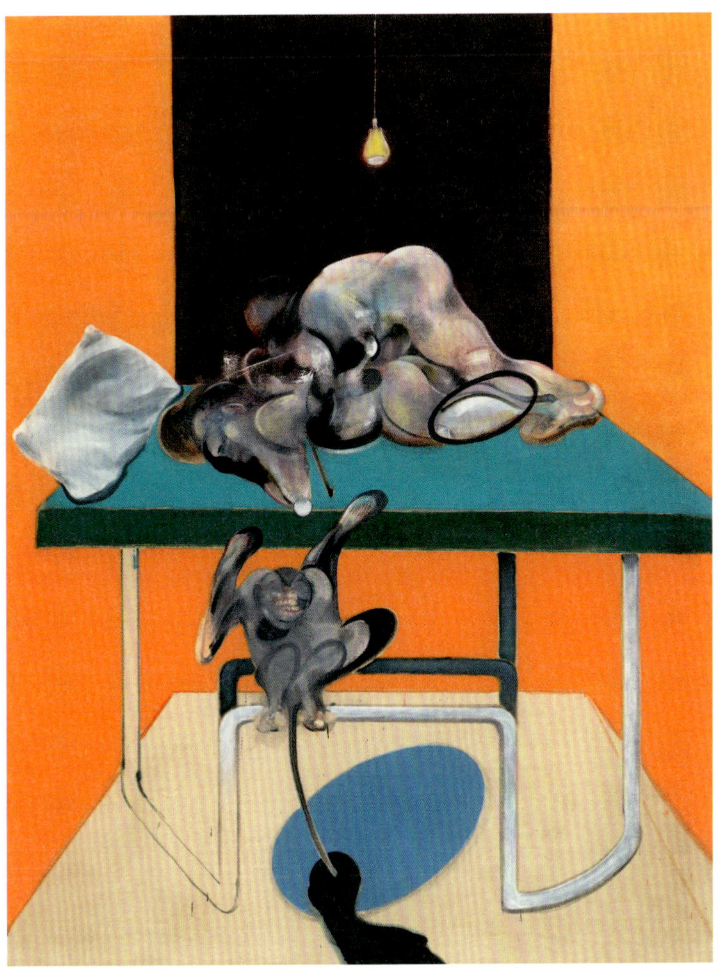

7. *Two Figures With a Monkey*, 1973

Budge's *Hieroglyphic Dictionary* lists more than forty different monkey or primate gods. Perhaps significantly for Bacon, the god of virility, Baba, was depicted as a baboon.[11] The major deity Thoth, lunar god of wisdom, writing, and scribes, was rendered as either ibis-headed or baboon-headed. Baboons themselves were regarded as sacred,[12] and their mummified bodies have been found in temple sites. They are primates belonging to the monkey family that howl at sunrise, and it was probably this behaviour that linked them with the moon and the transition from night into day. As dimorphic animals the males have large canine and incisor teeth which, besides tearing flesh and plants, are used to display threatening behaviour, both to protect and attack; aggression can be a positive form of defence. The bared teeth in Bacon's painting *Head I*, 1948, are those of a baboon. Assuming Bacon had read his nature books, he would have known that the baboon's aggressive facial gestures are as much a warning as an attack; his adoption of the bared teeth as an exaggeration of Man's own aggression might be understood as a legacy of our ape ancestry. This image is powerful because we recognise its danger and react instinctively. If Bacon was sympathetic to our human-animal predicament – that we carry the burden of our animal past in our present lives – is there forgiveness? If he intended to convey equivocation, his ambiguity is successful.

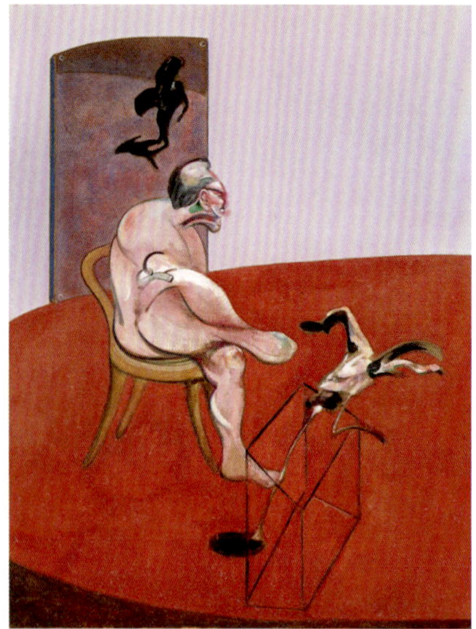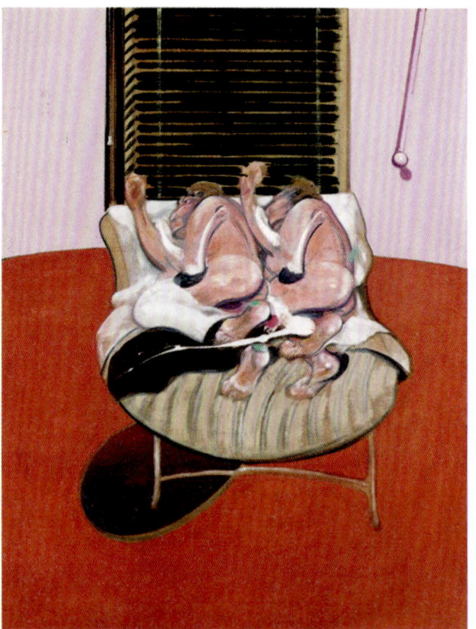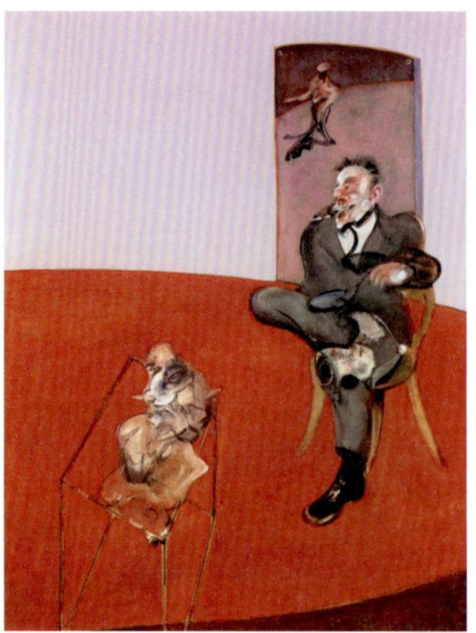

8. *Two Figures Lying on a Bed with Attendants*, 1968

Bacon turned to mythological subjects through paintings by Old Masters and his admiration for Aeschylus's plays. In his triptych *Two Figures Lying on a Bed with Attendants*, 1968, the centre panel features two male figures with ape-like heads who lie with fists raised in a phallic gesture. Bacon may have based these figures on the mythological Cercopes,[13] two roguish brothers who inhabited the forest, running wild and playing tricks, thieving and causing trouble; their crimes angered Zeus, whose punishment was to turn them into monkeys.[14] Bacon painted depictions of simian morphology between 1948 and 1973, but it was only in the last of these, *Two Figures with a Monkey*, 1973, [7] that he employed the monkey in its medieval meaning, as a 'personification' of lust. Its tail acts as a penetrative element and the leering face emanates transgressive glee; Bacon's culturally traditional monkey wittily narrates the lascivious monkey business he is witnessing. The identification of human drives like libido, gluttony, anger and aggression as bestial and uncivilised had been made for millennia: monkeys and apes, owing to their physical resemblance to humans, carried the trope. The 'chained monkey' developed into a symbol of material and moral sin. One or two monkeys were often depicted, as tame pet monkeys would have been kept, chained to a heavy ball or stone weight, an allegory of Man, metaphorically chained to worldly appetites.

The term 'babewyn' is used by medievalists to refer to fanciful and hybrid creatures found in marginal illustrations on manuscripts and carved grotesque decoration. [9] Originally the term was used only for the apes that enacted scenes within the decorated borders around texts, but its use widened to include all sorts of fantastical hybrids. The word derives, via old French, from *babbuino*, Italian for baboon. The antics of apes and monkeys feature in many illuminated manuscripts where they ape Man or perform lewd acts. These were not solely for amusement; the scenes, like morality plays, bore warnings on how not to conduct life. Scandalous behaviour had consequences before the law and in the promised afterlife. Bacon's pictures are, to an extent, a continuation of the theme, only his stance is not moralising but factual.

Bacon explained to Jasia Reichardt that his interest in monkeys stemmed from the fact that, like humans, they were fascinated with their own image, which they demonstrated 'with an abandon and relish rarely equalled by that of men'.[15] In Christian culture such conduct was frowned upon and designated as the sin of

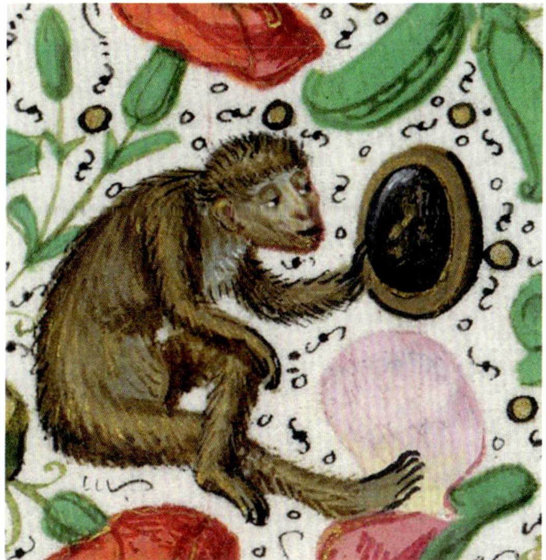

9. Monkey regarding a mirror; detail from *The Isabella Breviary*, 1480s/90s British Library Collection, Add. 18851, f. 270.

In medieval culture, Luxuria, the personification of intense sexual desire, lust, holds a mirror as a sign of vanity. Monkeys and apes stood in as symbols for lust enacting Luxuria's gestures and her power to seduce.

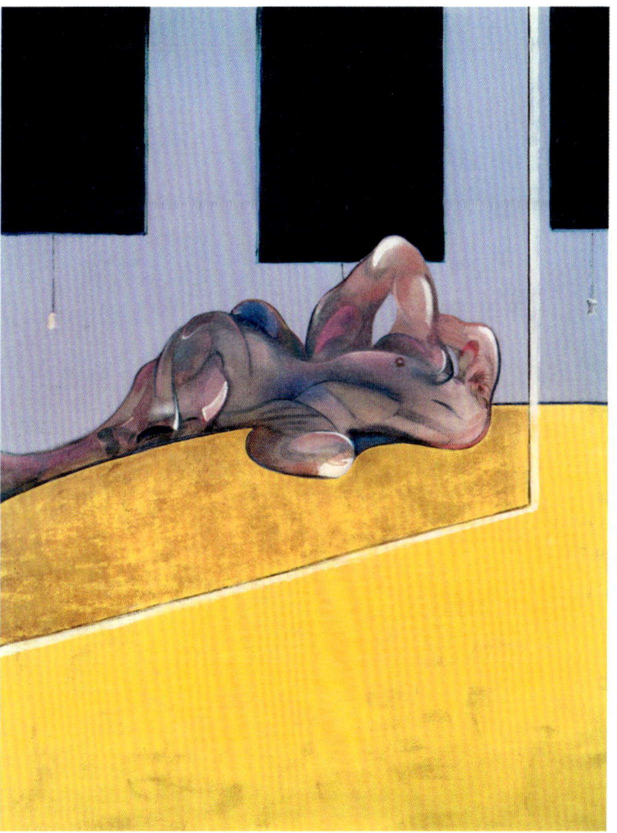

10. *Lying Figure in a Mirror*, 1971

vanity. Often women were accused, and by association mirrors became a symbol for the sin; thus, mermaids and monkeys who hold mirrors project the same message. If mirror-gazing and the fascination with one's own reflection is narcissistic, the recognition of the self, unexpectedly reflected, can surprise and even shame or shock. Bacon employed reflections in his paintings both as a means of doubling and as an act of provocation: to cite an example that also turns the viewer into a voyeur, the crime in *Lying Figure in a Mirror*, 1971, is enacted solely in its mirror reflection.

From the publication in 1859 of Charles Darwin's *On the Origin of Species*,[16] followed by *The Descent of Man*,[17] the degrees of closeness of apes and monkeys to Man became an urgent subject of cultural enquiry and scientific investigation. Bacon owned two copies of *On the Origin of Species*, and he was probably familiar with both *The Descent of Man* and *The Expression of the Emotions*,[18] an early scientific book illustrated with photographs.

> 'Once you were apes, and even now, too, the human being is more ape than any ape'. – Friedrich Nietzsche.[19]

The theory of evolution shook Western society, bringing apes and their significance to the fore. Bacon's *Statue and Figures in a Street*, 1983, [11] is a comment on Man's predicament. Shadowy silhouettes of men and ape-like beings pass a vast sculpture, a monumental, classical, male figure. But the classical ideal is decayed, ignored, while Man trudges on, unheeding. Bacon addresses the Ape-Human borderline. His

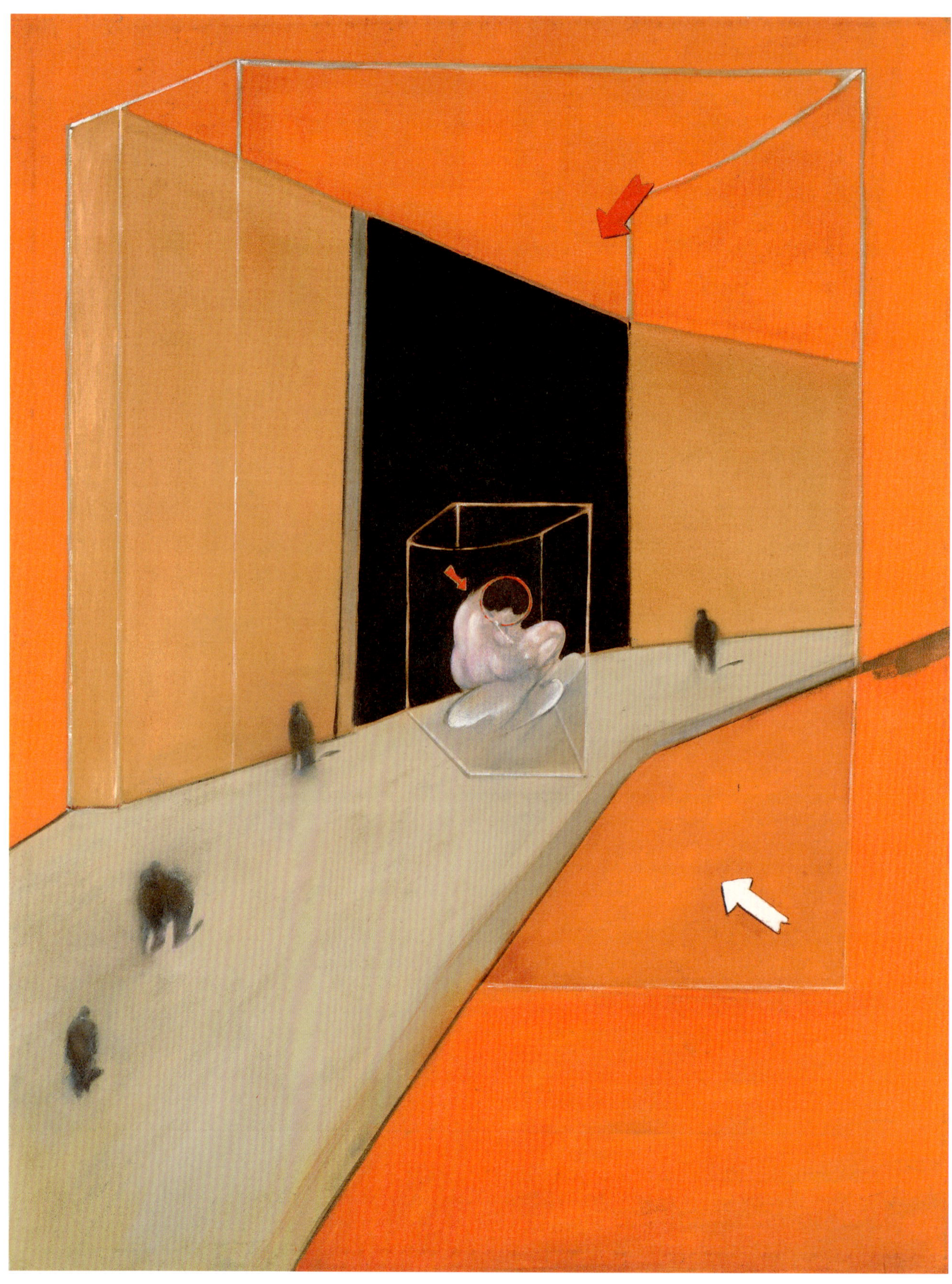

11. *Statue and Figures in a Street*, 1983

paintings of monkeys and apes reflect his understanding that he and all humans are a type of ape, and that apes themselves are not insensate. Bacon's fascination with monkeys and apes was also likely to have been influenced by his reading of Nietzsche's *Thus Spake Zarathustra* and *The Gay Science*,[20] in which the position of apes and humans within a hierarchy of evolving biology forms part of Nietzsche's thinking on Man's ability and determination to evolve beyond his current status to become an Übermensch. Nietzsche was writing after the translation of Darwin's seminal publications: Man's creation story no longer needed God. Questions of speciesism and disbelief in God or an afterlife chimed with Bacon's atheism, but the importance of authenticity remains central. Bacon's determination to be his own man as an artist and a member of society who is authentically himself is a step towards Übermensch status.

Bacon's translation of movement, gesture, and evocation of emotion and spirit is an attempt, perhaps influenced by Nietzsche, to be truly human, and not to be just an ape. Yet through his study of their physicality and expressive movements in photographs and books, and by watching them at the zoo, Bacon was appreciative of their natural, unrestrained mode of being; he also empathised with their vulnerable status as captives. Conversely, Nietzsche's apes are mythological or symbolic beings rather than true animals. In the 1880s the study of exotic animal behaviour was not well advanced; Nietzsche's interpretation of Darwin's theory of evolution was insubstantial and wavers, but ideas about simians and their biological similarity fired the imagination of writers in multiple genres.

Bacon's apes and monkeys were not culturally isolated. The subject of Man's biological closeness to simians was taken up by a variety of authors after Darwin and continued to be a part of the cultural landscape of Bacon and his contemporaries. Stories like Rudyard Kipling's *The Jungle Book*, 1894, were popular in the Edwardian era and would have been known by Bacon and his siblings. In one tale the main character, Mowgli, a boy raised by wolves, is captured by a tribe of monkeys, the Bandar-log. Kipling explained that he had based *The Jungle Book* partly on ancient Indian tales; his monkeys, arrogant and frightening, were bound to impress a young reader. Another feral boy, this time living in the African jungle, was Edgar Rice Burroughs's *Tarzan of the Apes,* 1912, an adventure story that Bacon would also have known. Bacon's sister Ianthe Knott recalled that she and her siblings were read Aesop's Fables. Eight of the fables concern monkey characters; one, *The Monkeys and Their Mother,* had been incorporated into medieval culture and was an early story printed by Chaucer.

The theme of Eugene O'Neill's play, *The Hairy Ape*, 1922, is the status of a physically strong working man, displaced in modern, urban industrialised society. The protagonist Yank is likened to 'a filthy beast' and suffers a crisis of confidence at the insult; he behaves like a depraved animal and is finally killed by a gorilla that he had, in sympathy, freed from captivity. A French translation of this expressionist work played in Paris in 1929 and Paul Robeson took the part of Yank in the 1931 run of the play in London. Bacon may well have seen the play in Paris or London, possibly with Eric Allden in 1931.[21]

O'Neill's 'Yank' had been anticipated by T. S. Eliot's ape-like character, 'Sweeney', a brute who represented for Eliot a base type of male. Eliot's poetry and plays had a direct effect on many of Bacon's paintings; Sweeney had first appeared in 1918

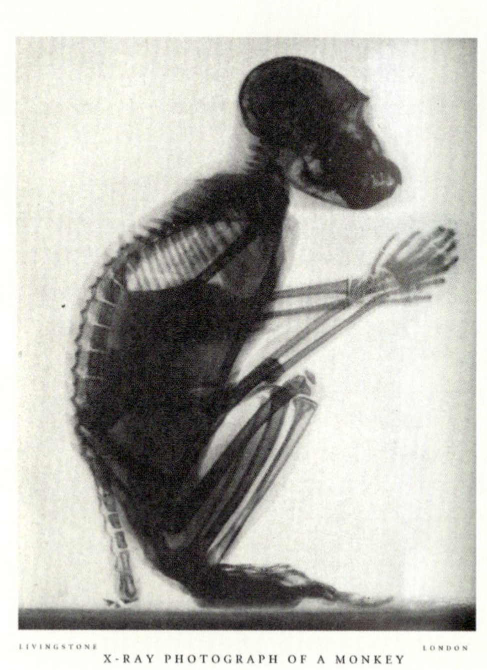

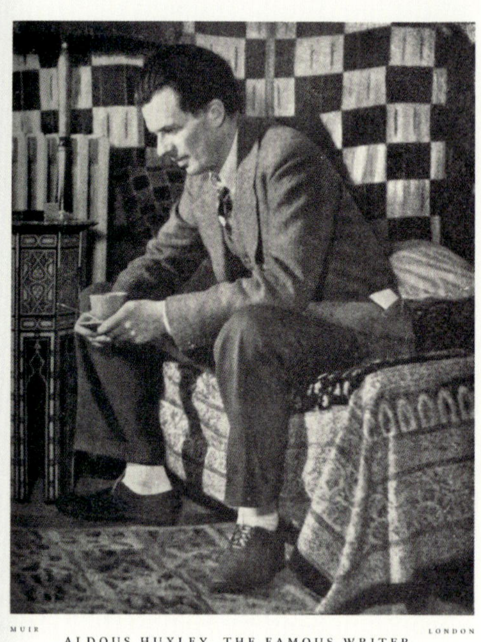

12. Double-page spread from *Lilliput*, June 1938, juxtaposing a photograph of Aldous Huxley with an X-ray of a monkey.

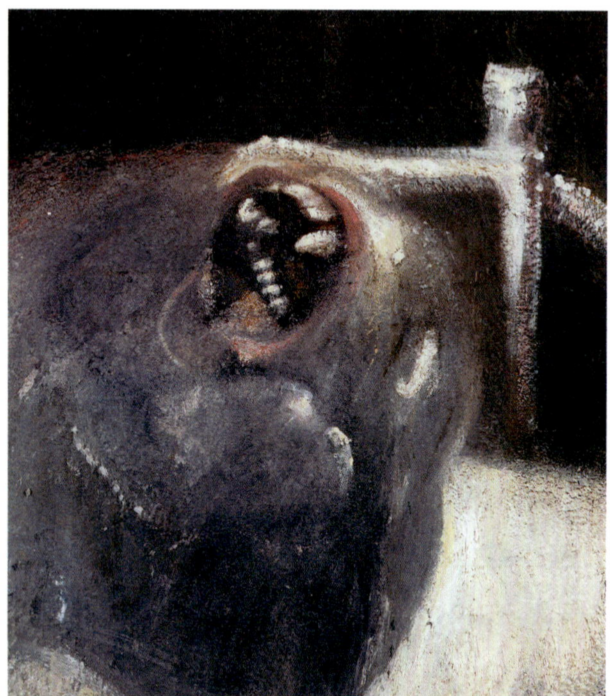

13. *Head I*, 1948 (detail)

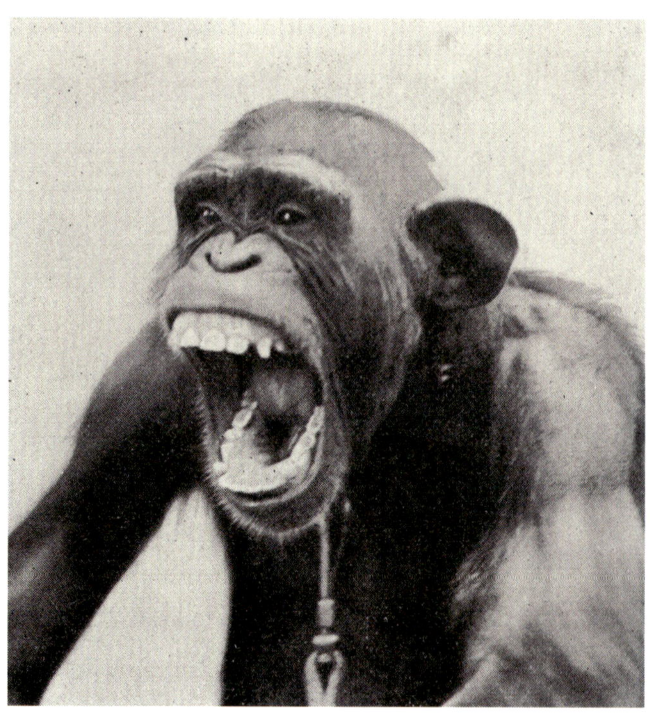

14. 'Yawn', plate from R. M. Yerkes, *Chimpanzees: A Laboratory Colony*, 1943

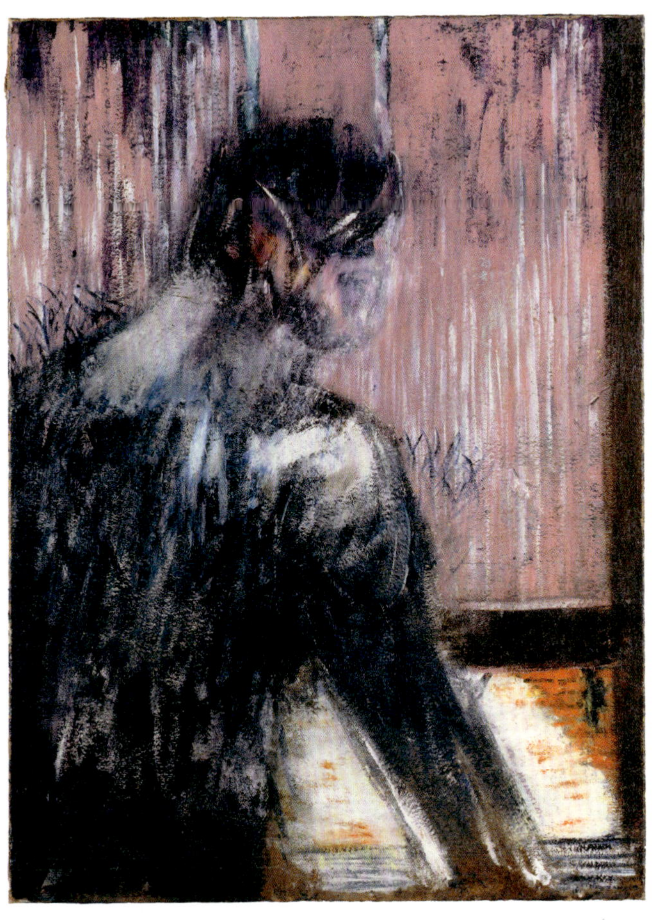

15. *Man Standing,* c. 1945

in *Sweeney Among the Nightingales* and *Mr. Eliot's Sunday Morning Service*, then in *Sweeney Erect*, 1919: he is a main character in both *The Waste Land*, 1922, and the second section of his unfinished play published as *Sweeney Agonistes: Fragments of an Aristophanic Melodrama*, 1932. Bacon is likely to have seen the 1934 production of *Sweeney Agonistes* in London by the experimental Group Theatre or the 1935 Group Theatre revival, directed by Rupert Doone, in which the cast wore masks. Artists Henry Moore and Rupert Shepherd collaborated in these productions. Thomas Huxley had shown in 1863 that, anatomically, humans are apes. In 1948 his grandson, Aldous Huxley, published *Ape and Essence*, a novel about a dystopian post-nuclear-war future in which society is morally and, due to the effects of nuclear fallout, physically, degraded. Huxley's narrator, echoing Nietzsche, states: 'Today, thanks to that Higher Ignorance which is our knowledge, Man's stature has increased to such an extent that the least among us is now a baboon, the greatest an orangutan or even, if he takes rank as a Saviour of Society, a true Gorilla.'[22]

Bacon's first simian intervention in a surviving painting was in *Head I,* 1948, although he claimed that *Painting 1946* had begun as 'a chimpanzee in the grass'.[23] *Head I,* 1948, combines human characteristics with a chimpanzee's mouth, based on a photograph in R. M. Yerkes, *Chimpanzees: A Laboratory Colony*.[24] [14] *Man Standing,* c. 1945, was a precursor; the 'hairy', beast-like figure (Hitler) has an imprecise human face. Bacon was using simians as both symbol and metaphor, but where the boundary lay is blurred. The extent to which he sympathised with the animal nature 'within' the

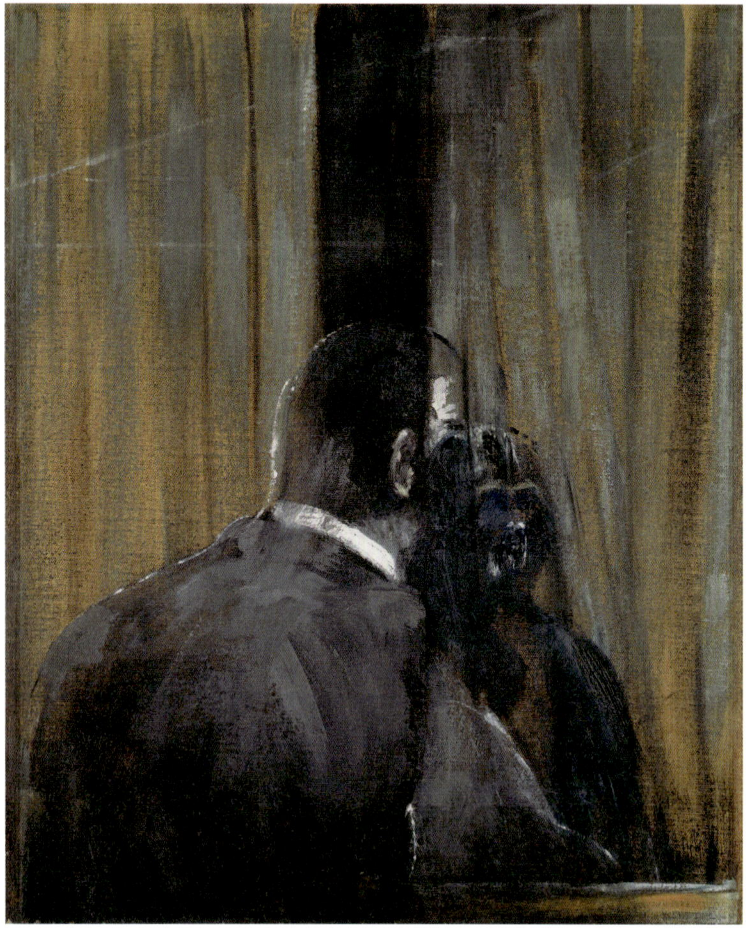

16. *Head IV (Man with a Monkey),* 1949

human, or associated his own emotions with the imagery, is unknowable. Also in about 1948, Bacon had reworked his 1946 painting *Study for Man with Microphones,* which, after he had abandoned it, was sold as *Gorilla with Microphones*. The chalky-white unclothed figure does not look like a gorilla, yet its bulk gives an impression of a hairless one; Bacon implies a bestial character to a naked man as he had to a clothed one in *Man Standing,* c. 1945, by giving the figure a furred aspect.

 Head IV (*Man with a Monkey*), 1949, reflects Bacon's reading of Amédée Ozenfant's *Foundations of Modern Art*, 1931,[25] of which he had more than one copy. An idiosyncratic book, encompassing Ozenfant's version of the history of Modernism and his personal philosophy, with an eclectic mix of illustrations of machines, African peoples and archaeological artefacts, it was intended to stimulate the thinking of art students. Bacon borrowed its photographic imagery on several occasions.[26] A photograph of an orangutan is placed opposite Ozenfant's potted history of post-French revolution cultural and scientific development; he mentions Lord Bacon under philosophy and the inclusion of Darwin as an example of freedom of thought may account for the ape illustration. An uncaptioned photograph of a man dressed in a suit carrying a young gorilla follows discussion of 'the triumph of agnosticism' and Darwin's Theory of Evolution.[27] Ozenfant asks: 'What is Man?' / 'The evolution of an ape, which was itself a stage in the slow evolution of a first cell.' / 'What created that first cell?' / 'Chance.'[28] This had a specific resonance for Bacon, as did the page's

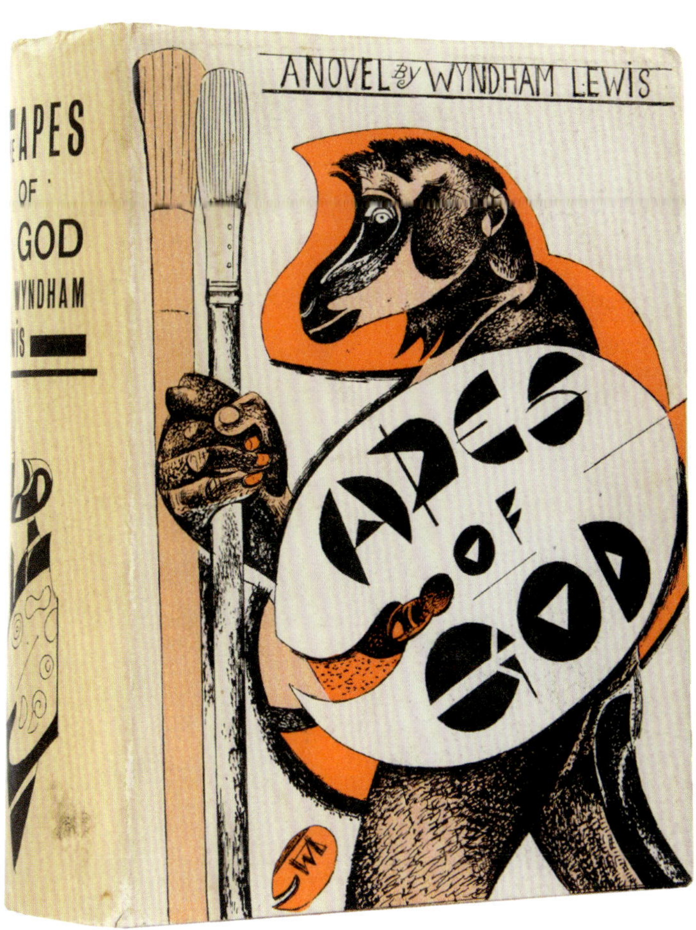

17. Wyndham Lewis, *The Apes of God,* 1930; dust jacket designed by Wyndham Lewis

footnote, which reads: 'Juan Gris, rationalist, remarked: "What astonishes me most is that series of accidents that made me into a man …". '[29] *Head IV* (*Man with a Monkey*), is a conspicuously ambiguous painting, for the boundaries between two bodies are indistinctly defined; was Bacon thinking about human nature and our animality, or 'chance', as defined by Juan Gris?

The artist and author Wyndham Lewis, who was aware of Bacon's paintings from 1946 and wrote two perceptive reviews of them in 1949,[30] doubtless recognised that Bacon's mordancy regarding the human condition was similar to his own. Lewis's books may have contributed to Bacon's views. It is likely that Bacon knew Lewis's 1930 novel *The Apes of God*, in which Lewis uses the concept of apes as mimics to satirise the Bloomsbury Group and London cultural society – the 'Apes of God' whom Lewis regarded as hypocritical imitators of genuine creators. Bacon may also have read Lewis's *The Wild Body*, a collection of short stories with an explanatory section, 'The Meaning of the Wild Body', in which he says: 'There is nothing that is animal (and we as bodies are animals) that is not absurd.'[31] His philosophical musing focuses on the mind/body divide and examples of the divide that reveal the absurdity. Lewis identifies an incident as comic because '… the man's body was not him.'[32] His protagonist in the stories describes his body as 'forked, strange scented, blond-skinned gut bag'. Bacon's awareness of the peculiarity of human consciousness and its similarities to and differences from that of animals is abundantly expressed in his paintings.

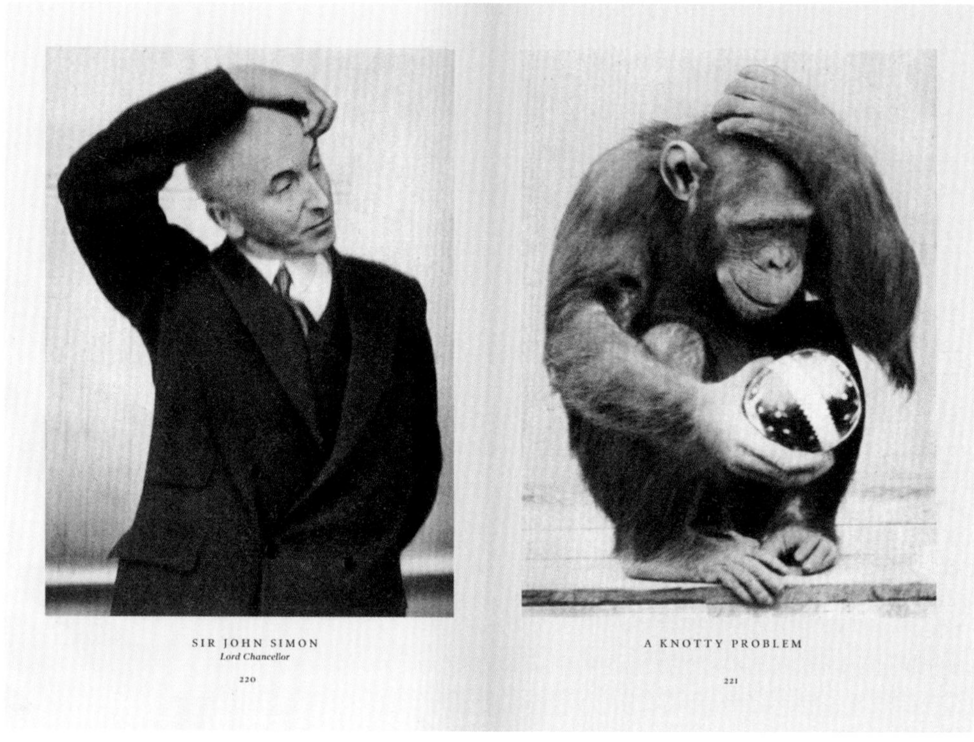

18. Double page spread from Stefan Lorant, *Chamberlain and the Beautiful Llama*, 1940. The similarity between human and simian gestures recurred frequently in mid-twentieth century popular literature. The arm gesture appears in many of Bacon's paintings.

This theme had also been addressed by H. G. Wells in *The Island of Doctor Moreau,* 1896. Wells explained that his novel was a response to Oscar Wilde's 'graceless and pitiful downfall' and a 'reminder that humanity is but animal rough-hewn to a reasonable shape and in perpetual internal conflict between instinct and injunction.'[33] Suffering, experimental animal-humans –Wells's Beast Folk, created by the insane vivisectionist Moreau, regress to their basic animal behaviour, go feral, and walk on all fours. Bacon would have known of the novel; he also collected copies of *Picture Post, Lilliput,* and *Paris Match,* whose pages frequently featured photographs of monkeys and apes not only in their own right but also juxtaposed with humans.

Bacon's long connection with Monaco and its environs would have ensured he knew of the Franco-Russian surgeon, Serge Voronoff (1866–1951). A controversial figure, Voronoff performed the first human xenotransplants in 1920; he proceeded from implants to cure thyroid to implants of slices of ape testes into human testes in the belief that the patient would be both sexually reinvigorated and enjoy a longer life. He had a successful clinic with satisfied clients before the Second World War. Voronoff also experimented with impregnating simians with human sperm. One of Voronoff's buildings was situated on the slopes below a house Bacon rented; looking over to the Mediterranean, Bacon would have seen the tops of the cages of Voronoff's experimental animals. The operations to revive men's virility were widely reported (and mainly ridiculed); a gin cocktail called Monkey Gland was created in Paris at Harry's New York Bar. Frustratingly, Bacon is not known to have commented on Voronoff or the animals on which he experimented, and it seems no one asked him; however, his avid interest in reports of crimes and sexual scandals would suggest he closely followed Voronoff's activities.

Hybridisation and Distortion

Bacon's claims to spontaneity, which were never questioned by his interviewers, are manifested in his extemporised painting techniques rather than the fecund springing of images from his imagination. An alternative model of how creative minds imagine scenes was recorded by Mary Shelley. In the introduction to the 1831 edition of *Frankenstein, Or The Modern Prometheus*, 1818, she wrote: 'I saw – with shut eyes, but acute mental vision – I saw the pale student of unhallowed arts kneeling beside the thing he had put together. I saw the hideous phantasm of a man stretched out, and then, on the working of some powerful engine, show signs of life and stir with an uneasy, half-vital motion. Frightful must it be, for supremely frightful would be the effect of any human endeavour to mock the stupendous mechanism of the Creator of the world.'[34] She chose a quote from Milton's *Paradise Lost* to indicate on the title page the meaning of her story: 'Did I request thee, Maker, from my clay / To mould me man? Did I solicit thee / From darkness to promote me?'[35]

This nihilistic question and the lament asked of his creator by Adam, the first man, are in essence the questions Bacon is asking. In Shelley's novel, on finding his creator Frankenstein dead, The Monster says: 'I, the miserable and the abandoned, am an abortion, to be spurned at, and kicked, and trampled on.' By shutting her eyes Shelley invented the concept of a patchwork collage of human parts, an all-human hybrid, a would-be Prometheus, the Greek God of fire whose name means forethought. Her Frankenstein lacks forethought and pays the penalty. In some myths, Prometheus creates Man from clay, steals fire to give humanity fire, knowledge and thus civilisation. His punishment from Zeus is for his liver to be devoured daily while chained to a rock, only for the liver to regenerate overnight and the process to be endlessly repeated. For Ancient Greeks the liver was the seat of the emotions and therefore of suffering. Shelley composed tragic consequences to cause Frankenstein's death and that of his creation; H.G. Wells's Doctor Moreau and his Beast-Folk suffered similar fates.

Mary Shelley was aware of advances in science and had read widely and conversed with radical thinkers of her time. She intended her story to be 'frightful' and to act as a warning. In doing so she adopted the same rationale that medieval Christian scholars employed to instruct their congregations. In many churches a 'Doom' was painted above the chancel arch, containing horrifying scenes of sinners suffering in Hell to the right and the blessed in Heaven on the left. The portrayal of doomsday in the form of monsters, demons, fire and brimstone warned of the perils of sinning. The word 'monster' is derived from the Latin *monstrum,* (portent), from *monere*, to warn. Monsters occurring naturally, like deformed births or malformed plants, were understood as demonstrations of the creative force of God. Omens and wonders were signs of celestial power on earth that were sent down to be heeded. To harness these beliefs, religious leaders employed craftworkers to turn abstract concepts into illustrations of the imagined beatific and malignant forces. Monsters then, the malformed, wrongly sized, or diseased, possess the power to shock, disgust and repel; yet with or without a belief system they are memorable. As Mary Shelley employed this 'Gothic' intensity, so too did Bacon: he aimed to make paintings with the visual potency to arrest the viewer.

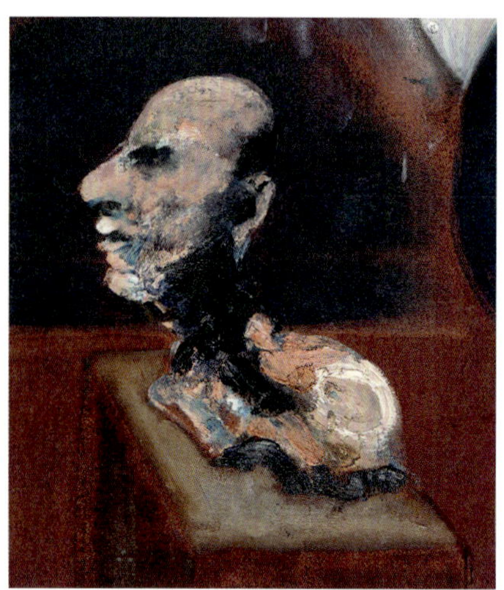

19. *Reclining Man with Sculpture*, 1960–61 (detail)

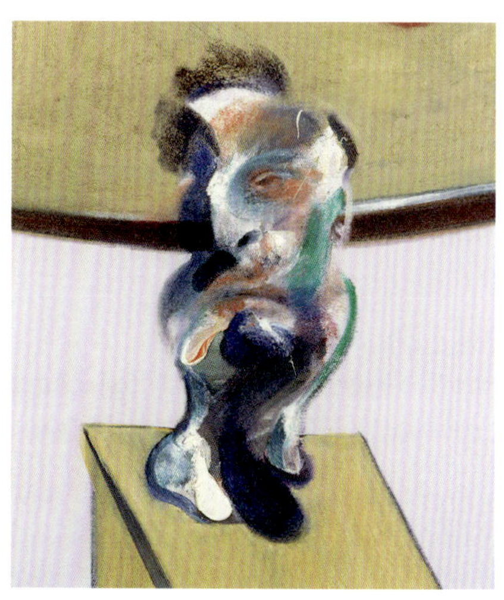

20. *Two Studies of George Dyer with Dog*, 1968 (detail)

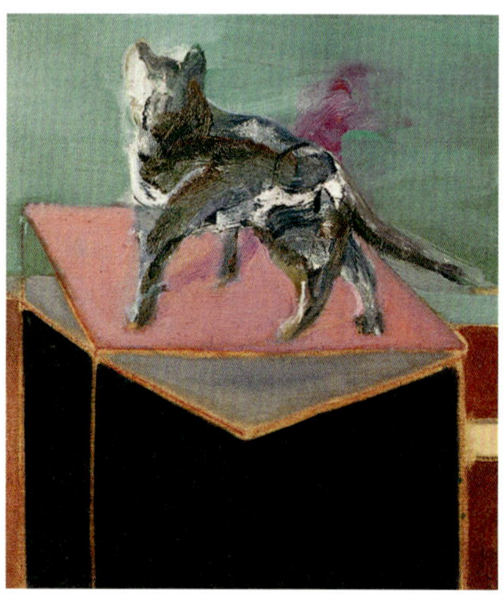

21. *Portrait of George Dyer and Lucian Freud*, 1967 (detail)

The myth of Man's creation from clay appears to be mocked by Bacon in his liquified modelling-clay-like heads displayed in *Reclining Man with Sculpture*, 1960–61, and *Two Studies of George Dyer with Dog*, 1968. In these paintings the sculptures serve as an incidental, an aside or stage whisper, alluding to the content of his painting. In the destroyed painting *Portrait of George Dyer and Lucian Freud*, 1967, a cat stands on top of a frame; Bacon's image source was a photograph, but in the painting we are unsure if the cat was intended as a ceramic model, a stuffed specimen or a sculpture: its ambiguous state is intriguing – like Erwin Schrödinger's thought experiment. Was Bacon referring to the mystery of quantum mechanics? He contended that such ostensibly inconsequential additions were merely formal devices to fill the foreground and that they bore no extra meaning. Yet they do augment any meanings, and in *Two Studies of George Dyer with Dog*, 1968, the 'meaningless' artefact is referred to in the title.

The sculpture in the foreground of *Two Studies of George Dyer with Dog* bears only a limited resemblance to Dyer, its neck and jowls dividing to form rudimentary haunches. In *Two Figures Lying on a Bed with Attendants*, 1968, the modelled head in the foreground of the right panel is, suitably perhaps, malformed or incomplete, with what appears to be a wound dressing on the injured nose. [8] Perhaps Bacon had been consulting his boxing books or repeating his use of falsified ectoplasm from spirit photographs. The head is as disturbing as the face of the attendant. It steps back from reality by rendering not a living person but a 'sculpture' that did not previously exist but was painted entirely from Bacon's imagination. Indeed, many of Bacon's figures seem to be moulded from a viscous, clay-like substance, forming a body into which life is to be injected. This could be interpreted as Bacon dissociating himself from the creative act or, in contrast, painting not as a record but as a work of fiction.

In 1933 Bacon was commissioned by Sir Michael Sadler to paint his portrait from an X-ray he had sent of his skull. Sadler had previously purchased Bacon's *Crucifixion*, 1933, which has a ghostly, X-ray-like aspect. The portrait in question is lost but in *The Crucifixion*, 1933, also bought by Sadler, higher on the canvas than the traditional skull at the foot of the cross is a semi-fleshed, semi-transparent skull, doubtless indebted to the X-ray of Sadler's head. On seeing an X-ray of her hand, the first ever taken of a human, Anna Bertha Röntgen is said to have declared: 'I have seen my death'.[36] Seeing

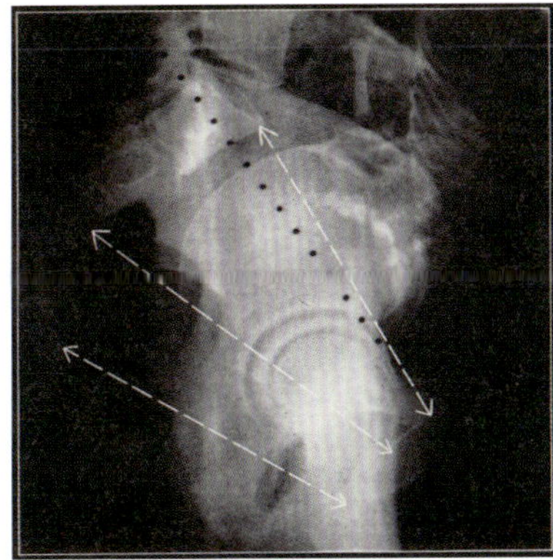

22. K. C. Clark, *Positioning in Radiography*,
plate showing use of perforated ruler

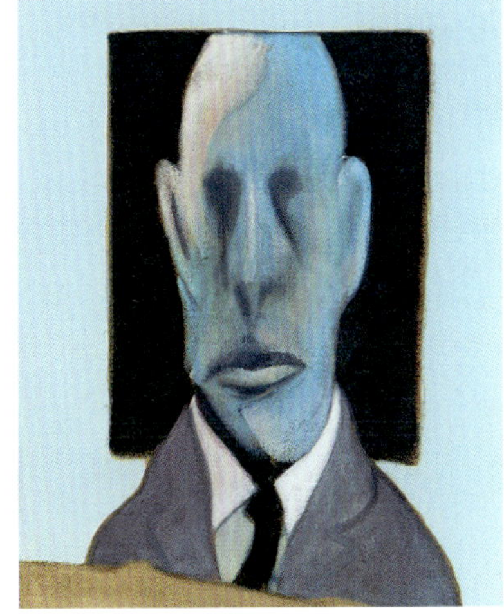

23. *Triptych 1974–77* (detail of centre panel)

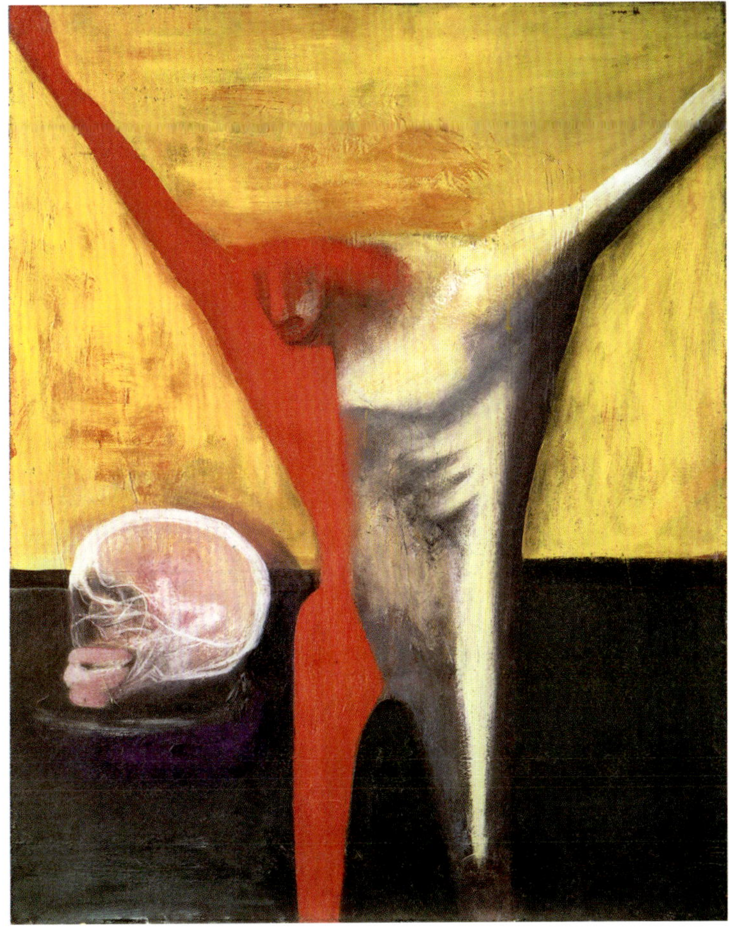

24. *The Crucifixion*, 1933

an image of one's skeleton still conveys a strange sensation and slight uneasiness about seeing what is supposed to be hidden. X-rays were discovered at the end of the nineteenth century and by the 1930s scientific investigations in the fields of genetics and mutations had progressed. Bacon would have been aware that the American Hermann Muller had in 1946 received a Nobel prize in Physiology or Medicine for the discovery that X-rays can cause, and be used to deliberately induce, mutations. X-rays were extremely important for Bacon and his paintings – they exposed previously hidden aspects of the human body. Bacon borrowed the visual language of X-ray medical investigation from a manual by K. C. Clark, *Positioning in Radiography*, from which he took patients' poses and the circles and arrows emphasising crucial areas and direction. He cannot have ignored the power of radiation to not only heal and reveal but to destroy, damage and distort human and animal bodies.

To the right of the centre panel of *Triptych 1974–77*, Bacon uses another modified photograph of a politician, Sir Austen Chamberlain, a plate in *Foundations of Modern Art* that Ozenfant used specifically to demonstrate distortion.[37] Ozenfant stated of distortion: 'It is meant to stand for the transfiguration which artists impose on the exterior world so as to give a more intense version of it.'[38] British statesman Sir Austen Chamberlain, holder of a Nobel Prize for Peace, British Foreign

Secretary and Chancellor of the Exchequer, had been strongly opposed to home rule for Ireland, and was, therefore, another figure who would have been a topic of conversation between Bacon's parents. Contrarily, Bacon altered the distorted image of Chamberlain into to an undistorted one, thus de-intensifying it; he was following, or at least referring to, Ozenfant's precepts.

Bacon's paintings are themselves hybrids, a mix of contrasting methods wherein we, as viewers, are required to be receptive to boldly stated passages alongside superimposed and contradictory elements of graphic instruction. A kind of seduction is occurring. Bacon's play of enticement or allurement and withdrawal, teases and fascinates, like hide and seek – now you see it, now you don't. In some paintings we see raw canvas (nothing to see here) and barely stated suggestions that are like false leads. The arrows and circles are graphics designed to be simply design, a reneging of the contract between the painter expressing a 3D scene into which we are drawn only to find the deal rejected by the narrator and ourselves reprimanded for filling in details that don't exist, or admonished that this is a 2D rendition. Bacon's hybridising was not confined to animals and people; ambiguity and mutability spread into furniture and its settings, landscapes, plants and closed/open spaces. Thrones morph into beds, patches of grass into rugs, a tuft of grass into an animate creature. The unstable nature of his vision creates hallucinatory, dream-like effects.

Birds and Furies[39]

The birds Bacon painted are always recognisable species, with the exception of the hybrid bird in *Fragment of a Crucifixion*, 1950. This winged creature with a human mouth was based on a flash photograph, taken by Eric Hosking, of a barn owl, rodent prey in its beak; (Hosking was the first to photograph birds in flight using electronic flash, which dramatised the owl's inherently ghostly appearance). But in *Fragment of a Crucifixion*, it has parts of *three* bodies. In creating this frightening apparition Bacon may have been recalling Geryon, the mythological three-bodied, four-winged, monster to which Clytemnestra likens Agamemnon, her soon-to-be victim husband, in Aeschylus's *Agamemnon*.[40] In Dante's *Inferno*, Geryon is the Monster of Fraud, dwelling between the seventh circle (violence) and eighth circle (fraud) of Hell. Bacon's ambiguous, screaming hybrid, suspended between two windows doubling as a cross, is simultaneously both crucified victim and malevolent, aggressive entity.

Bacon returned to the owl motif in five further paintings, in all of which paired owls are watching, like sentinels. *Owls*, 1956, [4] in which a pair of juvenile long-eared owls perches on sinister branches, is copied from a photograph in *Birds of the Night*, by Eric Hosking and Cyril Newberry, 1945, though their heads are also redolent of capuchin monkeys. The sinister bare branches are an unsettling lateral intrusion, with their animal-like grasping gestures, elbow-like joints and a yellow beaked 'head'. Bacon's owls are witnesses from these branches: they are birds of prey, the two pairs of eyes doubling the effect of observation. He probably encountered long-eared owls during his childhood in Kildare – they are the commonest owl in Ireland. Their ear tufts are long feathers, not ears, which are raised when alarmed, but they appear to be listening as well as watching. Bacon may have known the Vedic 'Parable of the Two Birds', where the mind's functions (or the self and soul) are explained with an analogy

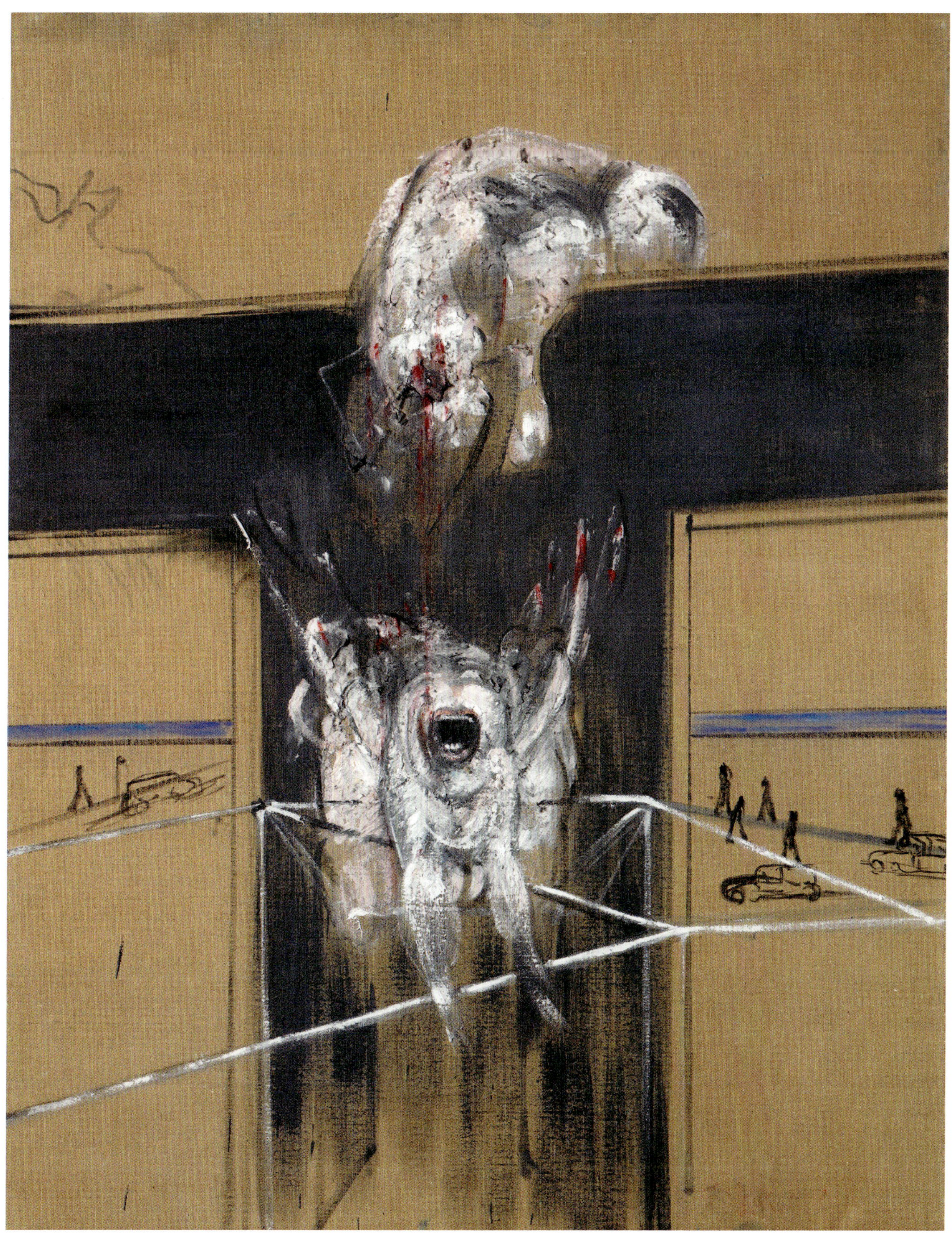

25. *Fragment of a Crucifixion*, 1950

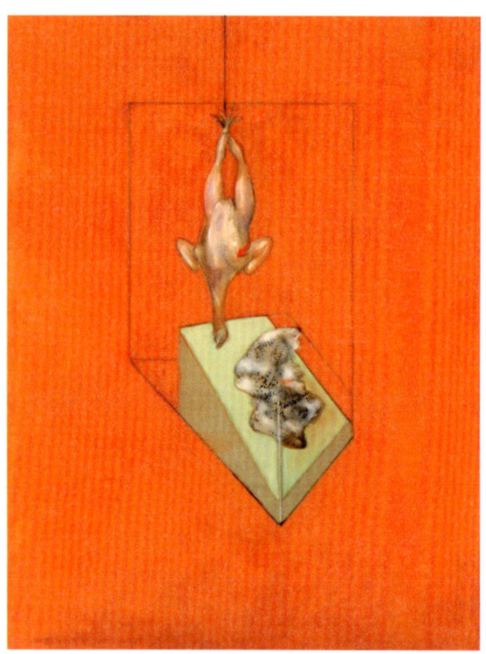

26. *Chicken*, 1982

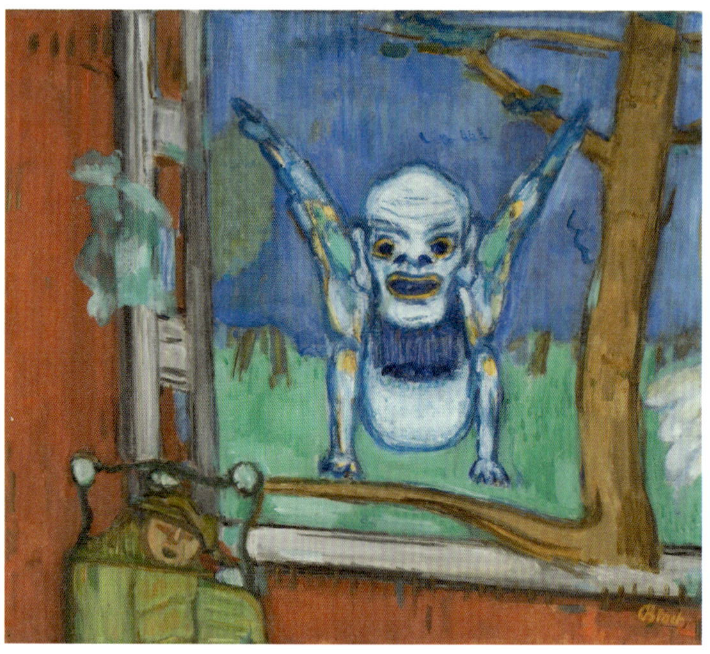

27. Martin Bloch, *Dream of the Dragon*, 1941
© The Martin Bloch Trust; photograph, Peter Mennim.

of two inseparable birds dwelling in a tree: one tastes the tree's fruits while the other only watches.

There are two paintings featuring birds within Bacon's oeuvre in which the birds have different statuses. In *Lying Figure in a Mirror*, 1971, [10] the swan and recumbent figure are an interpretation of Michelangelo's lost painting *Leda and the Swan*: the swan is Zeus in animal form.[41] The plucked chicken in *Chicken*, 1982, was originally the left panel of a triptych in which the right panel was a Fury. Bearing in mind Bacon's crucifixions, and one-time intention to paint an *Ecce Homo,* the chicken may be a cipher for Christ or Man. Bacon could have been reading Plato, who had defined Man as a featherless, biped animal; in response, Diogenes plucked a fowl and brought it to the *Akademia* saying 'Here is Plato's man'.[42]

The Furies were for the Ancient Greeks and Romans personifications of avenging spirits: projections of haunting guilt and fears of retribution. T. S. Eliot employs their benevolent aspect in *The Family Reunion*, 1939, in which they show Harry, who feels guilty over the death of his wife, how to cleanse himself of his guilt. For Bacon, the Furies or in later paintings, a Fury, represent his fears and, perhaps, his own aggression and resentment. As Howard Caygill discusses in 'Bacon's Cynegetic Vision',[43] Bacon's identification of himself as hunted, hunter, or both, follows the tradition of Aeschylus and hunting as a subject in the visual arts. In Classical art the abstract concept of an avenging spirit was described in terms of winged beings with a woman's body. Harpies, also female, were bird-bodied and human-headed. In the late inter-war period Bacon's friend and mentor Roy de Maistre ran an art school in London with the German artist, Martin Bloch. It is possible that Bacon saw Bloch's painting *Dream of the Dragon*, 1941 in which the creature hovering near a window has a marked affinity with Bacon's winged Furies. These Furies were always morphologically imaginary but animalian, and, in their later aerial form from 1974, appear to have been influenced by Max Ernst's Loplop bird paintings. By this time his figures had plain settings, although three exceptions have smudged floors. The solid colour surfaces do not convey disturbance or anxiety and had necessitated an alternative

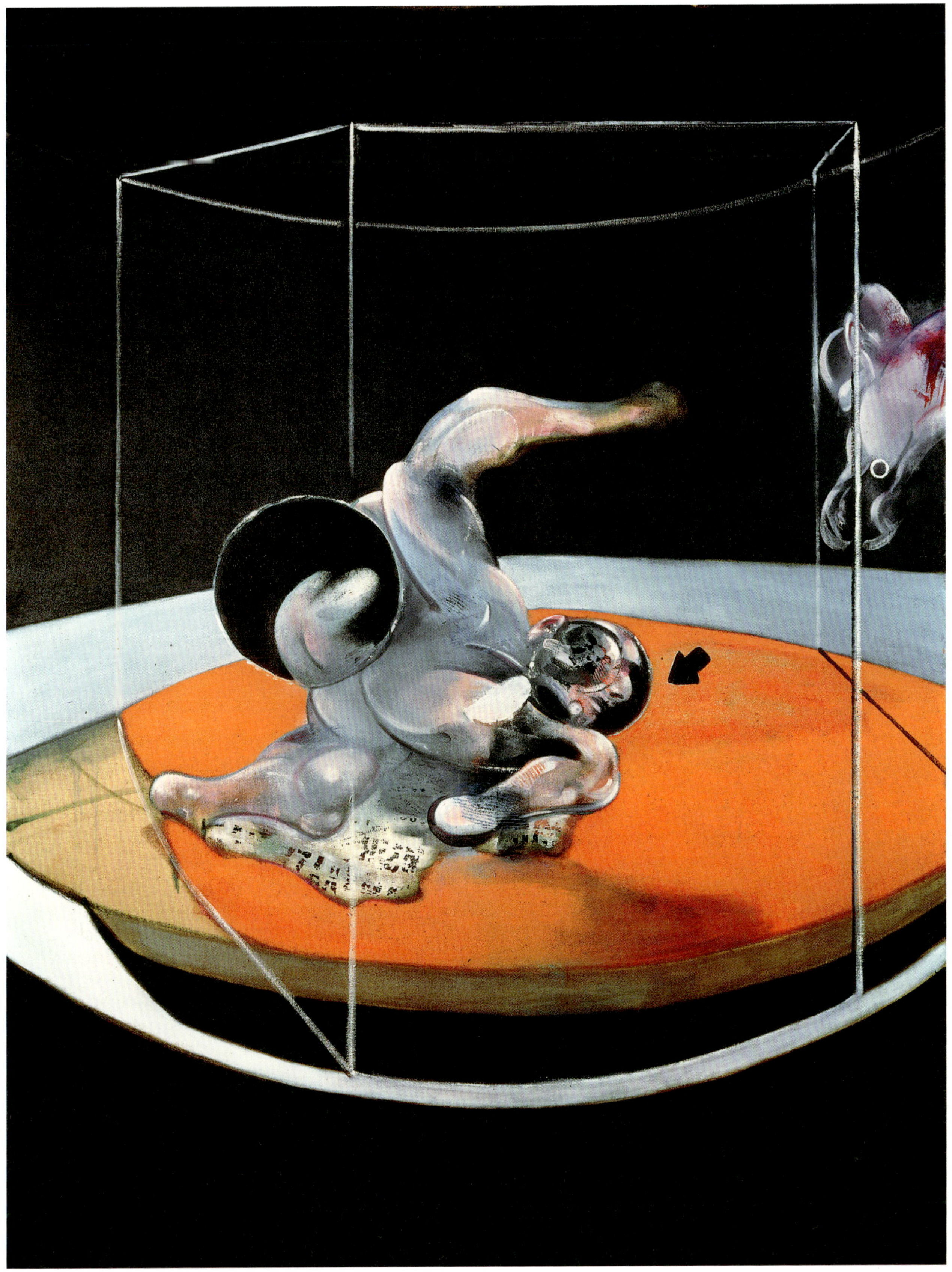

28. *Figure in Movement*, 1976

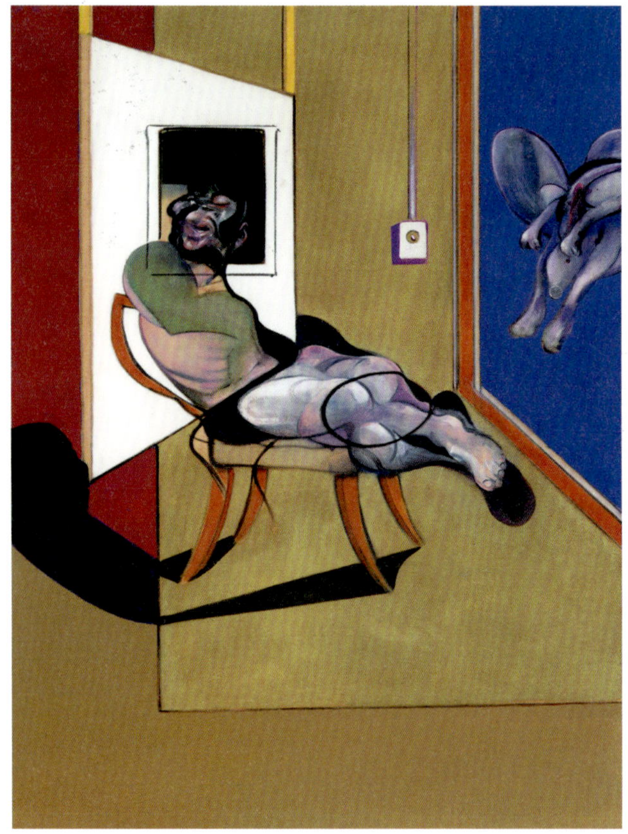

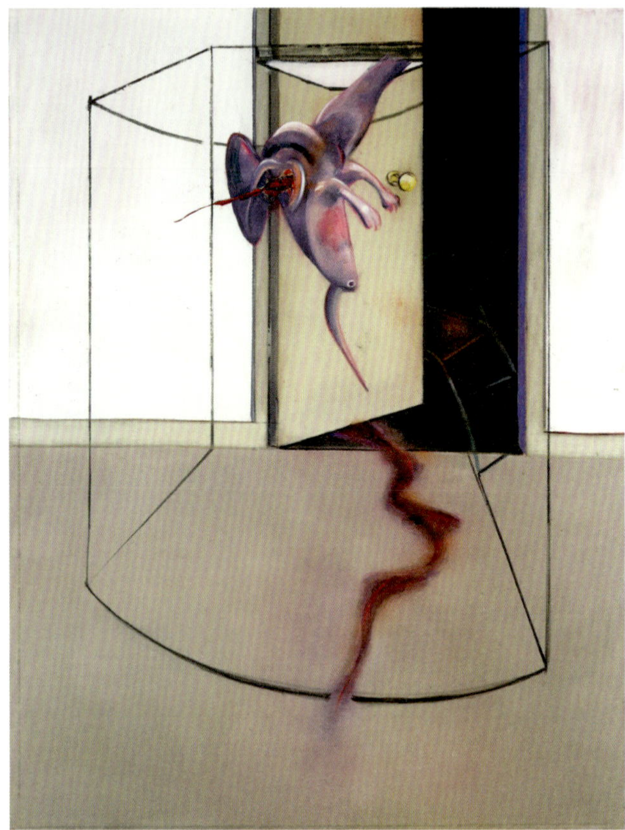

29. *Seated Figure*, 1974

30. *Triptych Inspired by the Oresteia of Aeschylus,* 1981 (left panel)

strategy: when Bacon needed an element to carry a sense of anxiety beyond the body of the figure, he introduced a Fury. Bacon's development of his Fury into an aerial being can be traced back to a sketch of c. 1936, in which a biomorph with two outstretched legs, seemingly based on a poultry carcass, is placed on a tripod. It was extended in the bio-forms of *Three Studies for Figures at the Base of a Crucifixion*, 1944, [102] through aerial internal organs with mammalian limbs in *Seated Figure*, 1974, to their final form which appeared first in *Triptych Inspired by the Oresteia of Aeschylus*, 1981.[44] In *Oedipus and the Sphinx after Ingres*, 1983, a Eumenides/Eryinys/Fury is about to enter the scene of Oedipus confronting the Sphinx. It advances through the air and, if Bacon was alluding to Sophocles's Oedipus plays, the Eryinys signals that Oedipus would die at a place sacred to the Eumenides.'[45] All seven of Bacon's later Furies are winged but featherless, with smooth leathery or offal-like skin. Although based on a sea bird, the featherless grey creatures invented by Bacon, despite being winged and in flight, resemble deep-sea creatures, with wings taking the form of lobes of liver.

In *Prometheus Bound*, Aeschylus refers to ornithomancy, the divination through birds' flight which was usual in Ancient Greece: '... I marked out many ways by which they might read the future, and among dreams I first discerned which are destined to come true; and voices baffling interpretation I explained to them, and signs from chance meetings. The flight of crook-taloned birds I distinguished clearly – which by nature are auspicious ...'[46] In the same speech Prometheus refers to 'the speckled symmetry of the liver-lobe' when further explaining his gift of divination to human-kind. In *Seated Figure*, 1974, and *Figure in Movement*, 1976, [28] the first winged Furies are featherless and have four limbs, but *Triptych Inspired by the Oresteia of Aeschylus*,

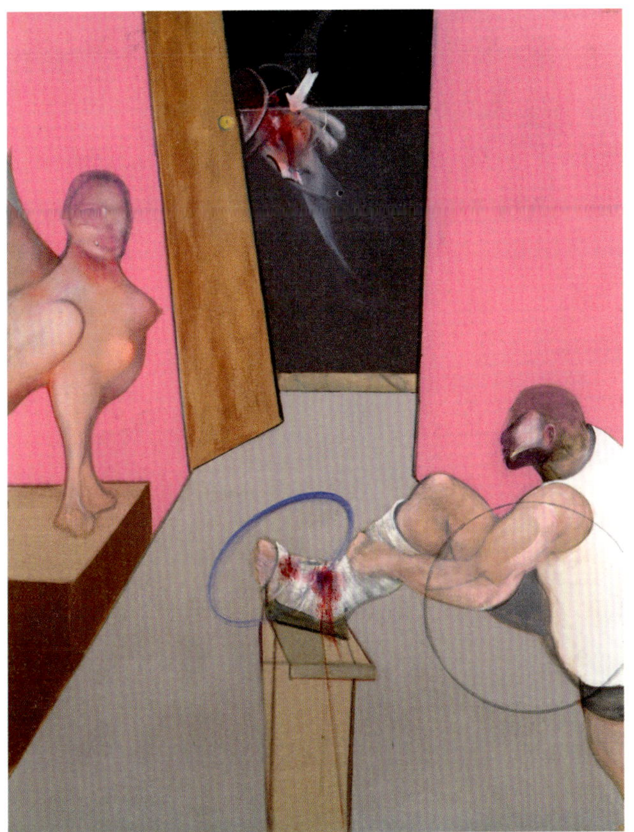

31. *Oedipus and the Sphinx after Ingres,* 1983

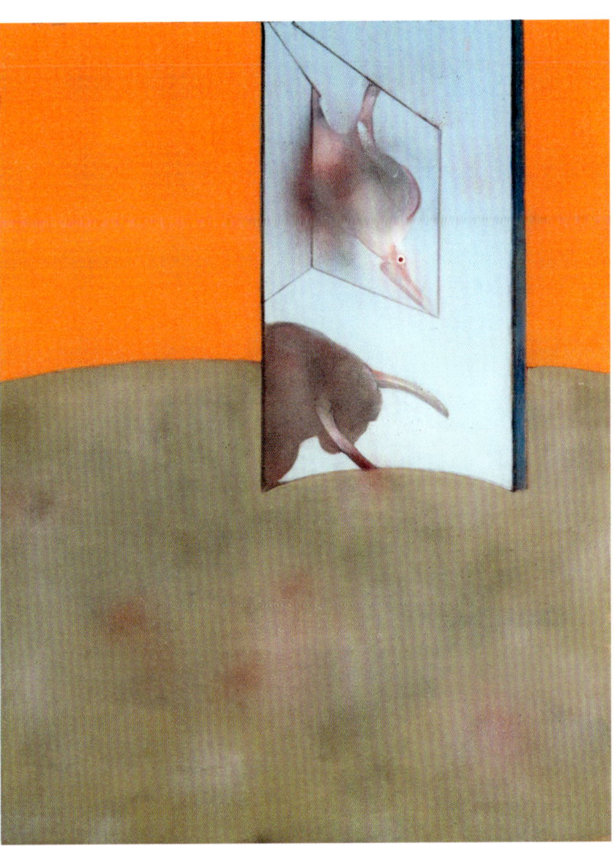

32. *Triptych,* 1987 (left panel)

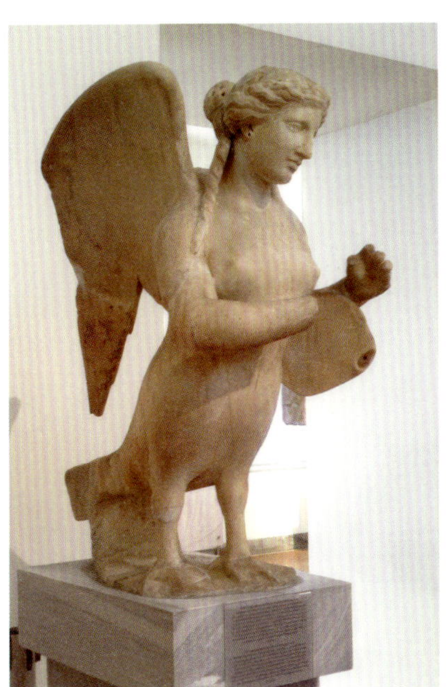

33. A siren. Funerary statue, Pentelic marble, coloured paint lost, c. 370 BC, National Archaeological Museum, Athens.

1981, marked the inception of six related Furies with a downward-pointing bill, based on a photograph of a brown pelican about to dive into the sea. Their bills have the aspect of weapons, and that in *Triptych*, 1987, echoes the horn of the shadowy bull beneath it. An intermediate bird form perches on a frame in the foreground of *Three Figures and Portrait*, 1975. [35] Possibly intended by Bacon to be a sculpture, it grins with a human mouth, like Tenniel's disquieting Cheshire Cat, and may be holding an egg. In *Oedipus and the Sphinx after Ingres,* 1983, Bacon modelled his bird-human hybrid sphinx on the c. 370 BC marble siren in the National Archaeological Museum, Athens. The funerary siren has smooth, blunt wings with a woman's head and arms and birds' feet, rather than feline paws. As he had modified Velázquez's Pope and Van Gogh's self-portraits, he proceeded to reimagine the painting by Ingres. The Fury is presented as injured; a strange detail – a patch of medical lint safety-pinned to its body – and the bloodied passage, combine to indicate that the efficacy of the avenging entity is to be questioned. Was Bacon saying that the old dispensation was waning? That what was once thought to be outlawed is less likely to be avenged or punished because the means of punishment are weakened? Or that the Eumenides have so many punishments to administer that they are exhausted?

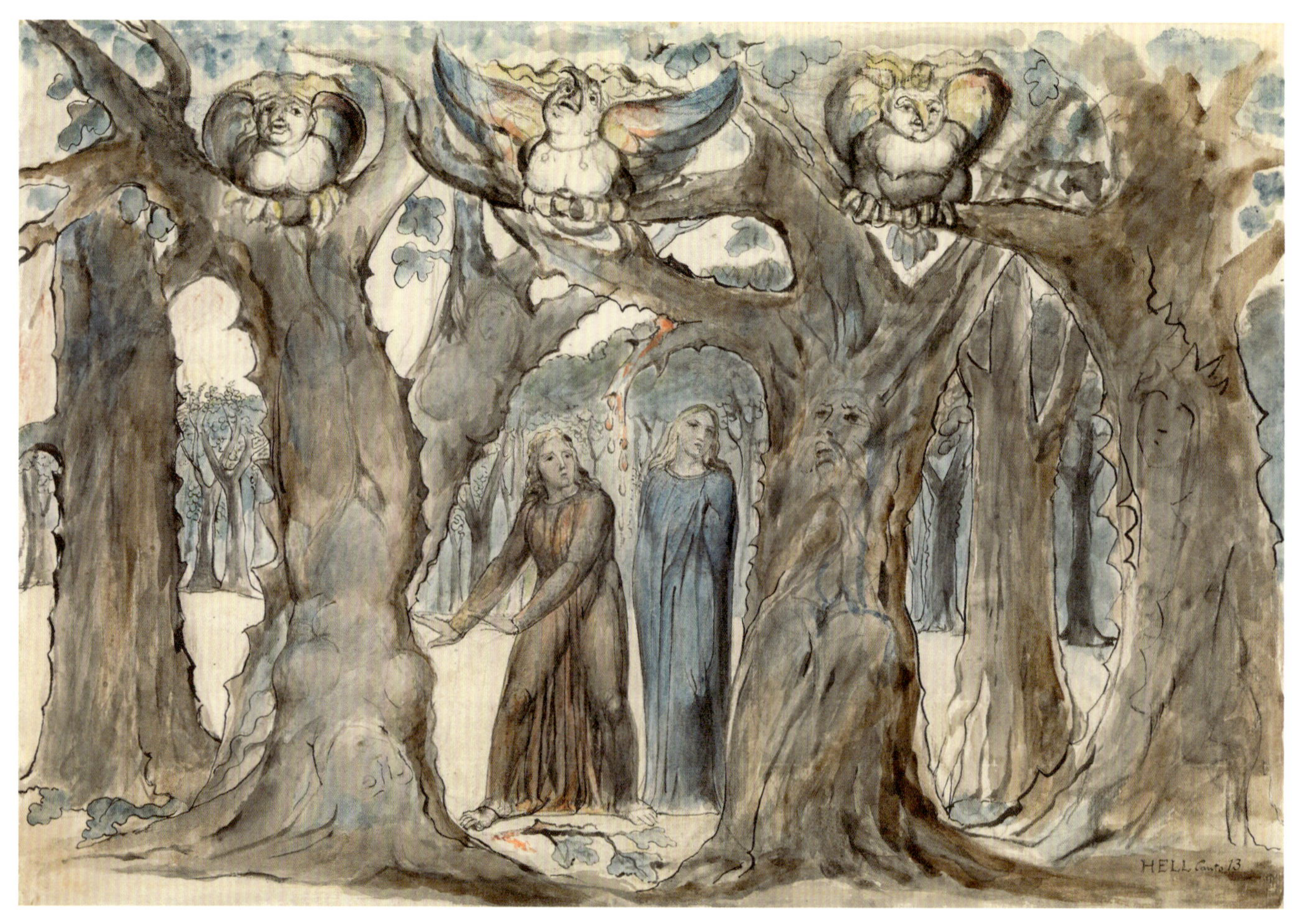

34. William Blake, *The Harpies and the Suicides* (illustration to *Dante's Divine Comedy*), 1824.

Harpies and sirens were both female, bird-woman hybrid creatures of Greek myth.
Blake's illustration of the Seventh Circle of Hell, where the violent are punished, is
shown to Dante by Virgil. Suicides trapped within trees are to be devoured by
harpies, which he depicts with beaked noses.

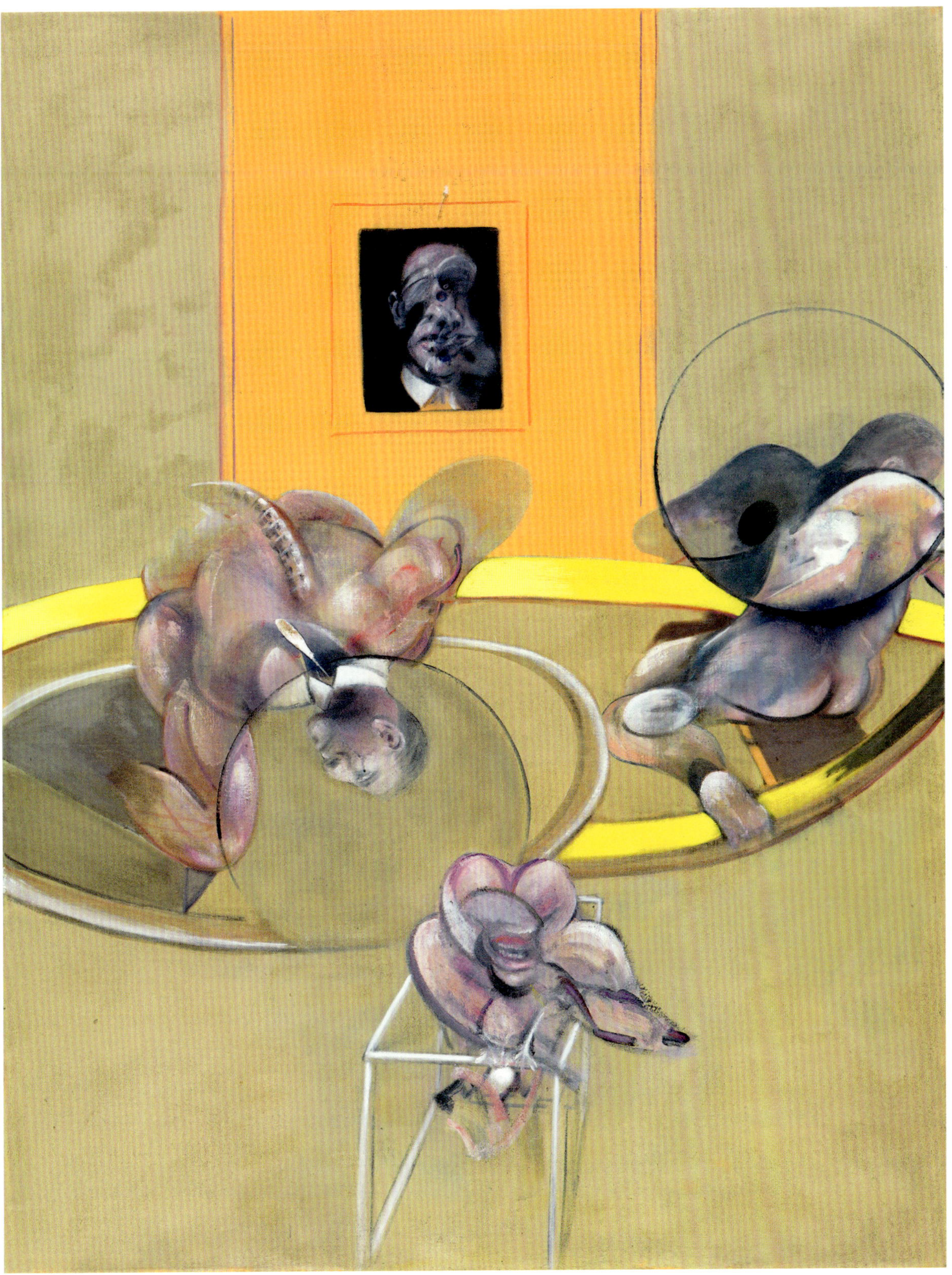

35. *Three Figures and Portrait,* 1975

Bacon created his own mythological harpies, which, unlike Blake's, have no visible female attributes. The implication of this Circle of Hell painting is George Dyer's potential punishment for self-murder.

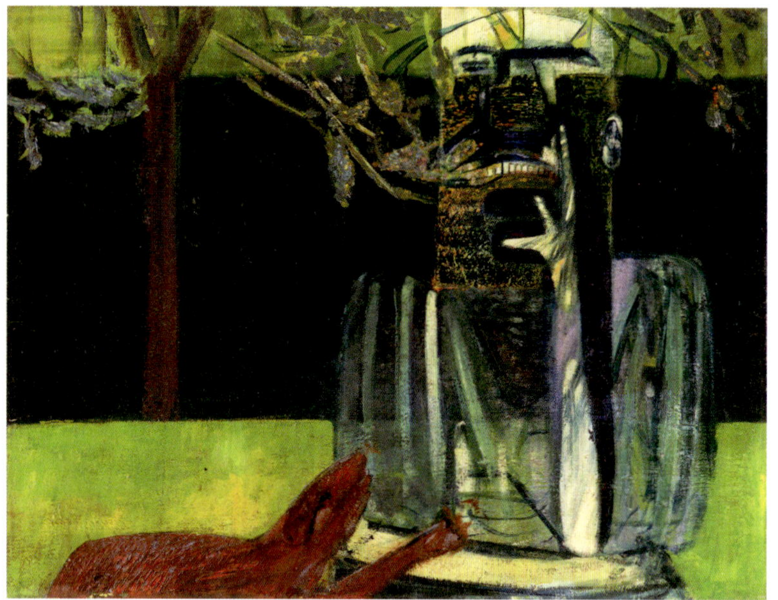

36. *Figures in a Garden*, c. 1935

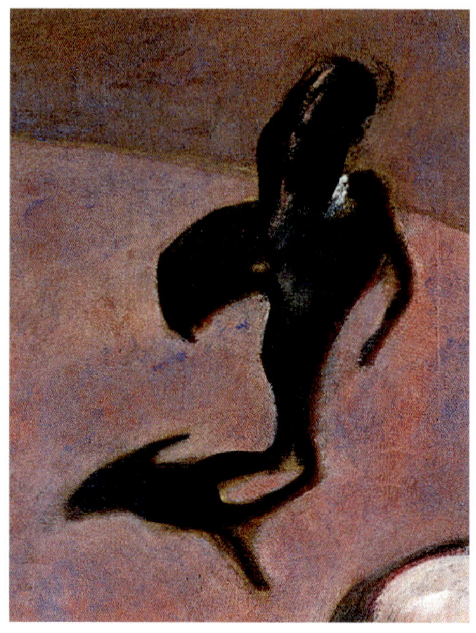

37. *Two Figures Lying on a Bed with Attendants*, 1968
(detail of left panel)

Shadows and Entities

Many artists painted Prometheus eviscerated, his liver consumed by an eagle, some depictions gorier than others. In privileging the liver, the Ancient Greeks examined the livers of sacrificial animals by hepatoscopy as a method of prognostication. Some of Bacon's figures have been partly eviscerated, but in *Portrait*, 1962, [44] *Portrait of Henrietta Moraes*, 1963, [41] and *Study for Portrait* (*with Two Owls*), 1963, [45] the guts develop into, or release, a discrete shadow-being or entity – dark, animalistic, emergent manifestations. According to Plato, the area in the abdomen where the liver was placed was also the seat of part of the soul. He described an image of the soul as a wild animal that was chained up with a man. Unlike, say, Munch, whose *The Scream* expresses anxiety in the form of the wraith's melodramatic gesture and the swirling sky and water, Bacon displaces the fear into a separate zone, one in which the traumatised 'soul' is represented as a shadow-being or a daemon.

In *Figures in a Garden*, c. 1935, a canine approaches an ambiguous spectral idol. It reaches up to the statue-like figure in a gesture reminiscent of Caxton's illustration for Aesop's fable, *The Fox and Grapes*. Although Bacon's statue/idol is static, its inchoate, shadowy formation renders it a powerful if enigmatic and rather awkward presence. From the emergence of the animated, morphing shadow in *Three Studies for Figures at the Base of a Crucifixion*, 1944 (in which a shadow is both a patch of grass and a rug), to their evolution into the silhouette entity in *Two Figures Lying on a Bed with Attendants*, 1968, Bacon's shadows function to unsettle. He wrote on a page of Eadweard Muybridge's photographs of a nude male boxing, 'Make shadow into separate unit.'[47] His shadows developed from discrete units into animated entities with a separate existence. In *Two Figures Lying on a Bed with Attendants,* one shadow-being has acquired a devil-like appearance and casts its own shadow. Neither the clothed nor naked George Dyer has a shadow that would be cast by his body, instead they are resituated in the two mirrors, where they exist in another dimension. 'Dressed George's' shadow is naked, but 'Naked George's' is pure silhouette; nonetheless, both entities have their own shadow. Might the two attendant Dyers indicate that Bacon had been reading Desmond Morris's recently published *The Naked Ape*?[48]

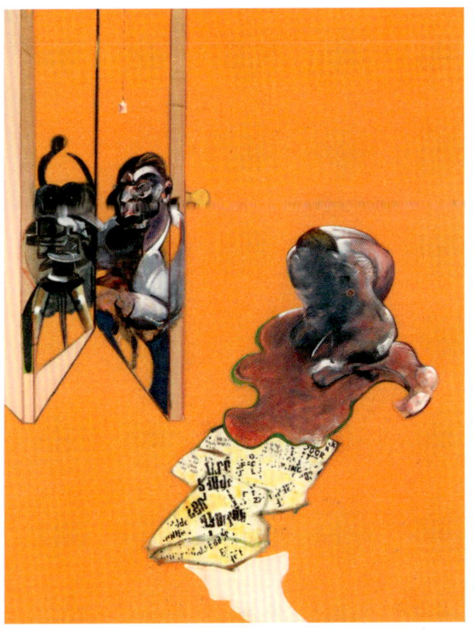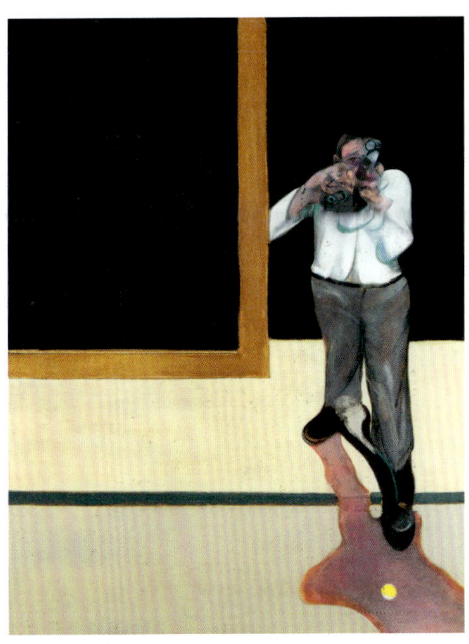

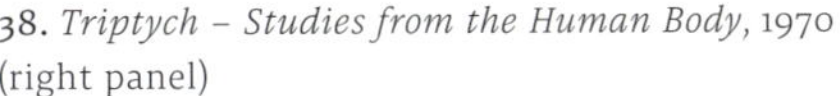

38. *Triptych – Studies from the Human Body*, 1970 (right panel)

39. *Triptych March 1974* (right panel)

In *Triptych – Studies from the Human Body*, 1970, the right panel has a full-length self-portrait standing side by side with a hybrid-anthropomorphic item of equipment. The tripod and cine-camera have assumed a sinister, living quality through their strange silhouette.[49] The tripod, which had originated in Bacon's iconography in 1933, here supports a two-lensed camera. Similarly, the standing figure who resembles Bacon in the right panel of *Triptych March 1974*, trains a cine-camera on the viewer. The three men in the triptych have pinkish flesh-like shadows which flow like liquid across a pavement and down a kerb. These animated shadows have forms that are semi-independent of the bodies which cast them.

As a child, Bacon's asthma attacks were treated by burning stramonium powders in his bedroom. Inhaling the fumes calms the lungs' lining, but the active content of the plant from which it is derived, *Datura stramonium*,[50] is a deliriant and hallucinogen known, anecdotally, to cause hallucinations and pareidolia. Having experienced such symptoms might have informed Bacon's depictions of distorted, living shadows and his extending the process into the forms of his 'shadow people'.

By turning shadows into quasi-living elements, Bacon increased their potential to extend and complicate his pictorial language; they augment what may be discerned from the main figures and setting. As he had borrowed the gestures of primates for his human figures, in a comparable exercise he shifted animal movement and forms onto shadows thrown by the figures, or even inanimate elements such as furniture. Bacon termed his flesh-pink shadows 'pools of flesh'.[51] Instead of figures casting their own shadows, contrarily he painted 'figures arising out of their own flesh.'[52] If the shadows of Bacon's figures in *Triptych March 1974*, are flesh, might the life within their bodies, their inner spirits, by implication be dead? He undermines logical assumptions, reversing normality, for unless dead, flesh is alive and potentially sentient. The haunting photographs of flash burn 'shadows' formed by the atomic bomb blast in Hiroshima record traces of living humans at the instant of death. The surroundings had been 'bleached' by intense heat and light; dark body-shaped patches were protected from the flash – extraordinary shadows of the Nuclear Age.

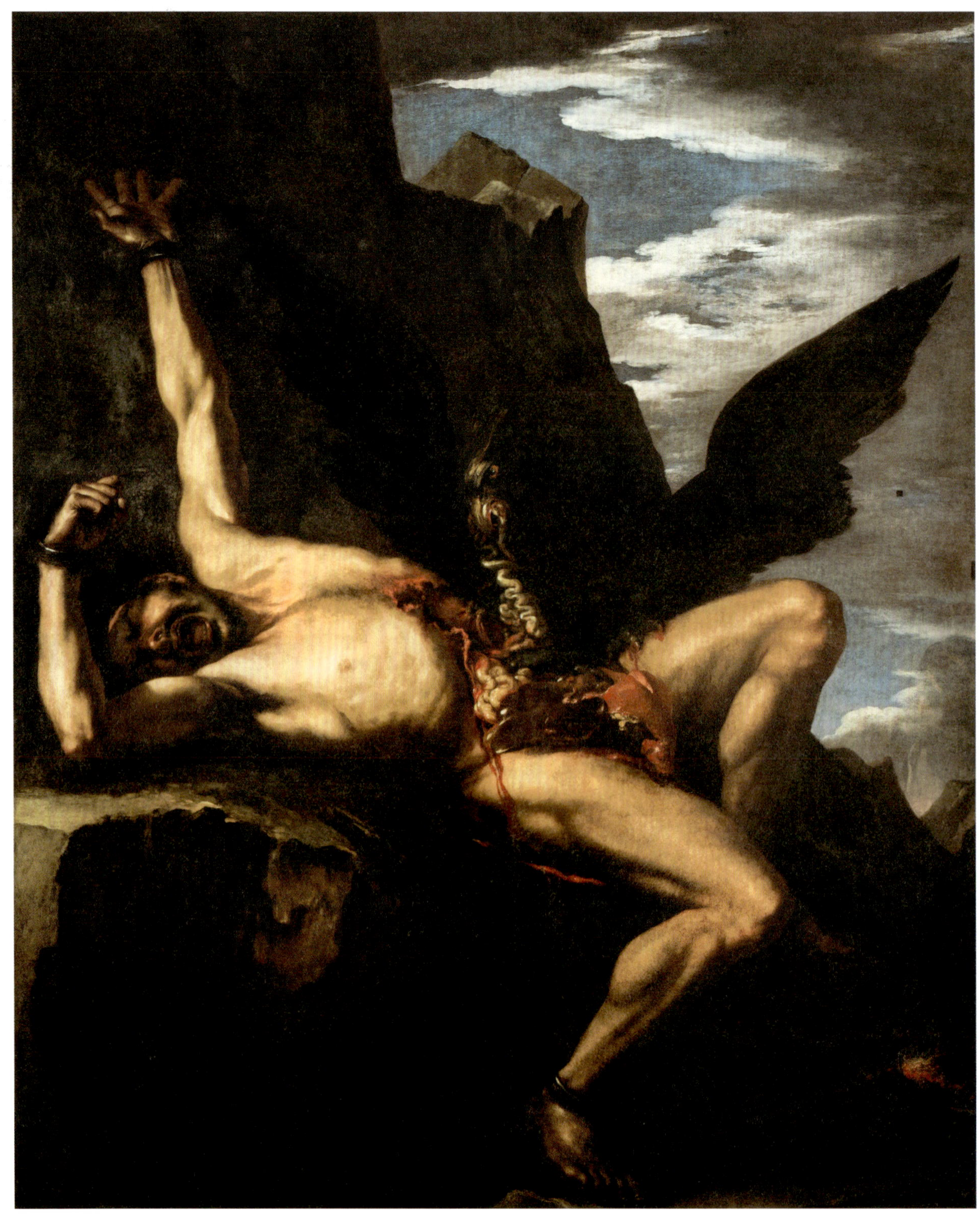

40. Salvator Rosa, *The Torture of Prometheus*, 1646–1648, Galleria Corsini, Rome.

The myth of Prometheus, bringer of fire and civilisation to humanity was dramatised by Aeschylus in *Prometheus Bound*.
The eagle of Zeus consumes Prometheus's guts daily; Rosa's depiction of live entrails gives them an identity. Bacon's
rendition of Henrietta Moraes's internal organs coming to life is an interpretation of the dark entity of her inner demon.

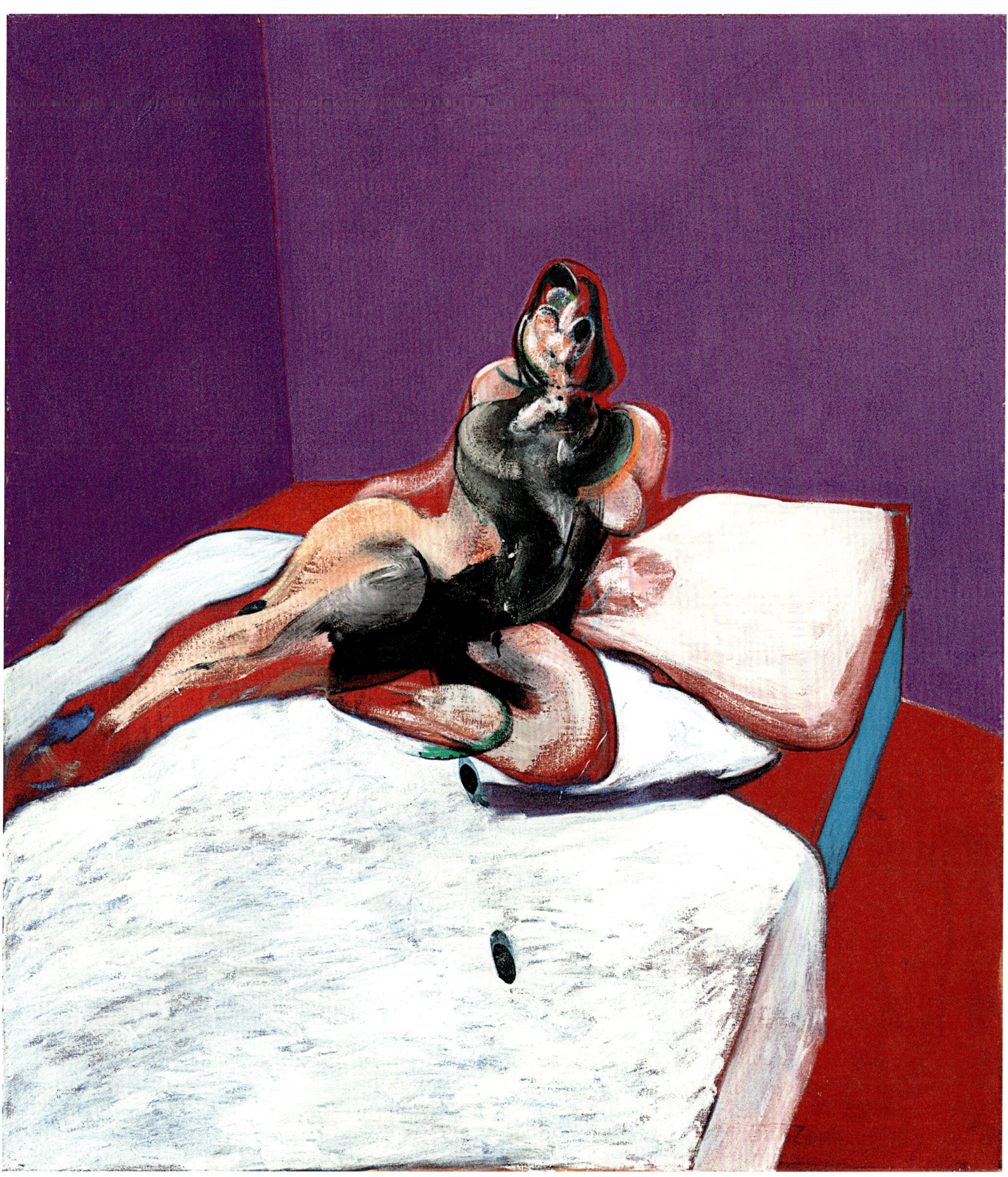

41. *Portrait of Henrietta Moraes*, 1963

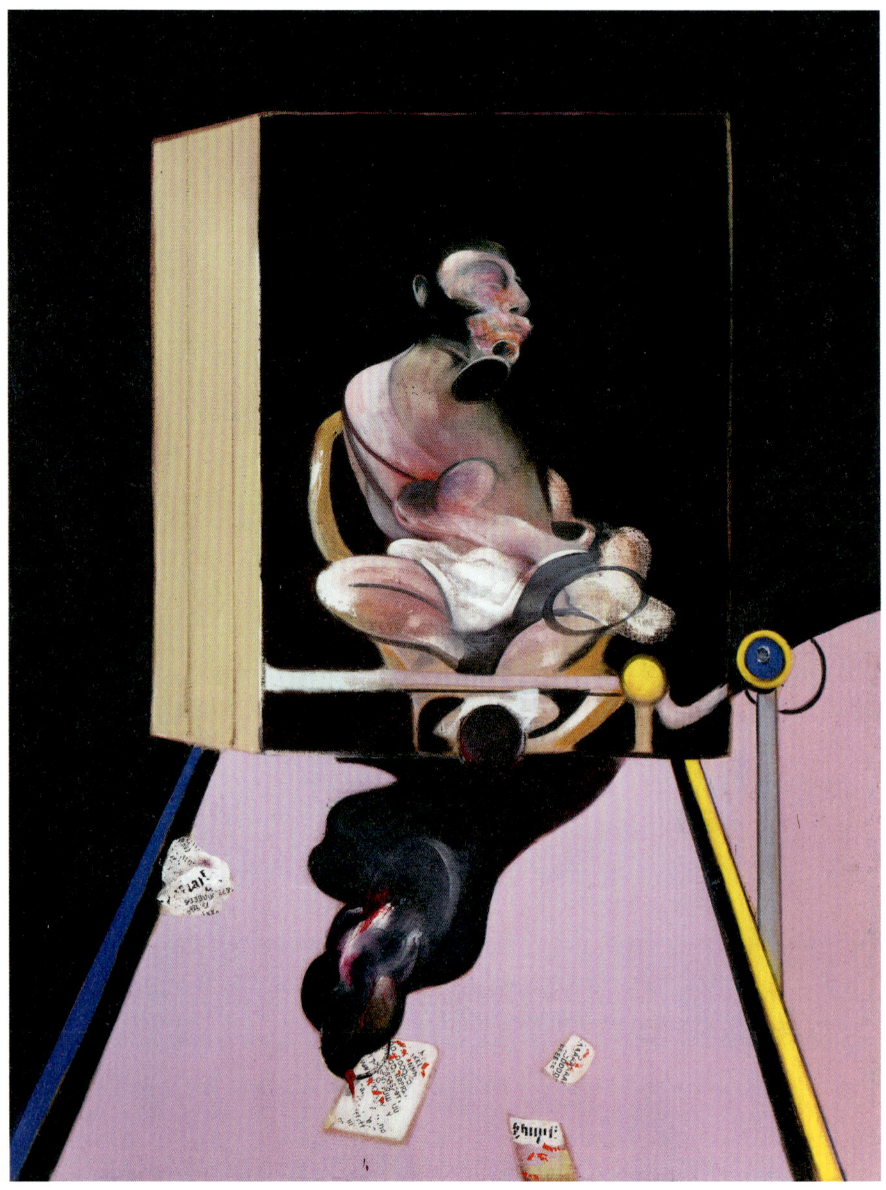

42. *Study for Portrait*, 1977

In many of the chairs and tables Bacon painted, their arms, legs and backs cast animated shadows that imply the furniture is on the prowl, perhaps in a surrealist pun. The 'living shadow' also invokes temporality; in a quiet room everything might be absolutely still, but shadows would move during the day or fall in different places when a lamp was turned on. In *Study for Portrait*, 1977, a shadow falls towards the foreground; it is a wounded shadow, an oddly poetic concept. George Dyer, who casts the shadow, had died six years earlier but was metaphorically still casting a shadow over Bacon's memories. Dyer had suffered with mental health and alcohol addiction problems, and Bacon, who made the painting in Paris, where Dyer had died, is recalling his lover's struggles by distorting and bruising Dyer's shadow into a turbulent injured form.

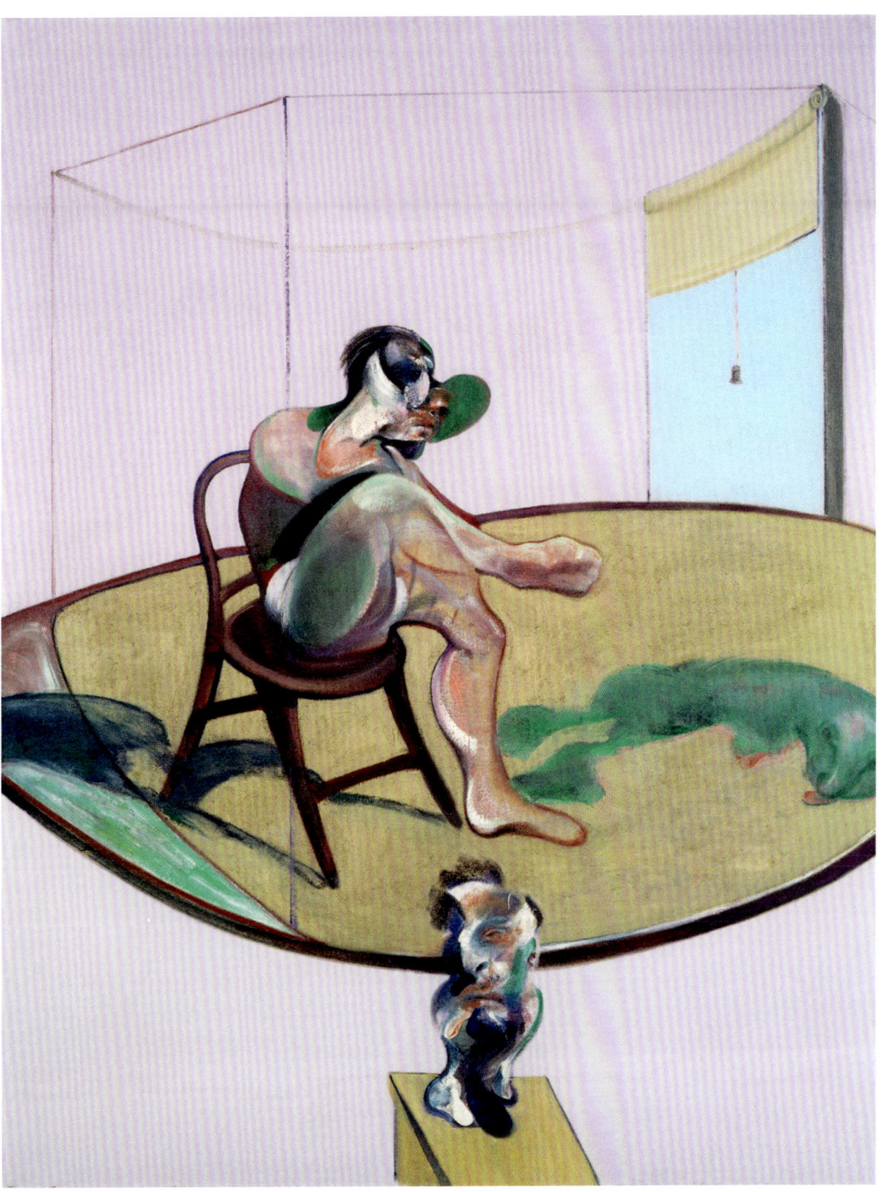

43. *Two Studies of George Dyer with Dog*, 1968

In *Two Studies of George Dyer with Dog*, 1968, the eponymous dog is represented in the form of a green apparition-like shadow, a hybrid dog/human shadow. The apparition's legs are almost attached to Dyer's foot, like Peter Pan's shadow. The green shadow is theatrically cast over an arena-like floor where it performs with what might be a pink tongue protruding; the entity-shadow does not look well. Bacon may have remembered from his books on mythology that the Romans believed they had a threefold soul, comprising Manes, Anima and Umbra. The Umbra or Shade 'hovered about the body as unwilling to quit it.'[53] As an admirer of Rodin, whose three identical bronze 'Shades' (*Les Trois Ombres*)[54] preside over his *La Porte de l'Enfer*, Bacon may have been inspired to devise shades for his painted figures.

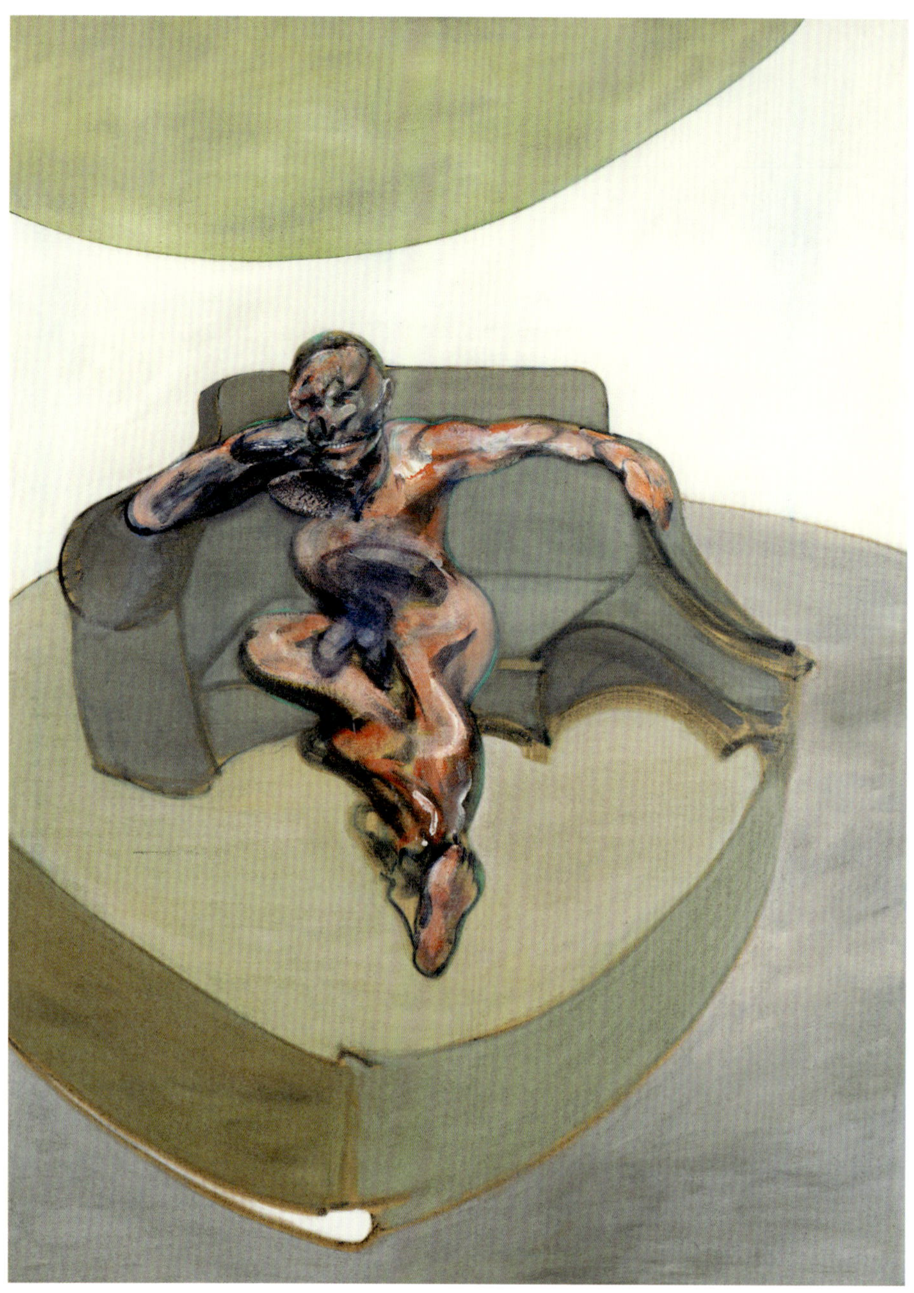

44. *Portrait,* 1962

In his most extreme portrayals of daemons, Bacon almost invariably had recourse to the presence of animals. In *Study for Portrait (with Two Owls)*, 1963, for example, in which the form that slides from the Pope's lap resembles a black angel, the horror of the scene – it is arguably Bacon's most violently distorted rendition of Pope Innocent X – is witnessed by two impassive owls. It would be the last of Bacon's paintings in which entrails spewed forth, and his penultimate Pope. The tentative 'Study for' of the title represents a typical Bacon time warp;[55] it is a kind of prequel, as though he were imagining himself to be Velázquez, trying out variations in preparation for his final magnificent work.

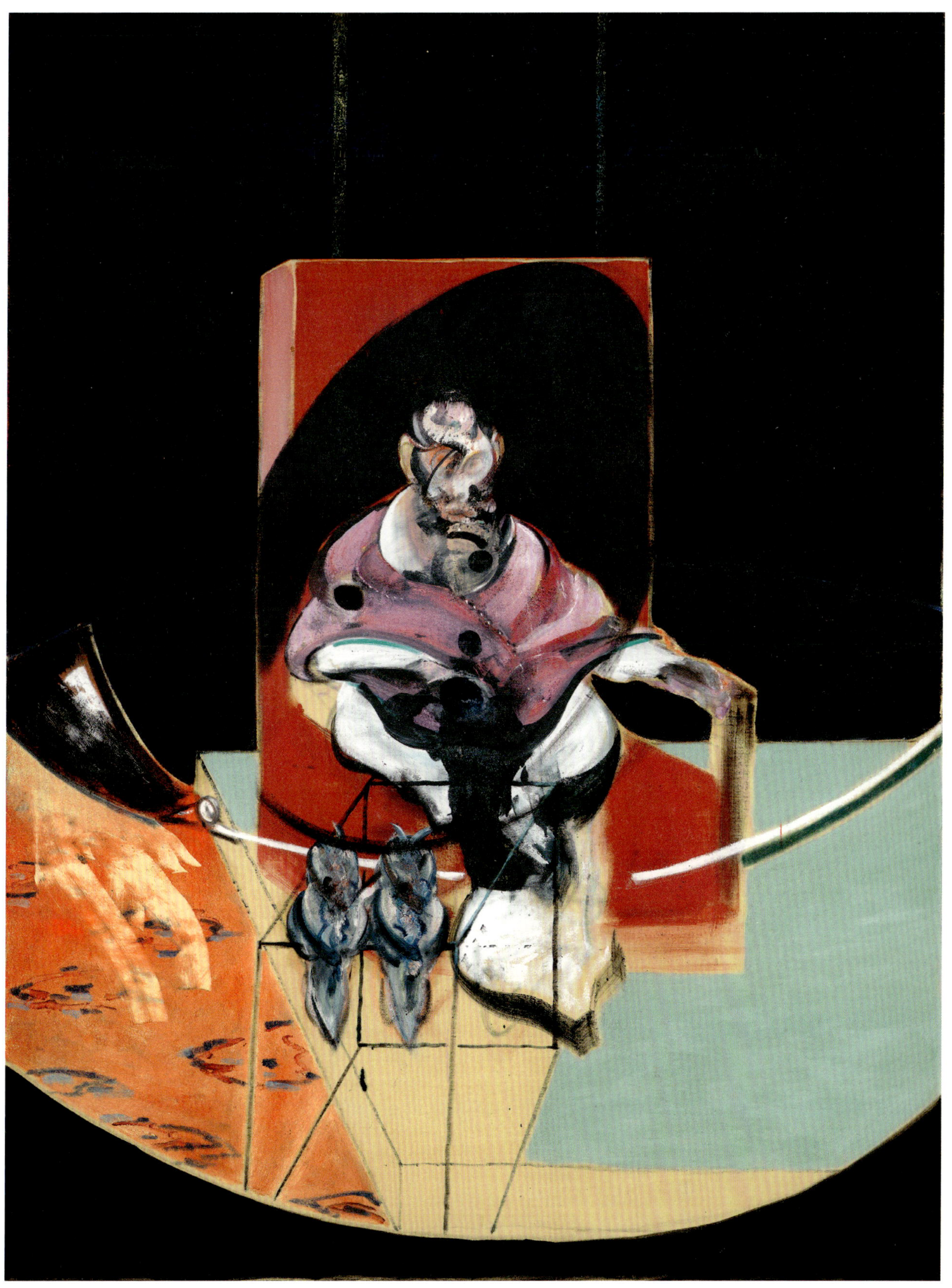

45. *Study for Portrait (with Two Owls)*, 1963

Endnotes

1. The principal exception, *Francis Bacon: Man and Beast* (London: Royal Academy of Arts, 2021), takes different approaches to mine. For the purposes of the present text, several of the categories of animals that Bacon painted have been omitted.

2. David Sylvester, *Interviews with Francis Bacon* (London: Thames & Hudson, 1997), p. 83; hereafter, *Interviews*.

3. *Interviews*, p. 136. In fact, Bacon recognised that he wasn't unusual in this, adding: 'I think it happens to every artist that things just drop in like slides.'

4. Pareidolia: seeing faces in inanimate objects; a tendency to perceive specific, often meaningful images in a random or ambiguous visual pattern.

5. *Interviews*, p. 82.

6. Ibid.

7. Of the extant paintings by Bacon, ten include apes or monkeys, ten a dog, six a bull and eight other mammals – horses, fox, cat, elephant, bear, camel, goat and rhinoceros. Birds are present in over thirteen paintings and eleven feature mythological Furies, whose forms Bacon invented.

8. These entries are extracted from Bacon's handwritten notes on the endpapers of a copy of V. J. Stanek, *Introducing Monkeys*, trans. George Theiner (London: Spring Books, 1958); Hugh Lane Gallery, Dublin.

9. 1 Kings 10:22

10. The Bacon's Books database at The Hugh Lane Gallery, Dublin, contains seven volumes on Egyptian art, including Hermann Ranke, *The Art of Ancient Egypt* (Vienna: Phaidon Press; London: George Allen & Unwin Ltd., 1936). In this book, we are told in the introduction, plates 48 and 49 show 'the oldest Egyptian religious image preserved to us', an alabaster baboon, the sacred animal of the God of Wisdom, Thoth, held in the Egyptian Museum in Berlin. In the captions Ranke uses the term cynocephalic but in his text he uses baboons.

11. Baba is a possible etymological origin of baboon, via the Latin babbuino. Interestingly, baba translates as 'father' in Arabic.

12. Papio hamadryas, (Latin). Thoth's attendant Astennu/A'ani, recorder in the judgment of the dead, was represented as a hamadryas baboon.

13. Cercopes is Ancient Greek for tailed; kerkos = tail.

14. The Cercopeses' name was adopted by taxonomists for the old-world monkey family, Cercopithecidae, which includes macaques, colobus and baboons. It may also be relevant that Bacon's triptych was painted shortly after the decriminalisation of homosexuality.

15. Jasia Reichardt, 'Developments in Style–V: Francis Bacon', *The London Magazine*, June 1962, p. 40.

16. Charles Darwin, *On the Origin of Species by Means of Natural Selection, or the Preservation of Favoured Races in the Struggle for Life* (London: John Murray, 1859).

17. Charles Darwin, *The Descent of Man, and Selection in Relation to Sex* (London: John Murray, 1871).

18. Charles Darwin, *The Expression of the Emotions in Man and Animals* (London: John Murray, 1872).

19. Friedrich Nietzsche, *Thus Spake Zarathustra* (London: Henry & Co., 1896); 4 vols. (Z:1 'Prologue' 3; cf. KSA 10:3 [1] 403).

20. Nietzsche's *The Gay Science*, which preceded *Thus Spake Zarathustra*, has a complicated publishing history. The English translation of the title was originally *The Joyful Wisdom*, and was only replaced by *The Gay Science* after Walter Kaufmann's translation of 1974.

21. The diaries kept by Eric Allden in 1930 and 1931 are lost, but it is known he was impressed by Paul Robeson's performance in 1924 when he saw him in New York in Eugene O'Neill's play *Emperor Jones*. It is highly likely that Allden, a regular theatregoer, possibly with Bacon, would have seen *The Hairy Ape* when Robeson starred in it at The Ambassadors in 1931, as we know he saw O'Neill's *Anna Christie* in 1937.

22. Aldous Huxley, *Ape and Essence* (London: Chatto and Windus, 1948). The novel's title is a quote from Shakespeare's *Measure for Measure*, in which Isabella complains: 'But man, proud man, Drest in a little brief authority, Most ignorant of what he's most assur'd; His glassy essence, like an angry ape, Plays such fantastic tricks before high heaven, As make the angels weep'.

23. Martin Harrison, *Francis Bacon Catalogue Raisonné* (London: Estate of Francis Bacon, 2016), p. 170.

24. R. M. Yerkes, *Chimpanzees: A Laboratory Colony* (New Haven: Yale University Press, 1943), plate 62.

25. Amédée Ozenfant, trans. John Rodker, *Foundations of Modern Art* (New York: Dover Publications, 1952). This was first published in France in 1928 and titled *Art*; Bacon owned both the 1931 translation and the Dover Publications edition; hereafter, Ozenfant.

26. Ozenfant, pp. 59; 243. The photograph captioned 'Sir Austen Chamberlain in a distorting mirror' accompanies a text on distortion.

27. Ozenfant, p. 174.

28. Ozenfant, p. 173.

29. Ibid. Given the importance of *Foundations of Modern Art* for Bacon, he must have been familiar with the Ozenfant

Academy of Fine Art, the school Ozenfant ran in Kensington from 1936 until 1939, when he emigrated to New York.

30. Wyndham Lewis, 'Round the London Art Galleries', *Listener*, 12 May 1949, pp. 811–12; 17 November 1949, p. 860.

31. Wyndham Lewis, *The Apes of God* (London: The Arthur Press, 1930). Bacon had taken Lewis's novel *Tarr* with him on a holiday in Ireland in October 1929.

32. Wyndham Lewis, *The Wild Body. A Soldier of Humour and Other Stories* (London: Chatto and Windus, 1927). A collection of short stories, with an explanatory section, 'The Meaning of the Wild Body.'

33. H. G. Wells, *The Works of H G Wells*, Introduction, vol. ii, Atlantic Edition (London: Fisher Unwin, 1924).

34. Mary Shelley, *Frankenstein, Or the Modern Prometheus* (London: John Murray, 1831).

35. John Milton, *Paradise Lost*, Book X, lines 743–45.

36. https://medicalmuseum.health.mil/index.cfm?p=visit. exhibits.virtual.xraydiscovery.index

37. Ozenfant, p. 59.

38. Ozenfant, p. 60.

39. In this essay the mythological deities that Bacon usually called Eumenides are referred to as Furies – the English translation of their Roman counterparts Furiea or Direa. In Ancient Greek culture the Eryinys were goddesses of vengeance thought to live in Erebus (the Underworld). So as not to incur their wrath, they were euphemistically referred to as Eumenides (Gracious or Kindly Ones). In Aeschylus's Oresteia, the third play, The Eumenides, concludes with the Eryinys' conversion into Eumenides by Athena.

40. 'Or if he had died as often as reports claimed, then truly he might have had three bodies, a second Geryon, and have boasted of having taken on him a triple cloak of earth, one death for each different shape.' *Aeschylus, Agamemnon*, trans. Herbert Weir Smyth (Cambridge, MA: Harvard University Press; London: William Heinemann, 1926) vol. 2, line 869 ff.

41. On Leda and the Swan, see Amanda J. Harrison, 'A Sudden Blow', *Francis Bacon: Monaco et la culture française* (Paris: Albin Michel, 2016), pp. 96–112.

42. Diogenes Laërtius, trans. R. D. Hicks, *Lives of Eminent Philosophers* (Cambridge, MA: Harvard University Press, 1925), vol. 2, book 6, p. 40. Loeb Classical Library.

43. Howard Caygill, 'Bacon's Cynegetic Vision', *Francis Bacon Studies II, Francis Bacon: Painting, Philosophy, Psychoanalysis* (London: The Estate of Francis Bacon Publishing, 2019), pp. 20–40.

44. In the film made in 1963 in Bacon's studio by RTS (Radio Télévision Suisse), Bacon discussed, in French, his *Study for Portrait (with Two Owls)*, 1963. As Bacon gestured towards the painting he spoke about the owls and asked for the French word for the Fates (rather than Furies), then clarified that he meant the characters in Aeschylus's plays. It could have been a slip (he had obviously been drinking alcohol), but, at this point, Bacon may have felt Furies and Fates to be one and the same – harsh, female, personifications controlling his destiny, delivering punishment for crimes, and that owls stood in as actors of a similar role. Bacon accepted the translation 'Les Soeurs' (the sisters), a term used in French for the Eumenides, although 'Les Fureurs' (Furies) or Euménides is more usual.

45. In Oedipus at Colonus, as prophesied by Tiresias in Oedipus Rex, Oedipus dies and is buried in the grove sacred to the Eryinys at Colonus.

46. *Aeschylus, Prometheus Bound*, trans. Herbert Weir Smyth (Cambridge, MA: Harvard University Press; London: William Heinemann, 1926), vol. 1, lines 485–500.

47. For Bacon's marked copy, see: Hugh Lane Gallery Database, RM98F:59.

48. Desmond Morris, *The Naked Ape* (London: Jonathan Cape, 1967).

49. The form is reminiscent of Jacob Epstein's *Rock Drill*, 1913, in its original state, and must also have taken account of Graham Sutherland's and Henry Moore's anthropomorphic standing figures of 1953; see, for example, Graham Sutherland, *Three Standing Forms in Black*, lithograph, 1953; Henry Moore, *Three Standing Forms*, bronze, 1953 (Solomon R. Guggenheim Museum, New York).

50. Mark Jackson, 'Divine Stramonium: The Rise and Fall of Smoking for Asthma', *Medical History*, April 2010; 54(2), pp. 171–94.

51. *Interviews*, p. 83.

52. Ibid.

53. Ed. Betty Kirkpatrick, *Brewer's Concise Dictionary of Phrase and Fable* (Oxford: Helicon, 1992), p. 645; first published in 1870.

54. The figures originally pointed to the phrase 'Lasciate ogne speranza, voi ch'intrate' ('Abandon all hope, ye who enter here'), from Canto III of Dante's *Inferno*.

55. For example, *Study from the Human Body*, 1949; *Study After Velázquez*, 1960: also note the similarly provisional use of 'fragment', as in *Fragment of a Crucifixion*, 1950.

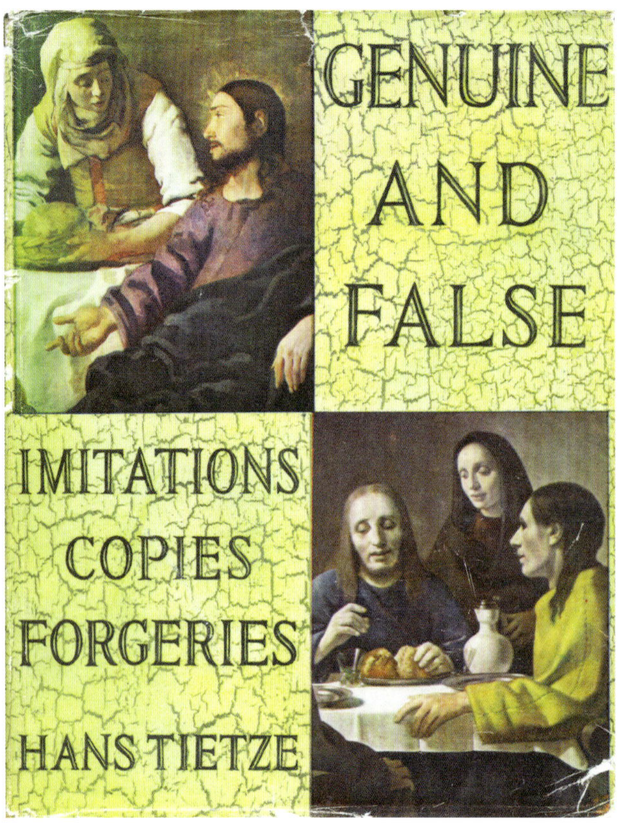

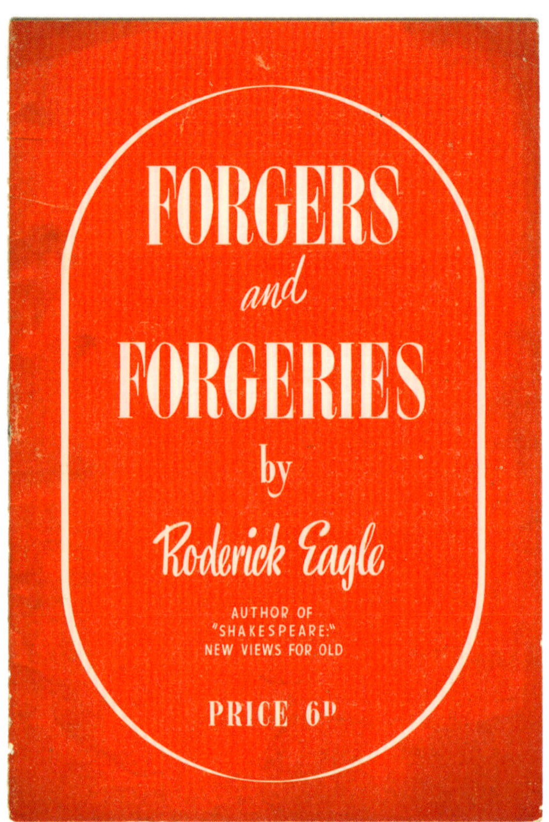

46. Art forgery, which has a very long history, was becoming more sophisticated by the nineteenth century. The cover of Hans Tietze's book (1948) shows Han van Meegeren's putative Vermeer, *Supper at Emmaus*, and his copy of *Christ in the House of Martha and Mary*. Roderick Eagle's booklet, *Forgers and Forgeries* (1944), was published, amusingly, for the Bacon Society.

In Whose Name? Some Thoughts on Art Forgery

Darian Leader

The fascination with the lives and methods of art forgers has tended to obscure study of those who sell, deal or attempt to deal in forgeries. Although historically it has sometimes been the forger themself who sells these products, this has been the exception rather than the rule, and the involvement of multiple figures at different stages of the process has complicated the question of culpability at both a personal and a judicial level. One of the curious facts here is how the sellers – unlike the forgers – may actually come to share a belief in the authenticity of the works, despite 'knowing' that they are fakes. How can this psychological situation come about?

Curiously, almost all studies of the motives of forgery sale have downplayed financial gain as the central feature. The effect of initial 'successes' in selling works for substantial sums may create circuits in which income has to be maintained, but other factors such as revenge on the art world or establishing one's own status as an important supplier or donor have tended to be seen as more significant here (Charney 2015). In some cases, indeed, works are never sold but donated to institutions: the Charles Courtney Curran forger Mark Landis would even gift at a loss, paying for frames and materials himself.

Yet if figures like Landis or the Samuel Palmer forger Tom Keating seemed to have little investment in claiming their works were genuine when scrutinised, those purveying the works may still insist on their authenticity. Experts may also continue to guarantee a work even after its legitimacy has been refuted, at one level perhaps to save their reputation but at another because the belief in it cannot be abandoned (Lenaian 2011). Provenance may be demonstrably fictitious yet is still passionately defended. How can two apparently contradictory beliefs be held simultaneously? And is there more to chance and circumstance that makes a forger work so closely with an agent or dealer? Is there a psychology proper to this situation itself?

Life itself begins with a forgery. Infants and children manipulate their self-image in order to conform to or to contest parental expectations, shaping themselves to become what they feel they are supposed to be or attempting to undermine this. Most often, there is a dialectic of conformity and resistance, as they comply in order not to lose parental love yet resist in order to exist and avoid alienation in ideals and behaviours that are imposed on them. Templates for conformity are based not simply on familial and social codes but on images of, for example, preferred siblings or other family members who seem to have some special status or endorsement. The child gravitates to such images while at the same time trying to assert themselves as different.

The fact that the creation of fictions and fictitious identities is such a common feature of all our childhoods means that we perhaps develop a sensitivity to questions of authenticity and deceit at a very early age. We want to be believed in, which essentially means to be loved, yet the problem is that to be loved we have to be and do things that might seem artificial. We learn how to play roles. Later in life, falling in love so often involves meeting someone who appears to have a belief in us, a feature of romantic relationships that is itself made central in so-called 'love scams' in which a con artist defrauds a mark through a fictitious romance (Blum 1972). In popular culture, novels, films and TV series continually depict a dancer, actor or performer who gets their big break by someone genuinely *believing in* them.

Although performing is often represented today as an expression of who one really is, the shadow of inauthenticity is rarely absent, as if to become the focus of other people's interest requires some form of deceit. Are we loved 'for ourselves' or for the roles we play, the places we occupy, the images we project? Echoing this dilemma is our entry into the world of speech and language. As Karl Popper observed, a child can only be said to speak when it can lie, that is, manipulate symbols and show that they are not simply passive vehicles of language. Speaking means knowing that we can lie, harbour our own internal worlds and be distinct from what others believe: we are owning words rather than being owned by them.

The ubiquitous 'imposter syndrome' experienced by so many testifies to the structural place that these themes occupy. People feel that they are playing a role and will be somehow found out or exposed, just as achievements are not felt as really belonging to us. The only thing that feels real is the potential shame of exposure or actual failure. And yet this only incentivises the creation of fictions: even if we decide to invest less in the fabrication of our own self-image, we want to believe in the image created by others. Our own belief is predicated on the belief we once hoped so desperately would come from our parents, so in believing in someone else we are implicitly reviving the phantasy of belief in ourselves.

There is one more crucial aspect of this childhood dynamic. As we learn that our parents are interested in more than us, and that our manipulation of images is in most cases limited, we may infer that other people have overridden us because of what they *have*, and this introduces the whole question of the role of objects and possessions as mediators. Someone else may be more important because what they have is better or bigger than what we have, and so it is not just about what we *are* for a parent but about what we might *have*. This could take the form of a literal object – that we might offer them as a gift or expect to receive from them – or the more abstract sense that there is something in us yet to be discovered. Frequently it will involve the effort to give the other person what we think they lack, what is missing from them, which makes our gift all the more important.

Myth and folklore put a premium on the weapons or tools needed by the protagonist to complete their mission, at the horizon of which is often obtaining the hand of one's beloved. In his study of the morphology of the folktale, Vladimir Propp discussed the importance of the variety of transactions here. A male figure, usually a son, is sent away from his privileged background by his father to complete some task, yet given nothing to help him do so (Propp, 1975). The magical instruments he needs are then supplied by a distinct donor figure, as we see today in the figure of Q in the James Bond franchise. But, and this is what interests us here, receipt of these weapons or objects occurs either by direct gifting or by a process of theft, where they are effectively taken through deception and cunning. The aim is the same, the method different: to acquire specially invested goods that will lead to a prize. An alliance thus allows outwitting of the more powerful third party.

How does the sale of forged art both exploit and inflect these patterns? Let's start with the question of belief. Although little studied, belief is not simply a property of a buyer or gallerist's relation to the presented work, but of the agent's relation to the forger. As the Rigbys pointed out many years ago, "Behind almost every successful creator of fakes in history has stood an artful dodger ready to handle the business end of a most promising partnership" (Rigby and Rigby 1944, p.419). We could evoke here the partnerships of Giovanni Bastianini and Giovanni Freppa, Alceo Dossena and Alfredo Fasoli, Elmyr de Hory and Jacques Chamberlin, John Myatt and John Drewe, or, more recently, of Pei-Shen Qian and José Bergantiños Diaz. Rather than assuming they simply worked in unison, sharing the same aims and values, a key variable is the agent's belief in the skills of the artist.

The difference from the childhood situation is that the skills being valued are precisely those of deceit, of being able to effectively copy someone else: one is not being loved *despite* one's deception but *because* of it. When it then comes to the buyer or gallerist, there is of course a comparable need to believe, reinforced by the desire to find what is missing, to complete the other person. As Mark Jones observes, 'Present Piltdown Man to a palaeontologist out of the blue and it will be rejected out of hand. Present it to a palaeontologist whose predictions about the 'missing link' have been awaiting just such evidence and it will seem entirely credible' (Jones 1990, p.11).

This is why van Meegeren's 'Christ at Emmaus' was so feted. He had found what Vermeer experts wanted to find, the 'missing link' that they had been searching for. As the Vermeer scholar Abraham Bredius put it, this was not just a brilliant Vermeer but *"the masterpiece"* of the painter's career. And this of course is exactly what many children become so sensitive to so early on: how to read parental desire, how to grasp what is missing for the parent and then, perhaps, to be able to offer it to them, whether this be through changes in one's very identity or through what one can offer as a gift. As one of Richard Blum's interviewees put it in his study of con artists, 'You've got to realise that the victim wants to believe you. The other thing, once you've got him moving, is to listen, because everyone wants to talk' (Blum 1972, p.42).

This listening will give the clue as to what the other person dreams of finding, which revolves around their own phantasies. As Blum's interviewee continues, 'the victim is, after all, just another con man too – and it's your money he wants'. Everyone wants to believe in something, and to supply to the other the precious object that will satisfy them. The gallerist, after all, wants to satisfy the client, to give them that special unique sale unavailable to anyone else, and to be *the one* to do so. That special hidden quality becomes materialised in the artwork offered. So there is a whole chain here of assumptions and expectations to be exploited. As Jones says, 'Bring an exceptionally rare Athenian coin to a classical numismatist and he will examine it with careful scepticism. Allow one of the greatest of all classical numismatists, Sir George Hill, a Director of the British Museum, to find such a coin *for himself*, mounted as a jewel around a lady's neck, and he will take its authenticity for granted' (Jones 1990, p.11).

But the key to understand this process is to recognise that the coin is always fake. The missing piece is always a fiction, and it is perhaps no accident that in the

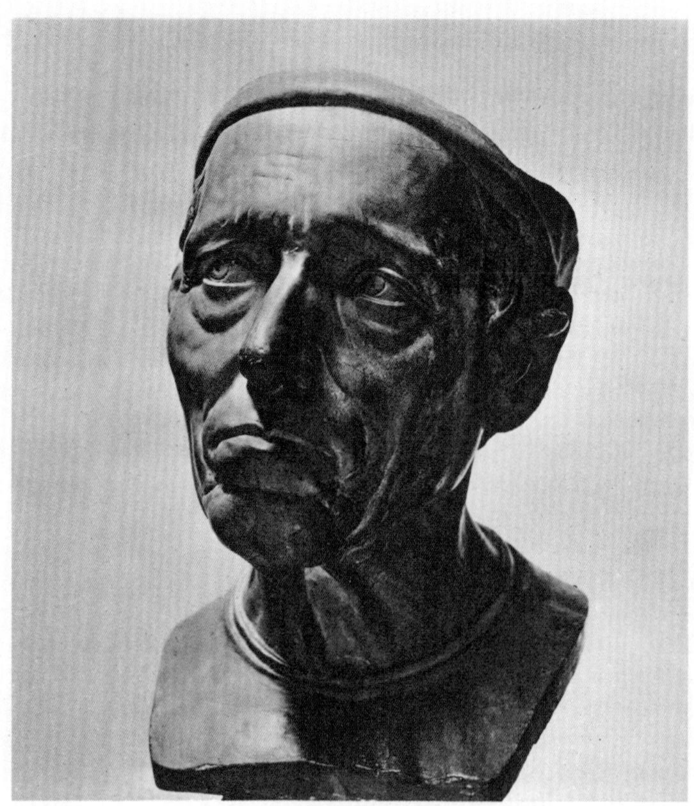

47. Page from Hans Tietze, *Genuine and False*, with a Giovanni Bastianini terracotta of
1864 that had been bought by the Louvre Museum in 1866 as a Renaissance head of
Girolamo Benivieni.

(Sculptor Giovanni Bastianini forged Renaissance statuary sold by his handler the
antiquarian Giovanni Freppa in the 1860s; Alceo Dossena's fake Classical and Renaissance
sculptures were made in the early twentieth century and peddled by art dealer Alfredo
Fasoli. Works by Bastianini and Dossena were bought by museums and private collectors,
and admired even after being exposed as fakes. Hungarian artist Elmyr de Hory's forged
modern paintings were widely sold to collectors by dealer Jacques Chamberlin in the
1940s and then by other agents; British painter John Myatt's many forgeries of modern
works were relentlessly sold by his handler and 'discoverer' John Drewe. The Chinese
painter Pei-Shen Qian's forgeries of American abstract expressionist works were handled
by Jose Bergantiños Diaz, and by others involved in the scam.)

vignette above the necklace is on a woman's body, as if to incarnate a body part that is purely imagined. The one object that will bring total satisfaction and completion is a phantasy element, something that cannot be embodied in a real empirical object (Greenacre 1958a, 1958b). That is why sometimes when gallerists sell a very high price work they take to be genuine, they may have the vague feeling that they have done something not entirely legitimate, as if the dimension of fiction haunts the most significant of transactions and marks the dissonance between an empirical object and a phantasy.

Art history is indeed filled with speculations about the ratio of fakes to 'genuine' works, and given the historical presence in major cities over several centuries of workshops specialising in producing fake works by named artists, this has been estimated at anywhere between 20 and 40%. Commentators have then taken this as a springboard to muse on the necessity of fakes to act as a counterpoint to what is real, or even to question the assumption that a work can in fact be real at all. The substantial market for fakes known to be fakes is taken to confirm this: people collect Bastianini works on their own merit today, just as William Henry Ireland's forgeries of his own forged Shakespeare manuscripts were once valued assets, like de Hory's fakes of his own fakes (Keats 2013, p.132).

It's a small town, and the dealer calls the car showroom, figures out what's going on, summons the police and the Duke is arrested. And then on Monday morning, the cheque clears. The Duke sues for false arrest and negotiates compensation with the dealer. So what is the con here? He has basically created a situation in which he is seen as guilty, as a conman, evidenced in the immediate resale of the car after a Friday evening cheque payment. According to all the laws of probability and expected belief, the cheque will bounce. So what the Duke is doing is escaping from these laws, from the network of significations and expectations that govern reality. Social codes and conventions are what make the plan work. And, in a nice irony, he becomes guilty at the moment of being proved innocent.

So, the Duke is cheating not simply the car dealership and the police but the system of codes and conventions that shape us, what analysts call the big Other. He is then released from jail not just with the money but with his own difference from the system, his status as exception, exactly what the system of codes would otherwise take away from us. He can cheat the system and escapes at the very moment he is being defined by it. Why shouldn't someone, after all, have the right to sell a car five minutes after buying it? This isn't usual or rational or expected, but why should we be obliged to behave as codes dictate? So the stakes of the con are very high, much higher than money in fact, since they involve the whole construction of human reality.

And this takes us back to the question of the stakes of art forgery. The initial salesman at the car showroom wanted to make the sale, and the Duke was a dream client, going for the most expensive item without asking for any modifications, tests, guarantees or accessories. There was a risk in taking the Friday evening cheque, but the benefits seemed to outweigh this. He wanted and indeed needed to believe in his client. But then the second salesman at the used car dealership, aware of the risk of purchasing a stolen car, had his own calculations to make. Everything pointed to an illegitimate transaction, and the information presented to him weighted towards assessing the situation as a scam.

Whose beliefs were really justified in all this? In the famous Gettier problem, we are asked to consider whether knowledge can be equated with justified true belief (Gettier 1963). Imagine that you're watching a tennis match in real time on TV and player A wins. Now an alien spaceship has landed on the roof of your building and is in fact transmitting a series of false images of a tennis match, in which player A wins. Your neighbour, on the contrary, is watching the streaming of the real match, in which player A wins. Now, you both 'know' that player A has won, but whose knowledge is justified, if we define knowledge as justified true belief? The argument goes that your belief that player A has won is not actually knowledge, because the causal chain that goes from the real match to the TV transmission to your brain has not taken place, although it has for your neighbour.

This might seem like a rather silly, abstract problem but it goes to the heart of many human dynamics, and can illuminate the problem of the belief in the forgery's authenticity that we posed earlier. What right do you have to question me, given the information I have given you? When a child explains themself with an account of the context and rationale of some misdemeanour, what right does the parent have to chastise them? They don't have any more information beyond what the child has told them so they must settle for this, even if, in many cases, they don't, generating rage and fury in the child. The parent has not obeyed the rule of belief construction: go on the information and evidence available.

This is well-known in legal circles. Someone is accused of a crime and although clearly guilty, defends themselves with great zeal, to the point of genuinely believing themselves innocent. What matters here is that they are innocent from the point of view of the information delivered: they have only said so much, there is only so much evidence, so although objectively guilty, the other has no right to accuse them, no right to know that they are guilty, and in judging them they are guilty *themselves* of some terrible crime. The true transgression is on the side of the accuser for overriding what they 'know', what they have been told by the person accused.

And this is exactly the logic of the puzzling sense of self-righteousness and actual belief in their wares shown at times by those selling forged artworks. Here is the work, here is the provenance, here is the expert report, and so – given this information – you can't base your judgement on any more than this, and if you

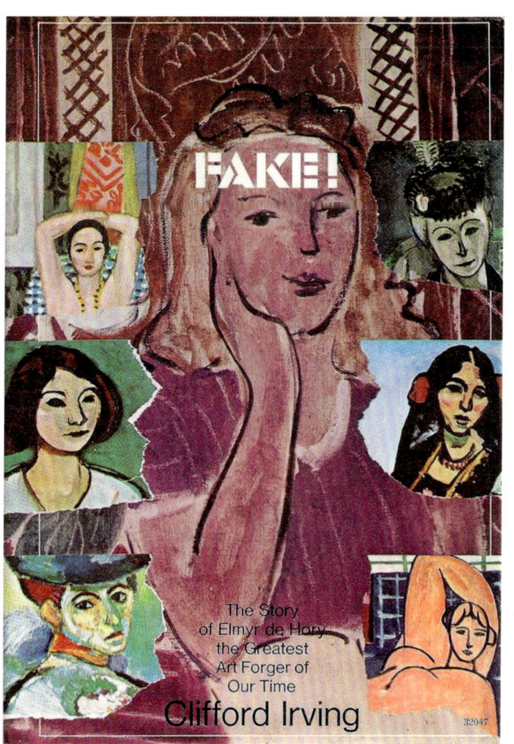

48. *Fake!* by Clifford Irving, 1969, with cover
showing some of Elmyr de Hory's faked 'Matisses'.

do, you're breaking the epistemic rules of engagement. At the horizon of these
interactions is the question of what the other person *has a right to know*. Within the
restricted parameters of the information provided, the forgery must be accepted as
real, and if it isn't, the fault lies with the other person. They have no right to know
that it's a fake.

When John Drewe carefully inserted false provenance details in the Tate and V&A
archives for works that John Myatt was forging, he was crafting exactly this reservoir
of background knowledge, engineering what others had a right to know. And so any
attempt to contest this would in itself be unacceptable, only reinforcing the sense of
righteousness that Drewe himself displayed. Like the deceptions constructed by the
Duke, the whole system of codes and conventions is at stake here, since the scams
relied on the effects of shared belief systems, which he then tried to differentiate
himself from. When we witness a forger's agent continue to try to sell works after
being exposed, this may well be a part of the logic of the situation: belief in the
works means belief in them as a person, in their difference from a system, in their
resistance to being defined and spoken by a system. So, the stake here is individual
subjectivity itself.

    And isn't this why forgers themselves have always proven so popular with the
public? Prison sentences are extraordinarily lenient, and afterwards a book deal,
TV series or movie are almost guaranteed. Van Meegeren was polled as the second
most popular person in Holland, and proposals were made for a statue of him to be
built (Keats 2013, p. 69). John Myatt became a well-known face on TV and presented
a Sky series on painting, Tom Keating got a book deal and a TV series on how to copy
the work of well-known artists, De Hory had Clifford Irving's bestselling biography
and an Orson Welles movie etc. (Charney 2015). Crime here is almost certain to pay,

and it must be the reflection and inversion of our most basic situation in life that the forger presents here. The lies we told when we learnt to speak become the very substance of the forger's life. The system of codes and conventions is undone, our wish to believe is exploited, but by the same token the Other is cheated: the all-powerful person at the dawn of our lives *and* the system beyond them is targeted. The child triumphs!

Let's conclude with one last aspect of the forger's deception which similarly resonates with a much more general experience. The forger's agent offers a work from a name: sometimes, in the case of forged autographs, it is nothing more than the name itself. But in the chain thus created, the buyer is accessing this name via a sequence of third parties, and, crucially, the forger's agent is speaking from the place of this name. When Tom Keating made his forged paintings, he claimed that he felt inhabited by the spirit of the dead artists he was copying, as if they were painting through him (Keating 1977). Now whether we choose to take this seriously or not, it is the name of the forged artist that legitimates the agent's – and not the forger's – position in speech here. They have a place from which to speak, as a purveyor of that name.

We could remember here the joke ascribed to Socrates, when insulted as to the absence of any family pedigree: 'Yes' he allegedly replied, 'but whereas your family's lineage ends with you, mine starts from me'. Making oneself the purveyor of works stemming from a famous name has the same effect: one is the bearer of Rothko or Bacon, and just as that name is hallowed, so is the one offering to supply the work. We could hypothesise here that this appropriation of a name is directly proportional to the agent's sense of an absence of a name, which would explain why so many forger's agents have had other, even multiple identities and aliases. The weight of the forged artist's name magnifies that of the agent, and the all-important chain of provenance in a way acts like their own missing family tree. And so we would guess that the identity problem is not simply with the forger but, more significantly, with the agent, with the one who uses the name of the forged artist as their compass and letter of introduction to the world. Their own importance is a function of this name, yet one more reason to keep on believing in the work. Their own identity is at stake.

There may be a problem here in the assumption of the father's name, and a relation with the mother based on illusion and fragile shifts in self-image. Rather than assuming one's name, one situates oneself in a fabricated lineage thanks to the names that culture invests. That's why for as long as artists retain their special status in society, they will create not just artworks but forged local lineages, taking up forgers into broader sequences of deception in which someone may be transformed from being the potential owner of a Bacon into the one who is, in effect, descended from him.

References

Richard Blum, *Deceivers and Deceived* (Springfield: Charles Thomas, 1972).

Noah Charney, *The Art of Forgery* (London: Phaidon, 2015).

Edmund Gettier, 'Is justified true belief knowledge?', *Analysis*, 23, 1963, pp. 121–3.

Phyllis Greenacre, 'The Imposter', *Psychoanalytic Quarterly*, 27, pp. 359–82, 1958a.

Phyllis Greenacre, 'The relation of the imposter to the artist', *Psychoanalytic Study of the Child*, 13, pp. 521–540, 1958b.

Mark Jones (ed.), *Fake? The Art of Deception* (London: The British Museum, 1990).

Jonathon Keats, *Forged* (Oxford: Oxford University Press, 2013).

Tom Keating, *The Fake's Progress* (London: Hutchinson, 1977).

Thierry Lenain, *Art Forgery* (New York: Reaktion, 2011).

Vladimir Propp, *Morphology of the Folktale* (1958) (Austin: University of Texas Press, 1975).

Sándor Radnóti, *The Fake: Forgery and its Place in Art* (Maryland: Rowman and Litttlefield, 1999).

Douglas and Elizabeth Rigby, *Lock, Stock and Barrel, The Story of Collecting* (Philadelphia: Lippincott, 1944).

Laney Salisbury and Aly Sujo, *Provenance* (New York: Penguin, 2009).

Geoffrey Wolff, *The Duke of Deception* (New York: Random House, 1990).

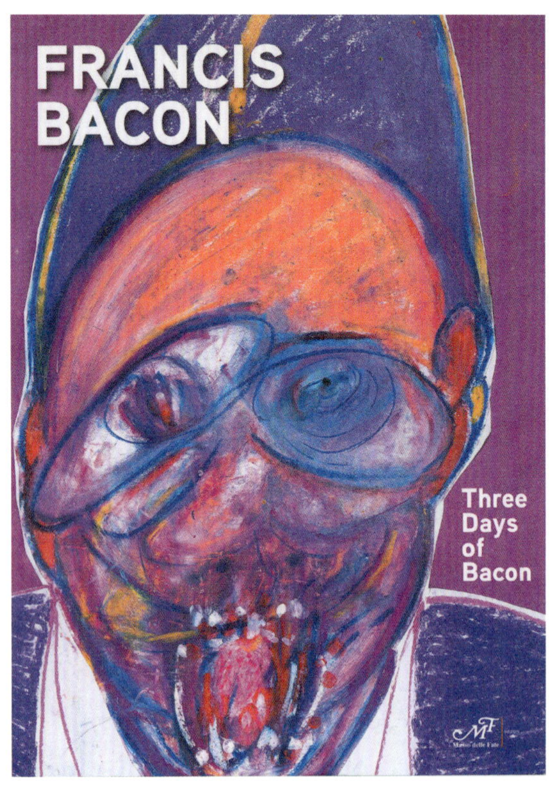

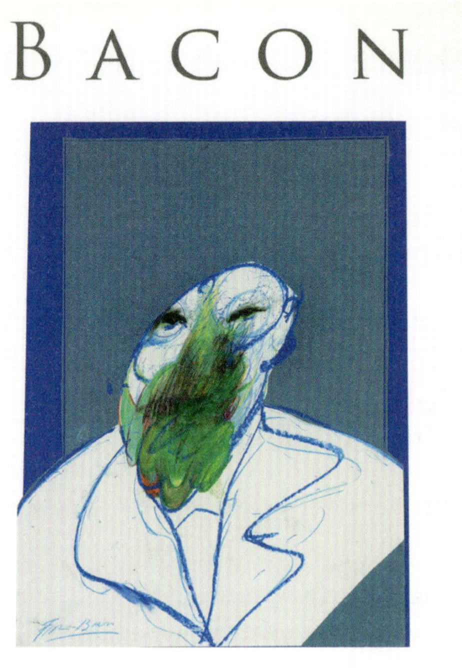

49. Covers of two purported 'Bacon' catalogues, the productions of Cristiano Lovatelli Ravarino

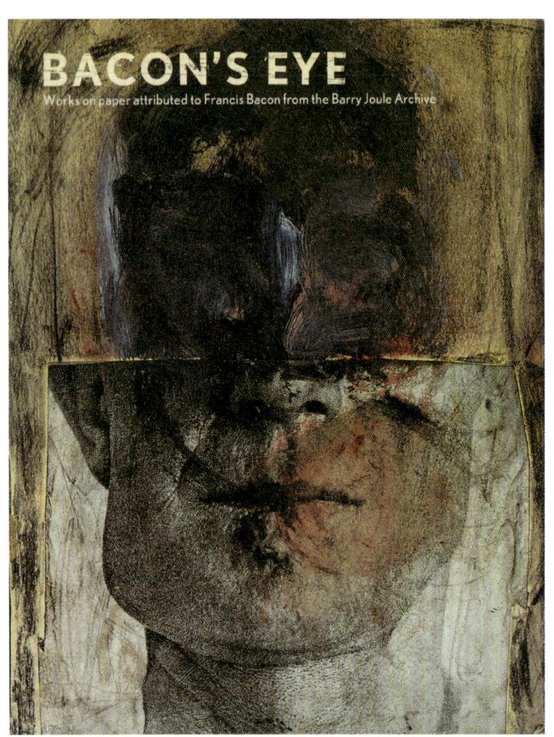

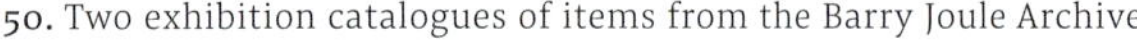

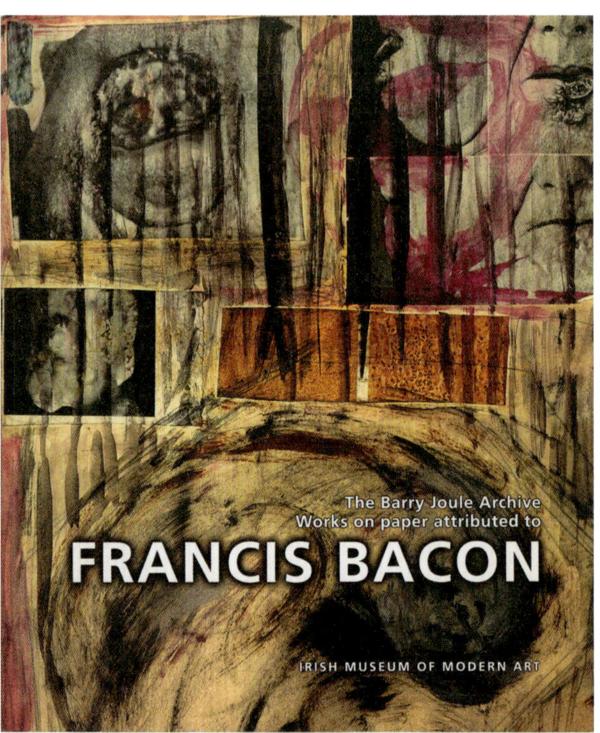

50. Two exhibition catalogues of items from the Barry Joule Archive

Postscript to
In Whose Name? Some Thoughts on Art Forgery

Since Francis Bacon's death in 1992, two bodies of forgeries have disrupted the serious study of Bacon's paintings and possibly confused non-specialists. Consequently, I asked Darian Leader if he would write about the parties mainly responsible, Barry Joule and Cristiano Lovatelli Ravarino. He declined on the grounds it would be unethical; it was an unreasonable request, since it would necessitate the psychoanalysis of individuals with whom he was unacquainted. Professor Leader's book, *Stealing the Mona Lisa* (London: Faber & Faber, 2002), investigated both the public's reception of art and its fascination with crime, his new essay has contributed significant insights into the minds and motives of art fakers.

The formation of the International Catalogue Raisonné Association (ICRA) in 2019 occurred at a moment when the viability of catalogues raisonnés was being called into question. With vast sums of money at stake, negative verdicts delivered by authentication committees began to be challenged by those able to afford the legal fees, and to this day ICRA meetings are attended by lawyers from the Art Lawyers Association (ALA). The problems and labyrinthine complexities raised by the processes of authenticating artworks can be instructively followed in the literature and conferences of these two associations. Yet when sustaining the market takes precedence over expertise and scholarship, the process of authentication can itself be abused: Richard Dorment's *Warhol After Warhol: Power and Money in the Modern Art World* (London: Picador, 2023), is a devastating exposé of the dangers.

The second catalogue raisonné of the works of Francis Bacon was published by The Estate of Francis Bacon in 2016. By definition, any paintings not included in the catalogue are not by Bacon. If a painting resurfaced of which Bacon's authorship appeared feasible, it would need to be authenticated; unexpectedly, perhaps, no such paintings have emerged since 2016. Less surprisingly, enquiries about hundreds of putative works have been submitted to The Estate of Francis Bacon. A high percentage of these exhibit overwhelming counter-indications: they are, for example, painted on the primed side, they are prominently signed on the front, the canvas is a size Bacon never used, and the imagery and technique are entirely inconsistent with any paintings in Bacon's oeuvre.

A few, however, at first sight, somewhat resemble a Francis Bacon painting. These continue to reappear on the market from time to time, and they take us back to the beginning of the systematic faking of Bacon's work. In Milan, about 1975, a group of art students was producing fakes of Bacon (and other artists) to raise money for left-wing party funds; they also considered their forgeries to be 'a blow against the bourgeois art market'. The main conduit for those that arrived in England was a London bookdealer, who also helped to fabricate the false provenances that are habitually attached to fakes.

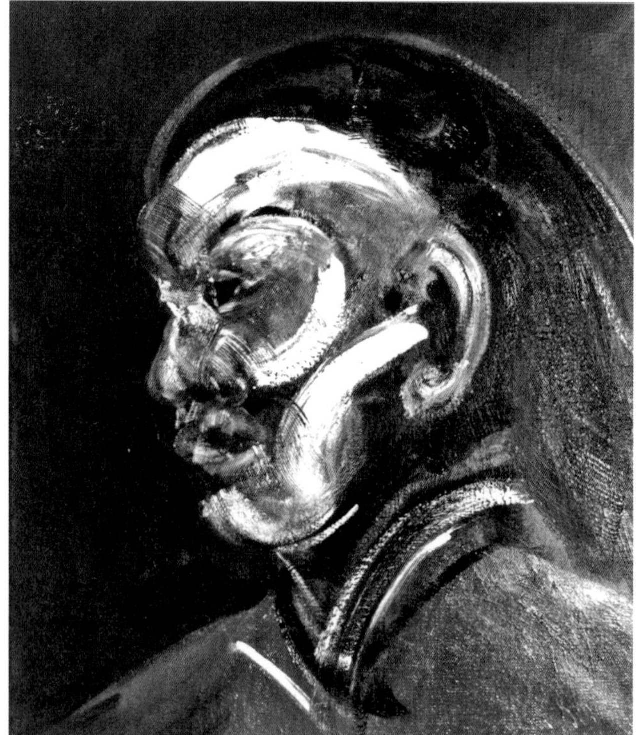
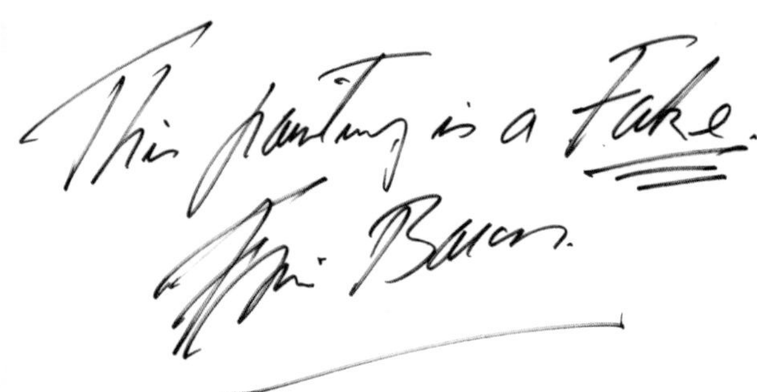

51. (recto and verso) Photograph of a fake Bacon painting, taken for Marlborough Fine Art, 1973

Naturally, the fakes were of concern to Bacon's gallery, Marlborough Fine Art; one of their directors, Tony Reichardt, explained to *The Observer*: 'We try to get any fakes destroyed, and inform the police and Interpol.' Bacon himself commented that, 'Most of these Italian pictures in my style are extremely bad', adding that 'I do take steps to get these false canvases off the market… I have even signed the backs of photographs of fakes, "this is a fake and not by me"'.

An example of the procedure Bacon outlined survives in Marlborough Fine Art's archive. [51] Although the print is only in black and white, the image serves to illustrate the strategy of the Milan fakers, which was to absorb elements of several of Bacon's authentic portraits and re-assemble them in a new painting that bore, superficially, some resemblance to what would have been a hitherto unrecorded painting. In the example here, there is only a loose connection with panels from three triptychs of Henrietta Moraes.

As Bacon's reputation – and the prices of his paintings – soared in the 1970s, he attracted more of this unwanted attention. In April/May 1978, for example, there was a major theft from his studio. He was having extensive renovations carried out at 7 Reece Mews, and, not wishing to aggravate his asthma, he moved out to stay with his friends Denis Wirth Miller and Richard Chopping at Wivenhoe. Valerie Beston warned the builders that none of Bacon's possessions were to be disturbed, and they must not enter the studio; yet together with many archival items, one (or more) of the builders stole a large painting of a bullfight. The police were brought in, and the painting was eventually retrieved; when detectives returned it on 15 November, Valerie Beston noted in her diary that Bacon paid the reward and 'He cuts it up and puts piece in dustbin'.

At the same time, Barry Joule entered Bacon's life. He was useful to Bacon as a handyman and driver, but their relationship was more complicated than that. Joule's need to be associated with famous people was evidently more important to him than monetary gain from selling fakes. The work he produced in emulation of Bacon was almost certainly unknown to the artist himself, and, significantly, did not emerge until after Bacon's death. It is unnecessary to elaborate on this material here. A substantial part of *The Barry Joule Archive: Works on Paper Attributed to Francis Bacon* was donated to Tate, London, in 2002, but it was de-accessioned twenty years later, following the publication of 'Work on the Barry Joule Archive', by Sophie Pretorius, in *Francis Bacon Studies IV* (2021).

The drawings produced by Cristiano Lovatelli Ravarino are diametrically opposed to the putative preparatory sketches of Barry Joule's. Strictly speaking, Ravarino's productions are not fakes, as such, for they bear no resemblance to Bacon's paintings: instead, he created what might be termed a parallel oeuvre. He claimed he met Bacon in 1976 and that they became secret lovers. The vaunted secrecy helped cover his inability to adduce any evidence that he knew Bacon: the counterfeit drawings became interwoven with his fantasies of Bacon's behaviour on his undocumented visits to Italy. Some of the drawings he claimed Bacon gave him were published in an article he wrote for *bologna incontri* in 1980; they drew a sharp rebuke from Valerie Beston, who wrote to the Italian Institute: 'Francis Bacon would be very grateful if you would make a strong protest on his behalf to the Editor of Bolognaincontri Magazine for publishing a scurrilous supposed interview with him ...'
     Thereafter, little was heard of Ravarino's fraudulent activities until after Bacon's death. From 1996 a welter of publications started to emerge, and by 2009 the older, A4 size drawings (297 × 210 mm.) were supplanted by ever-larger presentation drawings on paper, executed in lurid pastel colours. Their juvenile, caricatural imagery bears scant relationship to anything by Francis Bacon, and in September 2021 the Italian authorities confiscated over six hundred of them, along with equipment used in their manufacture. The case also involved charges of money laundering and became protracted, although the verdict of the Italian courts is forthcoming at the time this book goes to press. Meanwhile, the Bacon bibliography is sullied by two bodies of inauthentic works that may mislead the uninitiated.

Martin Harrison

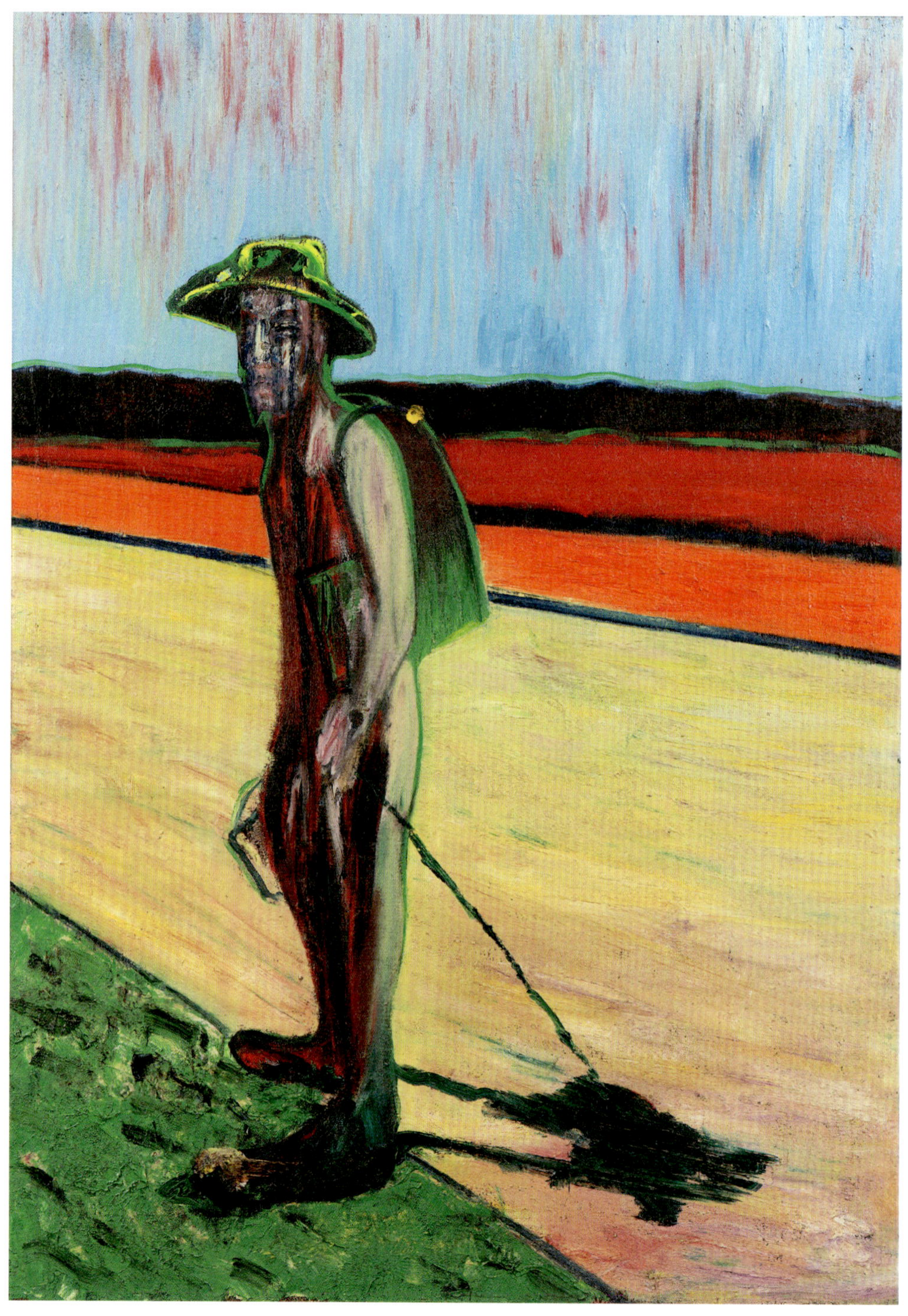

52. *Study for Portrait of Van Gogh V*, 1957

(As Dr Balaska reminded me, in his famous essay on Van Gogh's painting(s) of boots, Heidegger did not include an illustration. This is the only painting in Bacon's Van Gogh series that suggests worn shoes might have been in his mind. Bacon's first detailed depiction of footwear was in his *Self-Portrait*, 1956, and shoes became more carefully delineated in many of his paintings after 1961.)

The origin of painting: Bacon and Heidegger on appearance

Maria Balaska

'What does make a painting?', Michel Archimbaud asks Francis Bacon. 'No one really knows' Bacon replies (Archimbaud, 48). It is a question to which Bacon returns during his interviews and practice, also addressing it as a mystery ('the mystery of painting' or 'the mystery of appearance') (Sylvester, 105, 118).

The characterisation 'mystery' may puzzle us at first, especially if we are familiar with Bacon's overall aversion to metaphysical or religious interpretations (Archimbaud, 89). In fact, if we take Archimbaud's question as a question about efficient cause, there is no mystery whatsoever about where a painting comes from. It comes from the organ that paints (most usually someone's hand), the materials (traditionally the presence of paint on a canvas), as well as some mental event that comprises a combination of intention, skill, and one's response to external circumstances (accidents, or limitations of space, time, material, etc.). Answering this kind of question requires identifying certain events as parts of a causal chain that leads to an outcome.

But this is not how the question is meant. The question here is not about painting in the descriptive sense of the word, but about painting as a work of art. Hence, in the interviews a distinction is sometimes drawn between Bacon's own paintings and a painting that Bacon's cleaner or some child could produce (Sylvester, 92, 97, 118). The work of art puzzles us because there is achievement in it, an achievement of an unclear origin. This is expressed in a normative power that the work has not only over the spectator, but also over the artist, 'something more profound than what [the artist] had originally wanted' (Sylvester, 17), 'sometimes better than what you were in the process of doing' (Archimbaud, 82). As an artwork a painting is more than the paint, the artist's intention, skill, or external circumstances. In philosophical terms, we would say that these may be necessary but not sufficient.

'What makes a painting?' does not mean 'what causes it?' but 'what constitutes a painting qua artwork?'. The Greeks used the term 'arche' to designate something that is at the same time a source and an ordering principle: 'what is the origin (arche) of the work of art?' means 'what is the principle that best defines it?'. Thus framed, the question has had a long history in philosophy: Aristotle, Wittgenstein, Heidegger, Merleau-Ponty are only some of the philosophers who have reflected on the origin of the work of art.

In this chapter, I bring some philosophical voices, specifically (but not exclusively) Heidegger, in dialogue with Bacon's voice on the topic. The spirit of my endeavour is to envision a conversation between Bacon and a philosopher. Such a conversation can now only be one-sided, as I cannot know what Bacon would have responded to the philosopher's remarks. But because ideas come with their own space of possibilities, like a chess game that generates certain possibilities with every move regardless of the mental states of the player, it is possible to have a conversation with the concepts that guide Bacon, even if Bacon himself is not around.

What is appearance?

In his interviews with David Sylvester, Bacon characterises the mystery of painting as 'the mystery of appearance' and 'the mystery of making':

> Well, now, what personally I would like to do would be, for instance, to make portraits which were portraits but came out of things which really had nothing to do with what is called the illustrational facts of the image; they would be made differently, and yet they would give the appearance. To me, the mystery of painting today is how can appearance be made. I know it can be illustrated; I know it can be photographed. But how can this thing be made so that you catch the mystery of appearance within the mystery of the making? It's an illogical method of making, an illogical way of attempting to make what one hopes will be a logical outcome – in the sense that one hopes one will be able to suddenly make the thing there in a totally illogical way but that it will be totally real and, in the case of a portrait, recognizable as the person. (Sylvester, 105)

And later he adds: 'There are standards set up as to what appearance is or should be, but there's no doubt that the ways appearance can be made are very mysterious ways.' (Sylvester, 105)

What is 'appearance' and why is it problematised by Bacon? Let us start here with three possible meanings that the word can take.

(1) In a neutral way, 'appearance' can refer simply to what something looks like: 'shape', 'form', 'aspect', 'look', 'phenomenon' are some of its synonyms.

(2) The term can have a negative ring to it, when we juxtapose an appearance (what something looks like) to reality (what something *truly* is). For example, we sometimes say that appearances are to be mistrusted, and one should aim, instead, to represent something beyond its appearance.

(3) The term can be used in a positive and dynamic way to refer to the happening or event of appearing. Here the appearance of something refers to the case when it comes forth and becomes present.

When Bacon refers to the mystery of appearance and links this to the origin of painting, I believe he prioritises sense (3) of the word. Bacon links 'appearance' to a 'making' — here to painting. 'Making appearance' is a case of showing or bringing forth what something truly is, or as Bacon puts it, what is 'totally real' about the thing painted, 'transferring the essence of the image more poignantly' (Sylvester, 17). Making appearance does not mean inventing a form. Nor does it mean discovering a form. As a bringing forth it is neither merely active nor merely passive, it is both. Hence, he says that often, while he paints, something 'unexpected suddenly appears; it comes with no warning', 'almost in spite of oneself' (Archimbaud, 82) or in reference to the first version of *Painting 1946*: 'I was doing a landscape and I wanted to make a field with a bird flying over it. I had put a whole heap of reference marks on the canvas, then suddenly the forms that you see on that canvas began to appear; they imposed themselves on me.' (Archimbaud, 80–81)

Bacon is not interested in appearance as (1), the default idea that all things are perceptible (have a certain look), and he is critical of (2) which he associates with what he calls an illustrational account of appearance. The illustrational way of thinking about appearance is also what he calls the 'logical' way, in the sense of what is most usually and conventionally expected from a painting. Historically, painting has often been used as a case of recording. With the advent of photography, the illustrational function of an image, its role for documenting or representing reality, reaches its peak. Here the ideal of illustration links to a detached representation, an ideal inspired by science, a representation that attempts to remove any subjective colourings. This is no coincidence, as film and photography emerged from the scientific revolution and the transformative role of technology, not merely as new tools, but as a new way of perceiving the world.[1] Bacon's critical distance from the practice of documentation questions the nature of appearance and challenges what Sylvester refers to as 'the accepted standards of what appearance is' (Sylvester, 105): what is it to 'give the appearance' if it is not about giving the illustrational facts of the image?

When Bacon refers to what it means for a portrait to 'give the appearance', he mentions two desirable outcomes: that the portrait should be 'recognizable as the person' in question and that the thing painted will be 'totally real'. These two outcomes would clash if by 'totally real' Bacon referred to a portrait that looked real in the sense that it would trick us into thinking it was (a photograph of) the person in question. Instead, all we need at that level is for the subject to be *recognisable* as the person. In other words, this is not about mimesis or copying. To make the portrait 'totally real' means to bring out the reality or essence of the thing or person painted, not to create a perfect replica of the person.[2] But what does it mean to bring out the essence of an entity?

To start exploring this, it is important to draw attention to a problematic alternative that I think Bacon rejects. When art is distinguished from illustration, there is a temptation to think that appearance is not *at all* about the facts, that it is not about getting to the truth or reality of something (say, the subject of the painting) but only about expressing emotions.[3] But Bacon's preoccupation with true and real appearance resists the reduction of appearance to subjective feelings. Instead, Bacon seems to think that facts, truth, and a non-illustrational form are all crucial for art: 'an attempt to record a fact [makes the painting] much more profound' (Sylvester, 58). He expresses this clearly when he discusses what it means to do great art and its relation to recording.

> One of the reasons why I don't like abstract painting, or why it doesn't interest me, is that I think painting is a duality, and that abstract painting is an entirely aesthetic thing. It always remains on one level. It is only really interested in the beauty of its patterns or its shapes. We know that most people, especially artists, have large areas of undisciplined emotion, and I think that abstract artists believe that in these marks that they're making they are catching all these sorts of emotions. But I think that, caught in that way, they are too weak to convey anything. I think that

great art is deeply ordered. Even if within the order there may be enormously instinctive and accidental things, nevertheless I think that they come out of a desire for ordering and for returning fact onto the nervous system in a more violent way. [...] You see, I believe that art is recording; I think it's reporting. And I think that in abstract art, as there's no report, there's nothing other than the aesthetic of the painter and his few sensations. There's never any tension in it. (Sylvester, 58–60)

Whether Bacon is right about abstract painting is not what interests me here.[4] What interests me is his endeavour to maintain both a criticism of illustration and an account of appearance as a recording of the truth of a thing. The duality of which he speaks in the above passage is art's ability to reveal the world by moving us affectively. Hence emotions, sensations, and the senses are not independent of the true perception of the world. When they become cut off from the work of 'making appearance', then the result is 'too weak to convey anything'. Bacon also phrases the duality as follows: 'Isn't it that one wants a thing to be as factual as possible and at the same time as deeply suggestive or deeply unlocking of areas of sensation other than simple illustration of the object that you set out to do? Isn't that what all art is about?'. (Sylvester, 56)

The claim is not that there are different types of art, some illustrational, some entirely aesthetic, and some that attempt to be both factual and sensationally powerful. The claim is much stronger: the latter type of art is 'what all art is about'. But why should it be that appearance is more successful through a non-illustrational form? Why is painting a duality? Bacon connects this to how the world works in the first place: 'Now why this should be, we don't know. This may have to do with how facts themselves are ambiguous, how appearances are ambiguous, and therefore this way of recording form is nearer to the fact by its ambiguity of recording.' (Sylvester, 56)

Because the facts themselves are ambiguous, the idea that we can capture what they are by recording them from a detached viewpoint is misleading. To go back to the three meanings of 'appearance', if we take seriously the idea that appearance is dynamically brought forth, rather than simply documented or subjectively invented, then this must change how appearance is meant to link to reality in the first place.

From Aristotle to Heidegger: appearance as unconcealment

Phenomenology is an area of philosophy that challenges what I earlier called version (2) of 'appearance' by challenging the Cartesian view that there is a gap between appearance and reality, and that accessing the latter requires being sceptical towards the former. Phenomenology restores our trust to the phenomena as reliable guides to truth and the essence of things. Heidegger uses phenomenology to think about art. The question we began with, 'where does art originate?' is the guiding question of his famous piece *The Origin of the Work of Art*. Bringing some of his ideas in dialogue with Bacon's thoughts can help deepen our understanding both of Bacon and of Heidegger. I take both to be offering a dynamic reading of 'appearance' in art as a way to get to the essence of something.

In Heidegger's work 'making appearance' is called 'unconcealment' and it is internally linked to truth. In fact, Heidegger's 'unconcealment' is his translation for the Greek word for truth – a-letheia (ἀ-λήθεια) which literally means bringing out of lethe (out of forgetting, forgetfulness, or hiding), into the open. Discussing Van Gogh's painting of the (peasant's) shoes, a painting he saw on exhibition in Amsterdam in 1930, Heidegger writes about the artwork: 'The artwork lets us know what shoes are in truth' (2011, 102). Using the trivial case of shoes, Heidegger makes his point clearly, if not provocatively. How can an artwork's significance be distilled in making shoes appear as they really are? For one, shoes cannot be that trivial to understand. Secondly, what does it even mean to enquire about the a-letheia of shoes, what could be concealed or forgotten about shoes in the first place? And yet, when we are deeply moved by an artwork, we often express this in terms of how the artwork has managed to express the essence of its subject matter, whether it be a human face or an apple.

Similar to Bacon, Heidegger recognises the temptation to perceive the artwork's aptness as successful representation or illustration. In this scenario, a painting of shoes would be deemed successful to the extent that it accurately represented shoes, akin to a clear photograph of shoes taken under optimal lighting conditions. But, also like Bacon, Heidegger seeks a non-illustrational approach to the relation between art and truth.

> But perhaps the proposition that art is truth setting itself to work intends to revive the fortunately obsolete view that art is an imitation and depiction of something actual? The reproduction of something at hand requires, to be sure, agreement with the actual being, adaptation to it. [...] Agreement with what is has long been taken to be the essence of truth. But then, is it our opinion that this painting by Van Gogh depicts a pair of peasant shoes somewhere at hand, and is a work of art because it does so successfully? Is it our opinion that the painting draws a likeness from something actual and transposes it into a product of artistic production? By no means. The work, therefore, is not the reproduction of some particular entity that happens to be at hand at any given time; it is, on the contrary, the reproduction of things' general essence. But then where and how is this general essence, so that artworks are able to agree with it? (2011, 103)

To think about what it is to bring forth a thing's essence, I want to look at the Aristotelian concept of 'form' which is important for Heidegger. When Aristotle attempts to understand those beings that have been produced by techne (art or craft), he identifies 'form' as a crucial concept. Form (μορφή/morphē) is not just the subjective look that something has for a perceiver, nor what we moderns call 'sense data'. The form of a thing is related to how we address or define that thing, it is what Aristotle calls the *eidos kata ton logon* (εἶδος κατὰ τὸν λόγον), the shape according to the logos (2018, II. 1, 193b1–2). Today all we hear by 'logos' is 'logic' in the sense of 'rationality'. Hence, Jacques Derrida and the whole post-structuralism tradition has been so critical of mentions of 'form', dismissing them as expressions of logocentrism or even phallogocentrism.[5] But Aristotle has a much deeper and richer conception of 'logos', with several meanings that complement each other.

Derived from the verb legein (λέγειν) it primarily means the act of col-lecting, gathering together, as well as what results from this collecting. Second, it means order or ratio, the way the parts of a whole hang together, allowing for that whole to emerge. Third, it refers to the way we define something, the kinds of assertions we make about it. And, finally, it links to the end of an entity, its *telos* or function (logos means the reason of the being of something — its *raison d'être*). Thinking of these aspects together creates a much more complex perspective on what it means to make something appear, to give its form according to logos. It now means: to gather together meaningfully those elements that bring out the way an entity orders itself according to what is essential for it and what it is for, as this also comes out in how we address and define that entity.

Going back to Heidegger's remark that Van Gogh's painting tells us what shoes are in truth, we can now attempt an answer to our earlier question, what it means to give the essence of shoes (or anything else). By essence we do not mean some a-temporal definition or an elemental picture of the thing in question. In fact, there is no definition of any entity apart from the world within which it figures and the way it is addressed. Essence is presence: things only appear within a meaningful context, and that context gives those things their meaning. Therefore, to enquire about what something is, is to enquire about its presencing. Unless this dimension comes in, all we are left with are sensations, blobs of colour and sounds. Hence, Van Gogh's painting succeeds in making the essence of the shoes appear insofar as it also brings forth the world of a peasant within which those shoes figure, as well as the equipmental nature of those shoes within that world. This is also why, in the same text, Heidegger reminds us of a point he had made, in great detail, in *Being and Time*: entities always show up in connection to our practices, to how we are situated within a world.[6]

> [W]e never really perceive a throng of sensations, e.g. tones and noises, in the appearance of things [...]; rather we hear the storm whistling in the chimney, we hear the three-motored plane [...] and never hear acoustical sensation or even mere sounds. In order to hear a bare sound we have to listen away from things, divert our ear from them, i.e. listen abstractly. (2011, 95)

This is how I understand Bacon's reference to an inherent ambiguity of facts and appearances: the world is always already given to us within a meaningful and historical context that includes who we are and how we address things. This means that detached representation/illustration does not work here. To bring out the essence of an entity one needs to bring out the world within which it figures, what this entity is for, its place in particular practices, how it matters within that world, etc.

The violence of appearance: against aestheticisation

Some readers may have found it strange that what is at issue in art is truth and logos, as 'art presumably has [...] to do with the beautiful and beauty, and not with truth' (Heidegger 2011, 102). Truth is traditionally seen as the object of logic or philosophy, with a sharp distinction often drawn between what concerns the realm of the senses and what concerns cognition.

Bacon's work has often been seen exclusively in the light of arousing sensations[7] or negative affects, an aesthetic experience of 'ugliness', 'horror', 'shock'. This may

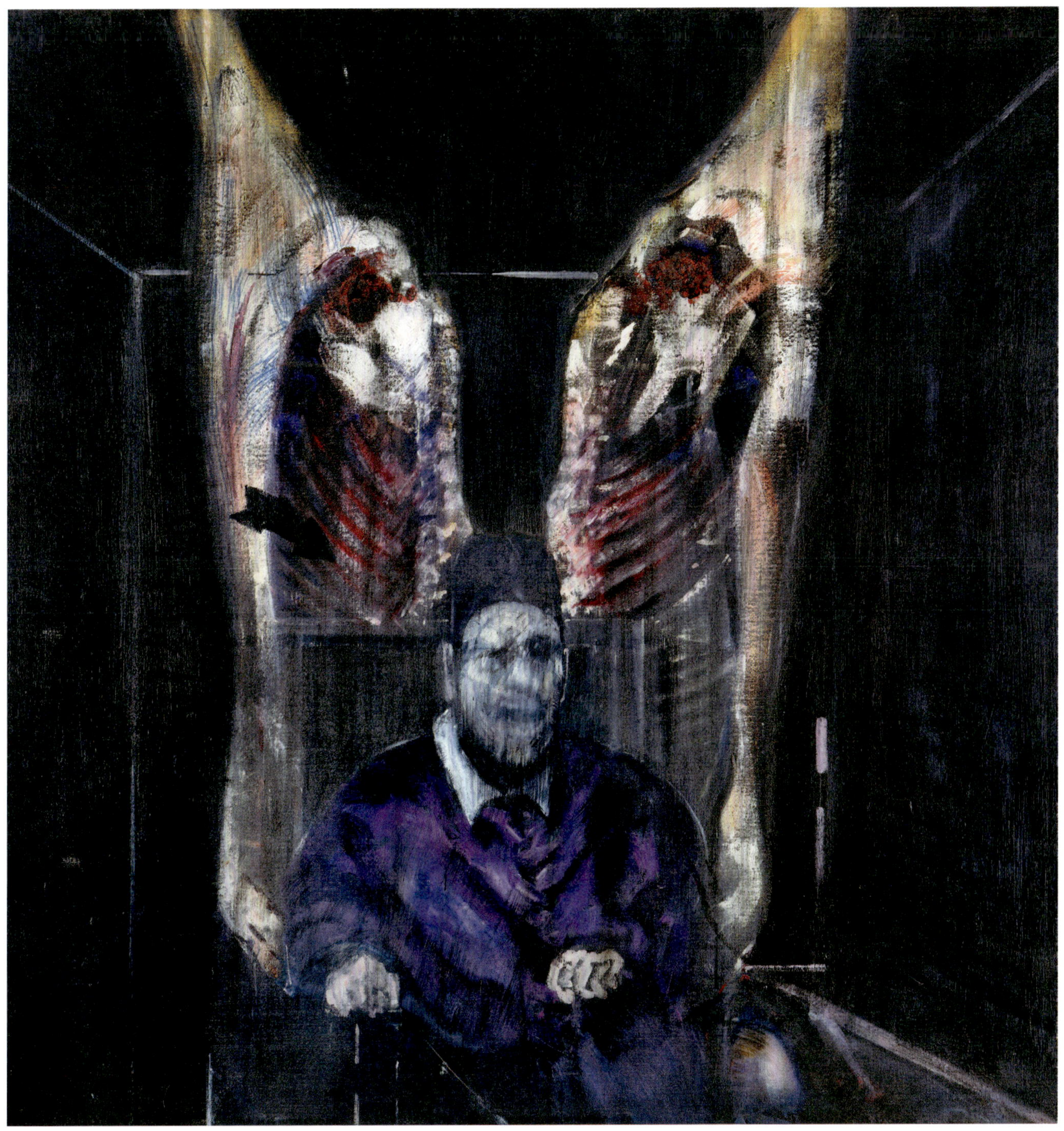

53. *Figure with Meat*, 1954

have been encouraged by Bacon's own choice of words when he describes his work[8] in terms of violence or as affecting the 'nervous system', but also by the scary or distorted atmosphere of some of his works, like *Figure with Meat*.

Here I propose a different reading of what may be perceived as violence at the aesthetic level, one that challenges the conventional distinction between positive and negative affects, beauty and ugliness, light and darkness. If, as I have tried to show, Bacon opens up a space for considering art as unconcealment, then the manner in which something affects us cannot be entirely divorced from the making of appearance. This interpretation is not far-fetched, by Bacon's own lights. When, while discussing portraits, Sylvester attempts to characterise the distortions that Bacon does to the faces of his subjects as an act of violence, 'an unconscious desire in the painter to inflict damage' (Sylvester, 43), Bacon resists this psychological reading. This is how Bacon characterises what he takes to be the violence of his work:

> When talking about the violence of paint, it's nothing to do with the violence of war. It's to do with an attempt to remake the violence of reality itself. And the violence of reality is not only the simple violence meant when you say that a rose or something is violent, but it's the violence also of the suggestions within the image itself which can only be conveyed through paint. When I look at you across the table, I don't only see you but I see a whole emanation which has to do with personality and everything else. And to put that over in a painting, as I would like to be able to do in a portrait means that it would appear violent in paint. We nearly always live through screens a screened existence. And I sometimes think, when people say my work looks violent, that perhaps I have from time to time been able to clear away one or two of the veils or screens. (Sylvester, 81–82)

Notice that the veil or screen here is not the appearance; the veil is reality itself – a statement that echoes Jacques Lacan's expression that reality is itself an imaginary construction, 'the grimace of the real' (1990, 6). Bacon uses the term 'violence' to describe his work, but not in the sense of an aggressive impulse towards his subjects. Instead, he de-psychologises the word: it is more like the kind of violence involved in presenting someone with a fact, he says. There is something violent about the presentation of how things really are. 'Violently' is a synonym for 'exactly' and 'clearly': 'How can I remake this thing once again more clearly, more exactly, more violently?' (Sylvester, 60).

According to my argument so far, to know what makes a painting we need to understand in what sense art is a work of truth. This was distinguished both from the idea that art is successful illustration (or mimesis) and the more modern idea that an artwork is a powerful portrayal of the artist's own feelings. These may well be elements of the practice, but when a painting succeeds – when appearance is made, transcending the original intentions or thoughts of the painter – then it manages to capture something of the essence of what it portrays.[9][10] To clarify this further, I will look at Bacon's *Study of a Child* as an example of the violence that Bacon refers to (the violence of unveiling, of a-letheia). [54] It is also an example of the restrictions of the psychologisation and aestheticisation of art, particularly when it rests on a simplistic distinction between positive and negative feelings (beauty versus

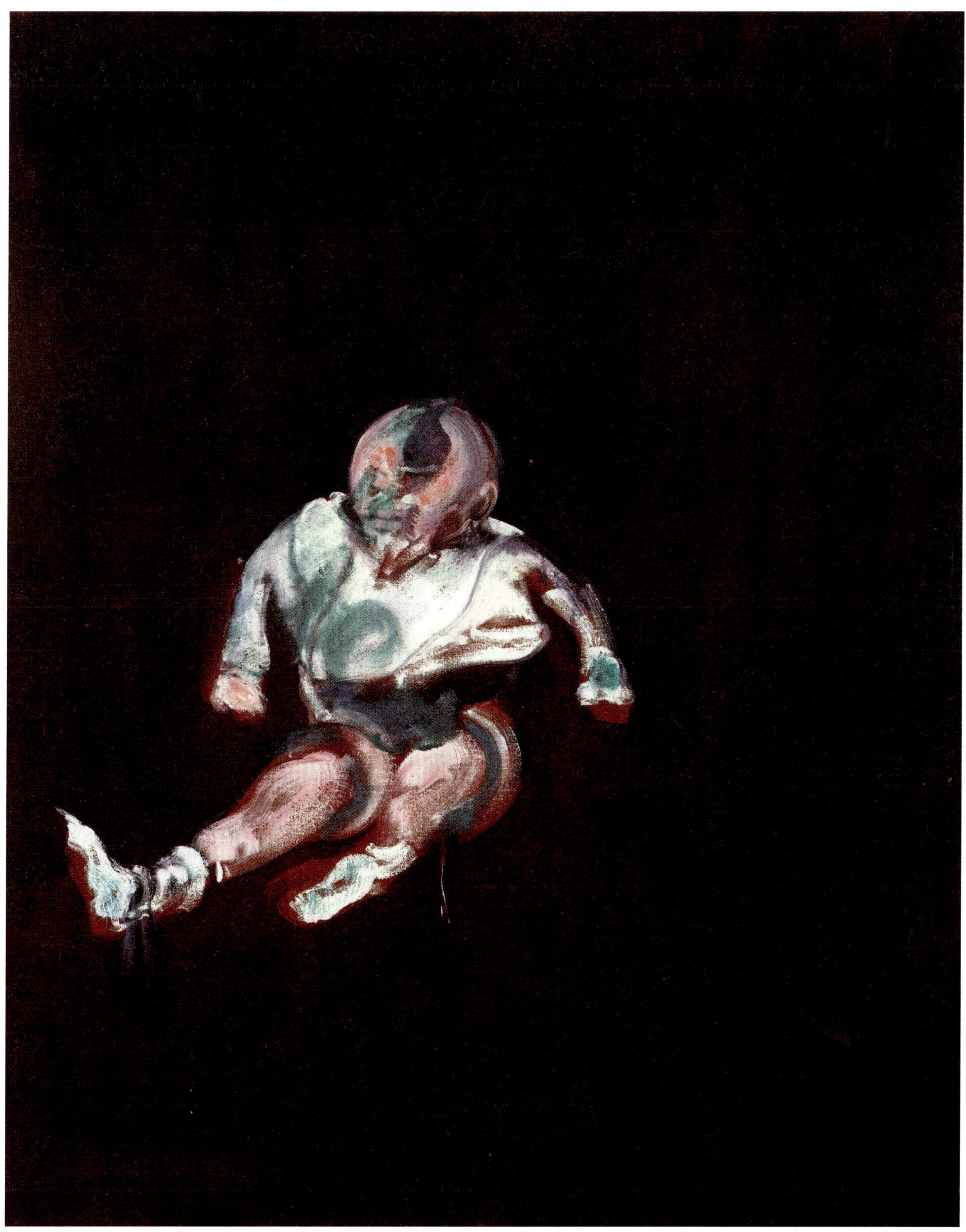

54. *Study of a Child*, 1960

ugliness). Like in the case of Van Gogh's shoes, I approach Bacon's painting as posing the question: 'what is a child?'.

There is a standard and conventional framework for depicting children. Typically, when we view a picture of a child, our expectation is to encounter beauty and cuteness: the plumpness of the face, the innocence associated with not having lived (and sinned), the smallness and fragility of the body. Here, the veil of reality consists in an association of children with something unreal, like the faces or bodies of angels. Bacon's painting of a child 'clears away [this] veil', inviting us to set aside our preconceived views on children and ask: what is a child *really?* The question takes us back to the philosophical difficulties I explored with Heidegger and Aristotle: what does it mean to give the essence of an entity? Distinguishing certain unique qualities, like the absence of signs of aging or the small size of the body, would be as futile as identifying a human being based on the unique trait of having earlobes, to use Hegel's example.[11] A child embodies what is possible for us humans. But we know neither what this human potential is (what we are for), nor whether a child will realise or squander that potential. Hence, looking at a child can generate not only a sense of awe at its pure potentiality, but also a great deal of anxiety around that potentiality. Generating an anxious wonder, a child is an enigma. It is this aspect of a child that shines forth in Bacon's painting.

Bacon corrected the initial title 'Falling Child' under which it was sold to Alfred Hecht in 1960, clarifying that the child was not meant to be falling. But as we read in the *Francis Bacon Catalogue Raisonné*, the image gives us reasons to interpret the movement of the child both as falling and ascending. This creates a dramatic sense of not knowing where the child has come from, or where it is going.

Instead, it appears as though it has been tossed onto a dark canvas, an 'unmediated picture field' (Harrison 2006, 624), lacking clear origin or direction, suspended between ascending and falling, as well as between adulthood (evidenced by the puffed-up chest) and infancy.

If we were to adopt a purely psychological interpretation of violence, we might interpret the addition of green paint atop the child's body and face as an expression of Bacon's negative or violent feelings towards children. This would completely miss the point. As Bacon emphasises repeatedly in his interviews, distortion can serve as a means to remain faithful to the essence of the depicted subject, whereas our conventional expectations regarding how something ought to be depicted can themselves constitute a distortion or concealment of the subject's true nature. As Bacon remarks: 'What I want to do is to distort the thing far beyond the appearance, but in the distortion to bring it back to a recording of the appearance' (Sylvester, 40). Here, the addition of the green paint is not an act of erasing or spoiling, but a reminder of the obscurity that surrounds the question 'what is a child?'.

If, as I am suggesting, Bacon's *Study of a Child* expresses the essence of the child as a dramatic suspension, a movement with an unknown 'towards', then I see no reason why this depiction of a child is less 'real' or 'accurate' than our ordinary perception of children as cute, sweet, and innocent[12]. If anything, the ordinary perception, the lazily sentimental approach to them, completely conceals the fact that the child is essentially an enigma.

It is undeniable that on a first level the world can strike us as pleasant or unpleasant, agreeable and comforting or disagreeable and threatening. But it would be a sign of a simplistic and impoverished notion of the human experience if we were to take this distinction as a sole guide to our emotional life (see Balaska, 2024), and an impoverished notion of art if we were to take it as a sole guide to its origin. Wonder can give rise to anxiety, and anxiety to wonder (Balaska, 2024); despair often lies behind feeling high; and a mental health specialist knows that where symptoms of mania appear, like an intense sexual drive, excitement and elation, depression often lurks.

Instead, I have drawn attention to the kinds of emotions that can arise in relation to 'making something appear': the 'violence' of unveiling, the 'feeling of life' when art 'brings [the thing] over at [its] most acute point' (Sylvester, 43), the deep sense of satisfaction that comes from seeing something clearly, from bringing it to light. Here, the intensity is neither that of high feelings nor of low feelings: it is 'the intensity of the reality which [the artist] is trying to capture' (Sylvester, 172).

References

Michel Archimbaud, *Francis Bacon: In conversation with Michel Archimbaud* (London: Phaidon, 1993), abbreviated as Archimbaud.

Aristotle, *Physics*, trans. C.D.C Reeve (London: Hackett Publishing, 2018).

Maria Balaska, *Anxiety & Wonder: on Being Human* (London: Bloomsbury, 2024).

Gilles Deleuze, *Francis Bacon: The Logic of Sensation*, trans. Daniel W. Smith (London: Bloomsbury, 2013).

Jacques Derrida, *Dissemination* (Chicago: Chicago University Press, 1991).

Sigmund Freud, 'Three Essays on the Theory of Sexuality' [1905], *The Standard Edition of the Complete Psychological Works of Sigmund Freud*, Volume VII, trans. J. Strachey (London: Hogarth Press, 1953).

Søren Kierkegaard, *The Concept of Anxiety*. ed. and trans. R. Thomte and A. B. Anderson (Princeton: Princeton University Press, 1980).

Martin Harrison (ed.), *Francis Bacon: Catalogue Raisonné* (London: The Estate of Francis Bacon, 2016).

Martin Heidegger, 'The Origin of the Work of Art' in *Basic Writings*, ed. and trans. D. F. Krell (London: Routledge, 2011), pp. 83–140.

Martin Heidegger, 'The Question Concerning Technology' in Basic Writings, ed. and trans. D.F. Krell, 41–57 (London: Routledge, 2011a), pp. 213–238.

Georg Hegel, 'Philosophy of nature, introduction' in *Hegel, The Essential Writings*, ed. F. G. Weiss (New York: Harper Torchbooks, 1974).

Gregg M. Horowitz, 'Scratching the Surface: Distance and Intimacy in Study of Henrietta Moraes Laughing' in *Francis Bacon: Painting, Philosophy, Psychoanalysis*, ed. B. Ware (London: The Estate of Francis Bacon and Thames and Hudson, 2019), pp. 42–55.

Jacques Lacan, *Television: A Challenge to the Psychoanalytic Establishment*, ed. J. Copjec (New York: W. W. Norton & Company, 1990).

Catherine Malabou, 'From Deconstruction to Plasticity: Morphing Francis Bacon' in *Francis Bacon: Painting, Philosophy, Psychoanalysis*, ed. B. Ware (London: The Estate of Francis Bacon and Thames and Hudson, 2019), pp. 71–93.

Maurice Merleau-Ponty, 'Cézanne's doubt' in *The Merleau-Ponty Aesthetics Reader*, ed. G. Johnson (Evanston: Northwestern University Press, 1993), pp. 59–75.

David Sylvester, *Interviews with Francis Bacon* (London: Thames & Hudson, 2016), abbreviated as Sylvester.

Ben Ware, 2019. 'Looking the Negative in the Face: Modernist Painting after Affect', in *Francis Bacon: Painting, Philosophy, Psychoanalysis*, ed. B. Ware (London: The Estate of Francis Bacon and Thames and Hudson, 2019), pp. 138–159.

Ludwig Wittgenstein, *Tractatus Logico-Philosophicus*, trans. D. F. Pears and B. F. McGuinness (London: Routledge, 1974).

Endnotes

1. Of course, both film and photography can also function in non-representational ways, and they very often do. However, this is a point about the technical possibilities of photography, namely that it allows for snapshots of reality that are detachable from the subjective viewpoint of the artist. The fact that a picture can be taken blindly, as it were, purely as a result of the camera's function, introduces the idea of an appearance that can emerge without a gaze. For a philosophical account of technology not just as a mere set of tools, but as a mode of relating to the world, see Heidegger, 2011a.

2. Despite his criticism of illustration, Bacon often used photographs for his work, and famously painted portraits from photographs of his models rather than from live posing. However, 'photographs are only of interest to [him] as records' (Archimbaud, 12), 'a means of illustrating something and illustration doesn't interest [him]' (Archimbaud, 12). Apart from the practical significance that photographs may have had for him, including the study of movement in the case of Muybridge, it seems also important for him that today it is impossible to do painting while completely bypassing photography. As Bacon discusses, the fact that an image can now be reproduced in such a direct way means that painting is forced to move beyond illustration, as other media (video, photography, etc) achieve illustration much better.

3. This mirrors what happened in the philosophy of language at the beginning of the twentieth century, when propositions were primarily viewed as empirical propositions, aimed at representing facts about the world. This prioritisation of representation led to propositions in aesthetics (and ethics) being treated as mere expressions of emotions – subjective cries of approval or disapproval, akin to 'Boo!' or 'Hooray!' – rather than propositions *about the world*. The ability of a proposition to reach out to the world, as Wittgenstein puts it (1974, 2.1511–2.1515), was derived from the field of aesthetics. As I discuss in the final section of this article, something similar has occurred with art, and more specifically with Bacon's art, which has often been treated in terms of a provocation of sensations and affects.

4. Bacon's attitude towards abstract painting was less dismissive than might be inferred from the Sylvester interviews. On other occasions he proved to be well informed about Abstract Expressionism and Colour Field painting, for example, confounding popular (mis)conceptions.

5. See Jacques Derrida, *Dissemination* (Chicago: Chicago University Press, 1991) For a view of Bacon's work as a re-elaboration of the concept of form, see Malabou, 2019. Malabou thinks that contra Deleuze and Derrida, form is central for Bacon. But it is not a Platonic kind of form associated with being. Instead, it is closer to a manifestation of becoming. She captures this distinction aptly through a reference to Heidegger's later concept of *Gestellung*, 'an installation into the aspect'. It is a presencing that captures the essence of something as a movement rather than a static universal, 'the movement that consists in coming to be lodged in an aspect the way one settles in a nest' (2019, 87).

6. In his discussion of what Cézanne was attempting to do through his painting, Merleau-Ponty puts this as follows: 'to make visible how the world touches us.' (Merleau-Ponty, 1993)

7. See Deleuze, 2013.

8. This is also reinforced by what Ben Ware describes as affective modernism, a problem he diagnoses in Deleuze's reading of Bacon's work in terms of the violence of the sensation but also, at least partly, in Bacon's own understanding of modernism. See Ware, 2019.

9. In his interview with Archimbaud, Bacon states at some point that what matters is not to know or understand the artwork, but to feel something. This is in the context of discussing whether it is important to know facts about the artist himself or the history of painting (art) more generally. Archimbaud asks for a clarification of this: 'do you mean that with painting the thing is to feel emotion?' Bacon resists that kind of summary of his view: 'I'm not sure that experiencing emotion is the most important thing as far as creativity is concerned. Perhaps it is for the person who experiences it, but probably not for the artist himself'. The way I read his dismissal of knowing or understanding is by going back to the point about duality. Art is neither an abstract mental exercise nor the simple provocation of powerful sensations. See Archimbaud, 78.

10. This is one way to understand the fact that Bacon used photographs to paint his portraits – obviously alongside the practical considerations he mentions, like having the time and space to study them, and also having the chance and time to study movement by looking at a sequence of pictures (see Archimbaud, 12). The distortions that Bacon's painting involves, the violence of removing screens happens best on and through the medium that is today meant to represent reality, namely photography. In other words, working from a photograph means working from and subverting the accepted standards of appearance. This also links to the point I make in endnote 2, that painting cannot bypass photography today, but must transcend it by acknowledging it. For a different, psychoanalytic view on

why Bacon paints portraits from photographs see Horowitz, 2019. Horowitz reads Bacon's preference to paint portraits through photographs in the Freudian-Kleinian context of reparation, the work of phantasy to impede the absence of his figures that he has imposed on them – by painting in their absence. I find this interpretation unconvincing both because of the bigger de-psychologised picture I have presented (looking to make something real by transcending illustration) and because Bacon also used photographs for his own self-portraits.

11. 'If nothing more than [a search for distinguishing marks] were involved, we might, e.g., take the lobe of the ear as the sign of man, for no animal has it; but we feel at once that such a characteristic is not sufficient for a knowledge of the essential nature of man'. Hegel 1974, 206.

12. Sadly, 'children' have not figured frequently in the history of ideas; however, there are thinkers who have drawn attention to aspects of being-a-child that we often overlook. For instance, Sigmund Freud highlighted their aggressive and sexual impulses, describing them as 'polymorphously perverse' (see Freud, 1953). Søren Kierkegaard shed existential light on children by addressing their attraction to what is monstrous and dark as an indication of their attraction to spirit, suggesting that children are already transcending mere interest in worldly entities and exhibiting an attraction to existential freedom (see 1980, 42).

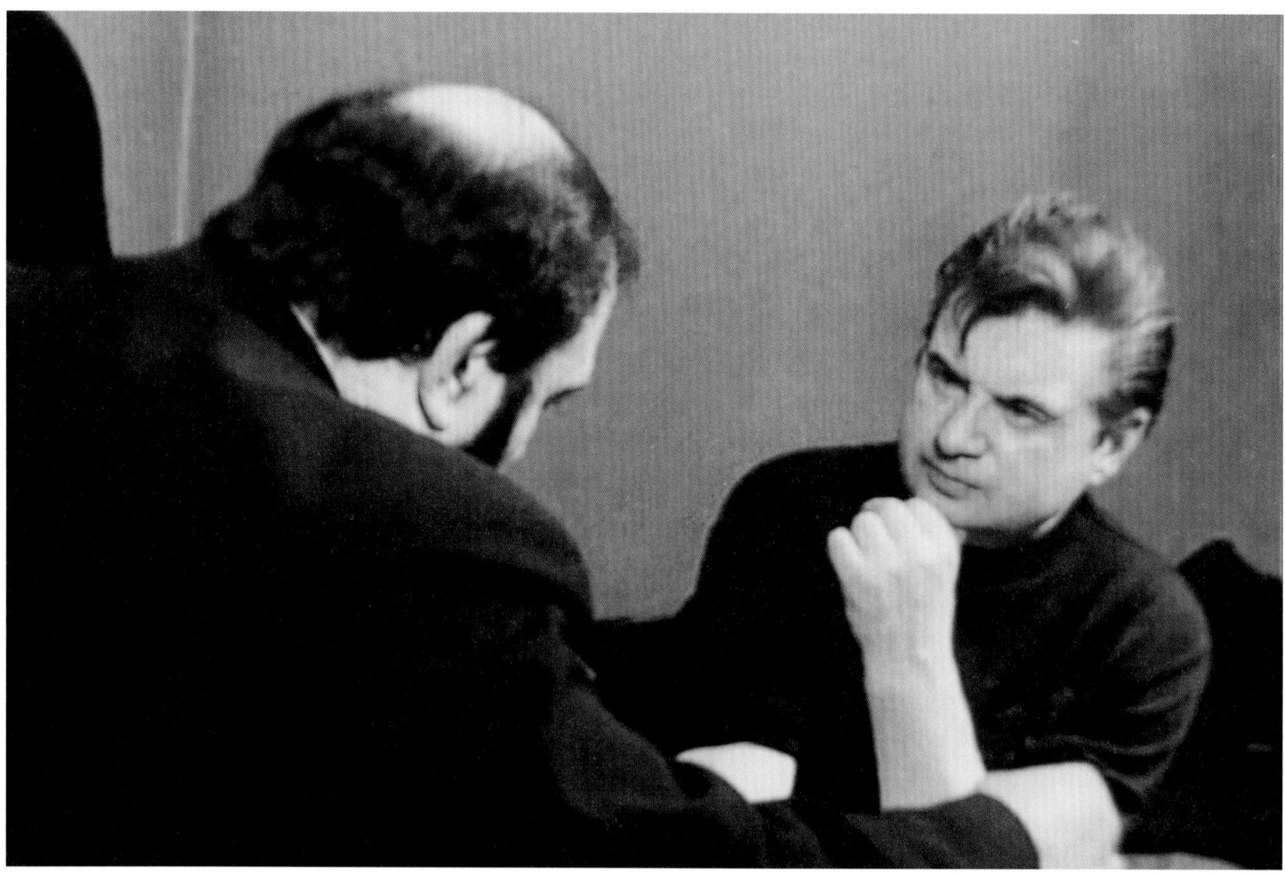

55. Bacon interviewed by Sylvester for BBC TV, May 1966.

```
p. 6

        age of about seven or eight - or probably even earlier
        than that - and they've been influenced by their
        environment, that all its spontaneity and vitality has
        gone and it just becomes very boring.  But of course
        the trouble with children's art is that it never, even
        at its best,    is    enough.

DS      Because the child hasn't experienced enough?

FB      This is one of the things I've often wondered.  If one
        lived one's life in some little place in the country
        and never really experienced anything, would one
        perhaps be still just as potent as an artist as from
        one's experience?      I don't know

DS      I think that, even if nothing actually happened to one,
        the fact that one had the need for it to happen, which
        one develops at a certain stage, and all the things
        that don't happen but which one has been needing to
        happen - that would already be a positive experience
        which the child hadn't had.

FB      Yes.  I agree.

DS      I mean, the marvellous example of what you're talking
        about is in fact Emily Bronte, to whom very little
        happened.    She knew her brother

FB      Yes.  The desire takes over, as it were, from the
        practice.

DS      Yes.  But when you talk about the potency which the
        image has when it's come from the unconscious and
        hasn't been corrected by the conscious thought, I
```

56. Leaf from typescript of 1982 interview, found in Bacon's studio. The paragraph at the top of the page was published in Sylvester's *Interviews* (p. 178), the second paragraph was published in a different form (p. 76), while the remainder of the page, including Bacon's enigmatic remark about Emily Brontë, that 'she knew her brother', was never published.

Lost Words: Unpublished Bacon

Martin Harrison

1 David Sylvester, *Interviews with Francis Bacon* (London and New York: Thames & Hudson, 1975). All editions are hereafter abbreviated as *Interviews*. The 1987 and 1993 editions were titled *The Brutality of Fact: Interviews with Francis Bacon*.

2 *Interviews*, 1993, p. 7.

3 We are greatly indebted to Martha Parsey, who continues to make films about Bacon based on these interviews. *Bacon in Paris* was made with David Sylvester in 1996 and the final film in her trilogy, *Bacon's Histories: Study for a Portrait*, is currently nearing completion. The extensive research for this version of the extracts was carried out entirely by Sophie Pretorius.

4 *Interviews with Francis Bacon,* 1975 et seq.

5 *Interviews*, 1993, pp. 6–7.

INTRODUCTION

Bacon's words are printed in bold type throughout.

Probably the most frequently consulted resource on Francis Bacon, among scholars and the wider public, is the series of interviews conducted by David Sylvester and published in nine parts between 1962 and 1986. The earlier of these were first published in book form in 1975 as *Interviews with Francis Bacon*.[1] The success of this book led to many further editions, which by 1987 incorporated all the later interviews; it was translated into many European languages, facilitating the wide geographical dissemination of the interviews, and remains in print today.

As Sylvester noted, three-quarters of the transcripts were jettisoned on grounds of 'editorial choice'.[2] The most illuminating of Bacon's remarks that were eliminated, and have remained unpublished, form the core of 'Lost Words'. The extent of the redacted material that had survived was first brought to our attention by the artist and film-maker Martha Parsey.[3] Parsey had met David Sylvester in 1993, while making the film *Model and Artist; Henrietta Moraes and Francis Bacon*; she was seeking his permission to use excerpts from the Bacon interviews. A friendship and collaboration ensued, and Sylvester granted her unlimited access to the six recordings of Bacon that had been made in the 1970s. Subsequently, Martha Parsey undertook the onerous task of transcribing and presenting the recordings, but her project foundered on legal and contractual problems with Sylvester's questions, which had to be withdrawn. They are similarly omitted from 'Lost Words'.

The *Interviews* were a remarkable achievement, and in order to fully understand the excerpts published here it is essential to refer to one of the editions published in 1987 or later.[4] The interviews were not, however, neutral, or entirely objective, for they were the outcome of what was essentially a dialogue, in which Sylvester's voice was as important as Bacon's. Sylvester was acutely conscious of the editing and re-sequencing he was required to carry out in order to make the interviews intelligible, and he described his guiding principles at length in the 'Preface' to the first edition; he retained the preface, with slight revisions, in later editions.[5] Sylvester had sensibly removed many of the tedious vocal tics – 'erm', 'yep', 'yeah' – from the earlier publications and that has been adhered to in 'Lost Words'. Similarly, if Bacon said 'I must say' twice, the repetition has generally been taken out here. Some of the problems that stem from transcribed recordings remain, but to have edited out all the grammatical solecisms would have risked inauthenticity; thus, although the results can sometimes be difficult to follow, we have erred on the side of retaining Bacon's voice.

The thematic, rather than chronological, arrangement of this new material will hopefully prove more convenient for readers; the dates of Bacon's responses are appended to every entry. Sylvester's presentation was in any case not linear, but rather a careful collage of remarks made at different dates, 'freely and radically rearranged.'[6] It should be noted that Bacon, too, exercised a certain amount of editorial control over what was published, although relatively few of his corrections or deletions have come to light. Latterly, the transcriptions seem to have been sent to Valerie Beston, of Marlborough Fine Art, who fed back Bacon's comments. On an isolated extant page of text from the interviews of 1984, Bacon was speaking about Linton Hall, the house in Herefordshire that his parents took in 1922. He happened to mention that on Saturdays he used to go shopping with his mother in the nearby market town of Newent; evidently, he reconsidered this ostensibly innocuous detail, probably because its cosy domesticity was counter to his reconstruction of a difficult upbringing, and he struck it out. There are also a few examples of Bacon editing a 1982 interview, [56] but unless further marked transcripts resurface the extent of the changes he made can only be speculated upon.

Given the massive contribution made to Bacon studies by the *Interviews*, it may appear ungracious to criticise aspects of them, but in some respects they have undoubtedly been misleading. That the questions he put to Bacon reflected Sylvester's views on art more than Bacon's is undeniable. At one point Bacon complains: **You seem to want me to be very discursive. Well, I can't be.** [1984] The very first question Sylvester put to Bacon in the first interview, recorded for the BBC Third Programme in October 1962, was: 'Have you ever had any desire at all to do an abstract painting at any time?'[7] This might have been intended to provoke a reaction from Britain's most resolutely anti-abstract artist, but Sylvester had interviewed seven American abstract expressionists in 1960/61, including Adolph Gottlieb, Franz Kline and Robert Motherwell, and it may equally have been an instance of an aficionado of these artists wondering how Bacon's figurative paintings continued to exert a fascination over him. One of the most repetitive of Sylvester's questions, 'Was that foreseen?', was invariably followed by Bacon's evasive, **No that was an afterthought**. [1973] It was a line of questioning that was never abandoned, to the point of tedium, and was never satisfactorily answered by Bacon; Sylvester surely harboured suspicions that Bacon was dissembling. It was not until many years after the final interview that Bacon's motivations began to be more thoroughly scrutinised, and the theory that 'the accident' drove his modus operandi was seriously addressed.

The first interview was recorded three months after the closure of Bacon's first major retrospective at the Tate Gallery, London. Marlborough Gallery had promised Bacon such an exhibition when he signed to them in 1958, and in 1964 they fulfilled another of their promises, to arrange a catalogue raisonné. Bacon was being successfully propelled into an elevated sphere of the art market and as part of that strategy the interviews with Sylvester were mutually beneficial. There may have been a tacit – or even explicit – agreement between interlocutor and artist that only art of the

6   *Interviews*, 1993, p. 7.

7   The last three words were omitted in the published version. Bacon's iconography was a secondary matter for Sylvester, who referred, for example, to a (distorted) man as a dog and misread a Eumenides as an elephant. Contrarily, I shall contend, in an essay now in preparation, that Bacon could be described legitimately as an abstract artist.

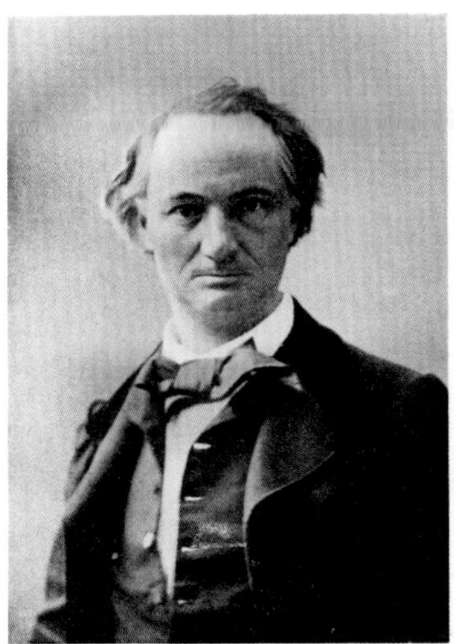

9 Nadar: Portrait of Baudelaire

57. Nadar: photograph of Charles
Baudelaire, from Peter Quennell, *Victorian
Panorama*, 1937. Bacon owned a copy of this
book, and the page reproduced here was
included in a Sam Hunter photograph of
Bacon's source images, taken in 1950.

highest order would be discussed. A pantheon evolved that encompassed
Michelangelo, Rembrandt and Velázquez, Degas, Seurat and Picasso, but
few 'lesser' figures. Daumier was never mentioned in the interviews,
redacted or otherwise, despite his importance for Bacon, while other
artists who had once advised him, such as Roy de Maistre, are similarly
absent. That Walter Sickert was briefly alluded to, only to be disparaged
for using squared-up photographs, was probably a case of Bacon denying
his erstwhile indebtedness. Again, while Yeats and Eliot occur frequently,
inexplicably, Baudelaire [57] is missing.

Cumulatively, the exclusions resulted in a skewed perspective on
Bacon. He seldom identified individual family members, although the
absence of his sister, Ianthe, or his cousin, Diana Watson, was possibly
because he wished to guard their privacy. The same reasoning may have
applied to former lovers, such as Eric Allden and Peter Lacy. Bacon was
unlikely to have initiated discussions about these people, and evidently
neither did Sylvester. For the most part, Bacon comes across as striving
to be co-operative, a testimony to the friendship between the two men.
Occasionally he called a halt to the proceedings when he was too tired,
or too drunk (or not drunk enough), yet for the most part he abandoned
his scepticism concerning the likelihood of saying anything worthwhile
about art. But he was alert to moments when the conversation was veering
towards the bathetic: **I'm talking bollocks** [1984] he muttered under his
breath at one point, or, in exasperation, exclaiming, **I think we're talking
nonsense now.** [1975] He also sought to avoid sounding pretentious: ...
anyway, the way *I'm* talking is talking in a sort of falsely grandiose way.
[1974]

It is important to note that Bacon's answers frequently addressed specific
historical contexts. For example, the interview conducted in December 1971
was recorded shortly after Bacon had returned to London following the
opening of his triumphant exhibition at the Grand Palais, Paris. Bacon, in
atavistic mode, had carefully curated the retrospective/historical sections
of the exhibition, and his comments on the paintings were based on
images in the catalogue; (the catalogues of the Metropolitan Museum of
Art exhibition in 1975 and the second Tate Gallery retrospective in 1985
performed the same function). This method aligned with a recurrent
thread in the interviews, periodisation, a system of classification that
reflected Sylvester's analytical stance rather than Bacon's. Artists habitually
opt to believe that their most recent paintings are their best, and to some
extent Sylvester was flattering Bacon by favourably comparing paintings
made since 1968 with those from the 1950s, even if the comparison was not
necessarily valid. Although he was prepared to try to respond to Sylvester's
leading questions about 'fallow' periods, Bacon was partly complicit in
the periodisation, agreeing, after some pressure, **I feel that between 1949,
except for a very few things, and 1960, I went through a bad trough.**
[1971] Yet Bacon proceeded, as was his habit, to contradict this generalisa-
tion by singling out more than 'a very few things' in which he perceived
lasting merit. They included **a painting from 1953 with two men on a bed,**
[*Two Figures*, 1953] and **the one you yourself had of the man sitting with
closed blinds.** [*Study for a Portrait*, 1953]. [58]

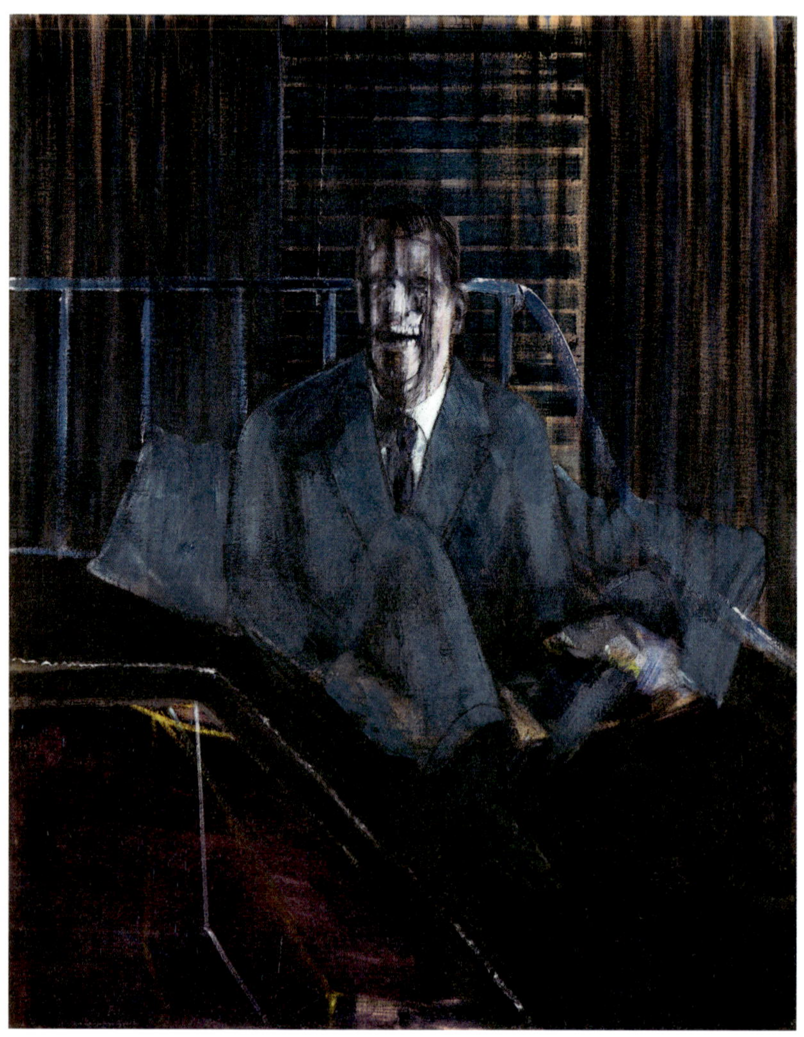

58. *Study for a Portrait*, 1953

8   'Fragments of Talk', David Sylvester, *Looking Back at Francis Bacon* (London and New York: Thames & Hudson, 2000), pp. 230–49.

After Bacon's death, with time to reflect and free from the artist's interventions, Sylvester reinstated some of Bacon's thoughts omitted from *Interviews* in a new book, *Looking Back at Francis Bacon*. These appear mainly in the section titled 'Fragments of Talk' and should definitely be consulted, not least because, with two partial exceptions, they are not repeated here.[8] What, then, might the present publication of the 'lost words' potentially disclose that is of value? It is itself selective, for among the material Sylvester rejected a large percentage was banal or repetitive, and therefore superfluous. If some of Bacon's statements printed here sound slightly familiar, it is because he had been asked the same question numerous times, yet some of his alternative answers carry subtly different implications that make it worthwhile to preserve the nuances. In other cases, it is unclear why Bacon's statements were expunged; his exegesis of one of his key paintings, *Study for Crouching Nude*, 1952, for example, is revelatory. [see pp. 86–87] To gain access to more than fifteen thousand of his previously unpublished words has been at times exhilarating and always informative.

I was born in Ireland and brought up as a Protestant and as you know, Protestants' obsession in Ireland is even more extreme and absurd than the Catholic one, because they are in the minority, after all; minority views are always more extreme. I don't think it's a thing we need to talk about, but I was just reading Jones's life of Freud[9] two or three days ago and, as you know, Freud was so anxious that psychoanalysis should not be thought of as totally a Jewish thing, so ... the Protestants were so violent that they didn't want to think of Catholicism as being only that thing that Ireland existed by. And that's the reason that Protestants are so rabid – and I was brought up as a rabid Protestant, with no beliefs of course. [1975]

And the people, they went to Straffan Lodge.[10] And the people who had a place called Straffan House were called Barton. And the Bartons were half French. And they are now the Barton & Guestier, who you find in Bordeaux, the great shippers of Bordeaux wines. And I know, of course I was too young to go to these things, but I always remember my mother telling me they used to have the most amazing dinner parties in this house, where they had eleven courses, which went on, they carried on the Edwardian tradition of these very long meals, and in between to revive themselves, they had sorbets, just to keep them going for the next meal. And that's about all I remember. Then, when I was about 16, I left Ireland and I came to London. [1984]

[Explaining that his mother was a scion of the Firth family, wealthy industrialists] ... And so, she had a bit of money, but ... And so that, I don't know if she was socially grand. You see, my father came from this family called Bacon. Whether they belong to the great tradition of the Bacon family, I don't really know. My mother very much wanted me to go into the whole thing. It takes so long to find, to go into this, to search out your family tree. If you give it to somebody, they generally tell you what they think you would like to hear. [1984]

[On his furniture designs] I sold one or two things. I remember somehow there was a very well-known German actress, whose name I can't remember now. And she was brought to my studio, and she liked the things very much. But you see, my things were very, very ... It was never any good, really, my designs, because they were so derivative. They were all derived from things that were being done in Italy, Germany, and France at that time. [1984]

Well, in this country, the first person who really started designing rugs was for Wilton's those type of rugs, was McKnight Kauffer and Marion Dorn. Marion Dorn was American. I'm not sure if McKnight Kauffer was American or not, but anyhow, they were the first people to start doing that. And then I did that afterwards. But I never looked back on them with any pleasure myself. I had a small studio around the corner here in a mews in Queensberry Place, and I designed them there. [1984]

9   Ernest Jones, *The Life and Work of Sigmund Freud* (first edition 1953–57).

10   Bacon's family, 'the people', moved to Straffan Lodge, Co. Kildare, in 1921.

11   Bacon is referring to the Anglo French Art Centre, London, an arts project that ran from 1946 to 1951. The two paintings he destroyed have not been identified.

... there were two paintings in the Anglo Art Centre that, there are not many paintings that I regret that I've destroyed, but there were two paintings in that Anglo Art Centre that I really now rather regret that I destroyed.[11] But going back to Michael Sadler, he bought that, and he bought that crucifixion, which, of course, not only was influenced by Picasso, but it was, to some extent, influenced by Masson. And anyhow, after he bought this, he asked me to do a portrait of him. And I wrote to him, I said, Well, I don't think I can do a portrait of you. And he then sent me a skull. And an Ektachrome, as it were, of his skull. And that painting, I don't know where it is now, and I did the skull beside a crucifixion. Where that painting is now, I have no idea. [1984]

[Roulette] I think I started that when I went down before the first, before the second [world war]. I went down about '35, '36. I went down to Monte Carlo, and I was there for a time. I also, after the war, I went back to Monte Carlo, and I lived there for about nine months or a year. I once went into the casino, and I was very lucky, for me. I took a villa on my winnings ... [1984]

And after all, in Ireland, there was the whole of the Sinn Féin period going on then. And we were living at this place called Farmleigh. And I remember my father said, if they come tonight, just keep your mouth shut. Don't say anything. Well, at my age, I wouldn't. Anyhow, they didn't happen to turn up. It was that time when they were burning down and shooting everybody in the houses. Well, that didn't happen. It might have even happened to us as we weren't Irish, as we were English, you see. And that could easily have happened, but it didn't happen. Then living through that, then after that, going to Berlin in 1927, '28, seeing something, the great distress, really. Although it was a city that was wide open, there was tremendous distress in Berlin at that time. And then leading on to the Second World War, starting, which, after all, the tension had been starting or had been going on all through the thirties. There'd been the war in Abyssinia with the Italians, and then the '39 war starting. I have lived, in a sense, through a continuous state of crisis. So that, whether that's reflected in my work or not, I don't know. It's not consciously reflected, but it may be reflected in me as I may, without knowing it, be aware of the violence of life in an extreme way, through the situations through which my life has passed. [1984]

Well, I like the good food I was brought up with it. My mother, living in Ireland, we used to have them ... We had very, very good, but very simple food. Things like oxtail and shepherd's pie and all those kinds of things which were absolutely delicious when they're properly cooked ... One of the most delicious game that I've ever had, which used to be quite plentiful on the marshlands in Ireland, was the snipe. And they were an absolutely delicious thing. And you know that's a small bird. And then the way they used to secure them with the bill, the way they used to do them in Ireland, you know how they use a skewer? They used to leave the head on and then skewer them through the legs with the bill. But it's a very, very delicious food. That was probably the best game we

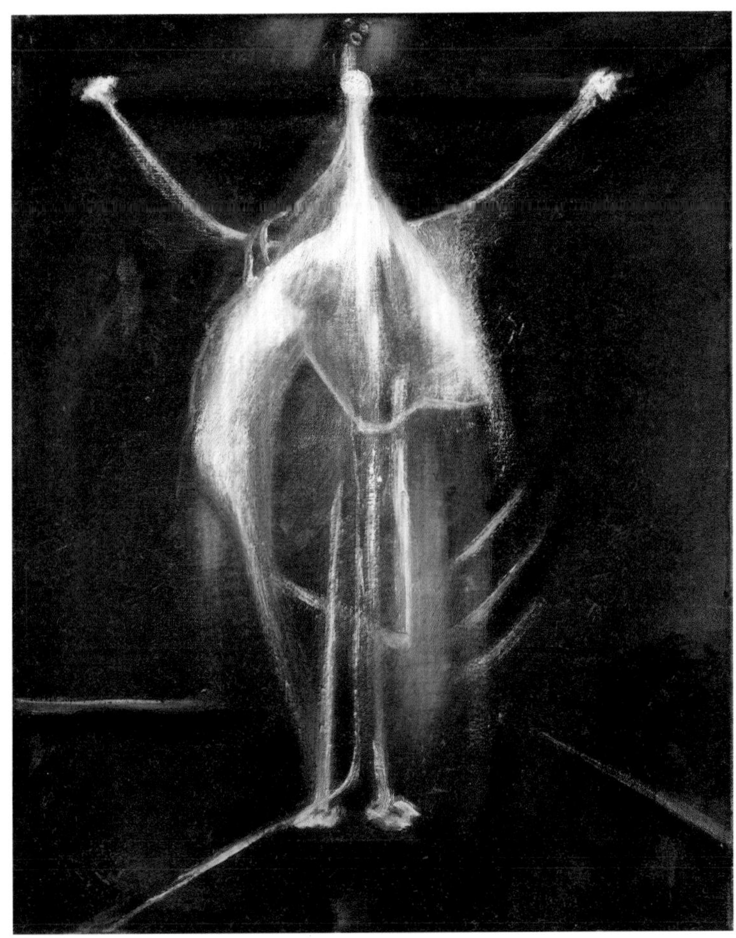

59. *Crucifixion*, 1933

ever used to have apart from pheasants and things. Well, pheasants to me don't mean all that much. I think I prefer chicken to pheasant … I love partridge, but then partridge is not very plentiful in Ireland … no grouse, no. There are lots of pigeons. It was just pigeon pie. It was absolutely filthy. But anyhow. I like stewed eels, but you didn't get eels in Ireland in those days. The Irish wouldn't eat them. [1984]

But the funny thing is, in those days, for instance, the Irish wouldn't eat sweet breads or brains or anything like that. And when my mother went to the butcher's, that she had been, to some extent, been in France for a certain time, and she knew how those things should be done. And so the butcher used to just give them to her because nobody else would touch them. They wouldn't touch oxtail, they wouldn't. They wouldn't touch a pig's foot or sweet breads. I don't think they would eat kidneys even. So, she used to get all those, the offal what's called, she used to get it for nothing. The butcher used to give it to her. Mind you, you probably have to buy a big joint to get that. But anyhow, he did because people didn't like them. But mind you, after all, eating is so much to do with what you're accustomed to, isn't it? The type of food you like is what you're accustomed to. [1984]

12   Bacon's exhibition at the Grand Palais, Paris, opened in October 1971; here he refers to a specific painting that he included, the only one from his 'Van Gogh Series'.

13   Neither Bacon nor Sylvester had a firm grasp of the titles or dates of the paintings, but in this case they were misled by a dating error in the 1964 catalogue raisonné; the painting to which Bacon was referring was in fact *Pope*, 1954.

Bacon was very selective in his judgments of paintings he had made in series, usually singling out only one for approbation, as in **I liked one of the Van Goghs, which was in the exhibition in Paris, of the variation on the road to Tarascon,** [*Study for Portrait of Van Gogh II*, 1957].[12] He continued to hold in high regard **one of the series of the Pope which was in the show which was painted in 1955** [*Pope*, 1954][13], and also **one of the Heads of Blake,** [*Study for Portrait II – after the Life Mask of William Blake*, 1955], adding that **I quite like the baboon.** [2]
[1975]

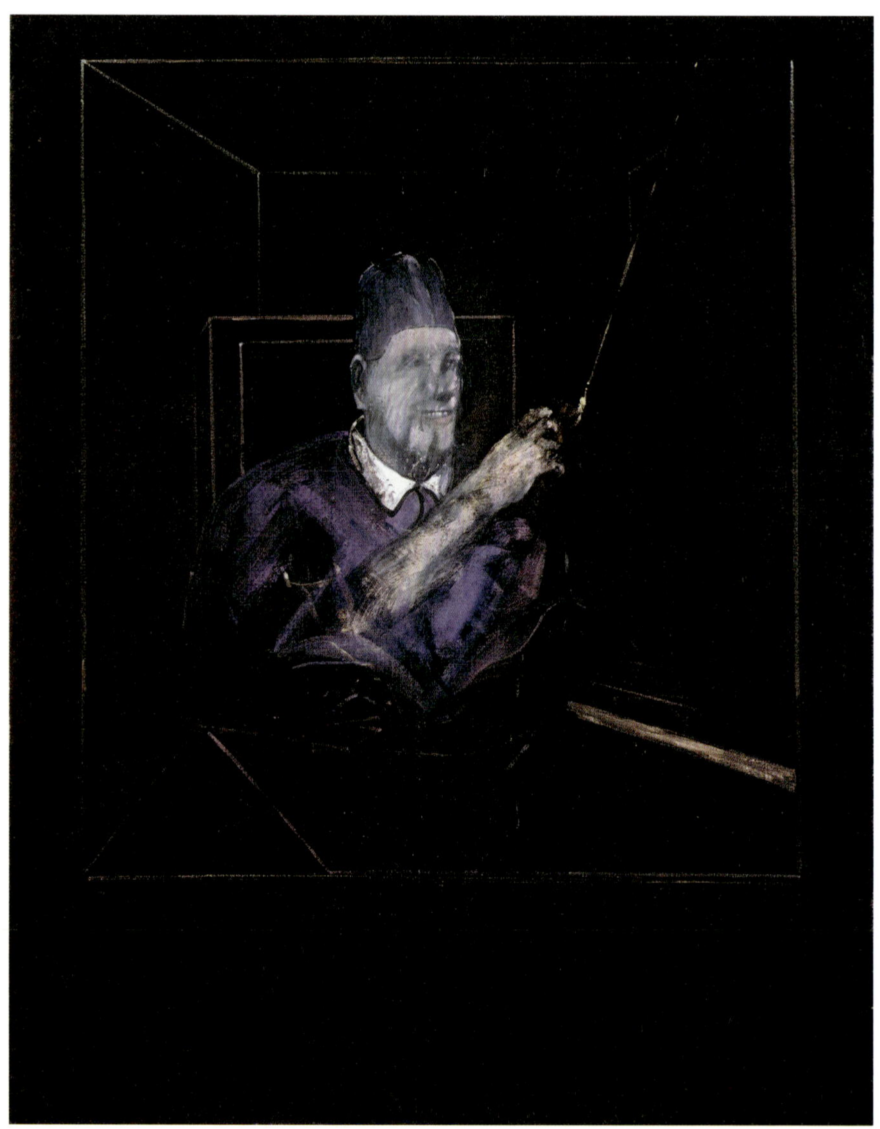

60. *Pope*, 1954

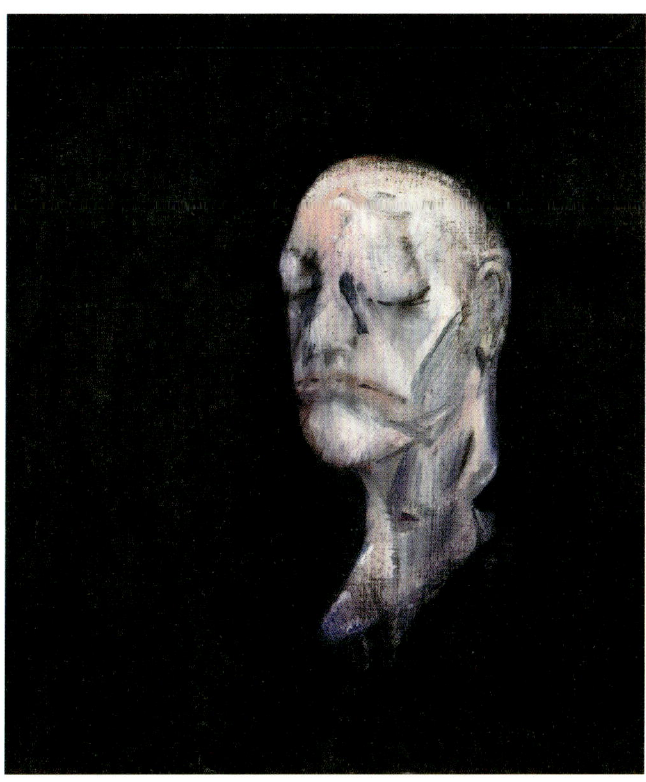

61. *Study for Portrait II – after the Life Mask of William Blake*, 1955

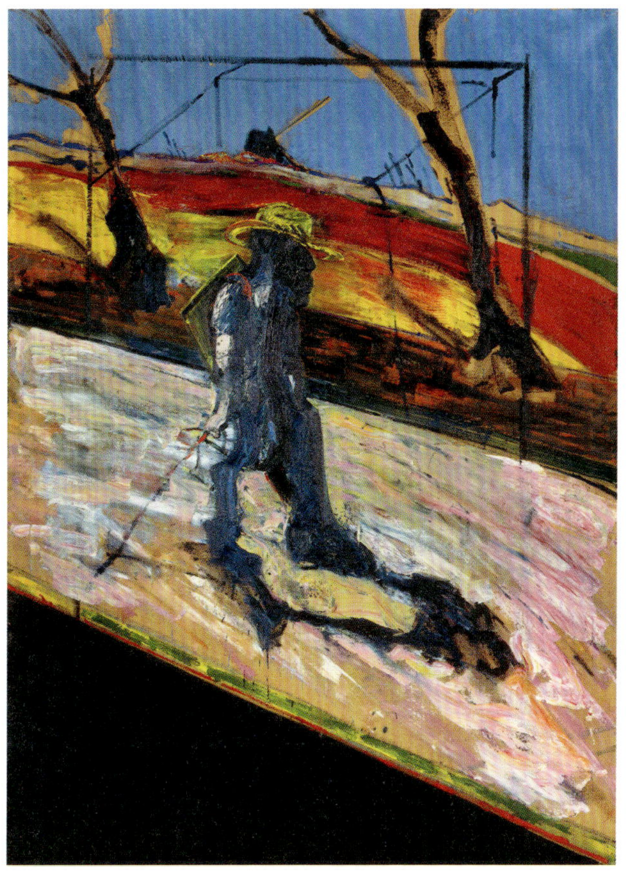

62. *Study for Portrait of Van Gogh II*, 1957

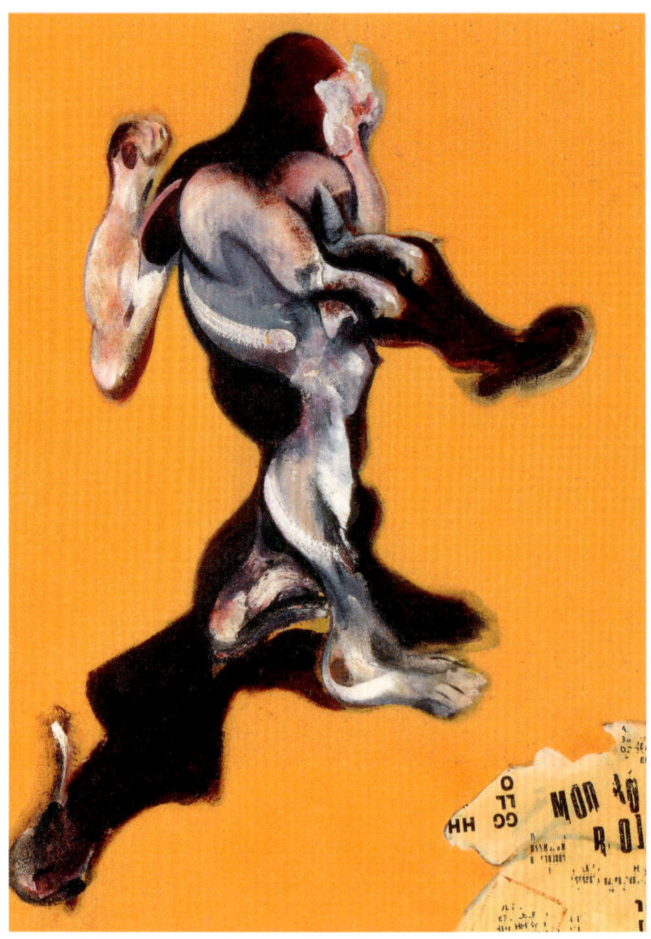

63. *Triptych – Studies from the Human Body*, 1970 (detail of left panel)

Turning to his more recent output, Bacon readdressed the question of the accident, eliding it into his ambiguous shadow-figures: **Well, one of the paintings, one of the groups of paintings that I like was the orange triptych ... I forget what it's called.** [He was discussing *Triptych – Studies from the Human Body*, 1970] **And this was a curious image that came about by accident because these predatory hands in a way came from, also from a photograph of a bird of prey coming down, and then suddenly ... I saw the shadow as though in a sense, as though it was two figures moving together. A bird going onto its prey in fact with these two little hands ... and then suddenly I saw the shadow as though, in a sense, as though it was two figures moving together.** Bacon stated, **All my paintings are problems rather than expressions.** The two melding figures was an enduring Bacon trope, and he tried again to explain his intention: **Well, one of the things is I've always hoped to make, and this is only perhaps a beginning statement, is to make a figure walking within its own shadow. So that the shadow and the image were identifiable not as two different things but as the, as it were, the shadow was part of the flesh that flowed out rather than being just a dark shadow against a lighter background. But I've always hoped one day to be able to incorporate the shadow and the image as one thing ...**[14] [1971]

14 For more on this theme, and Bacon's fluid gendering, see Sophie Pretorius, *Revisions: Francis Bacon in the Act of Painting* (2024), pp. 61–63; 124–25.

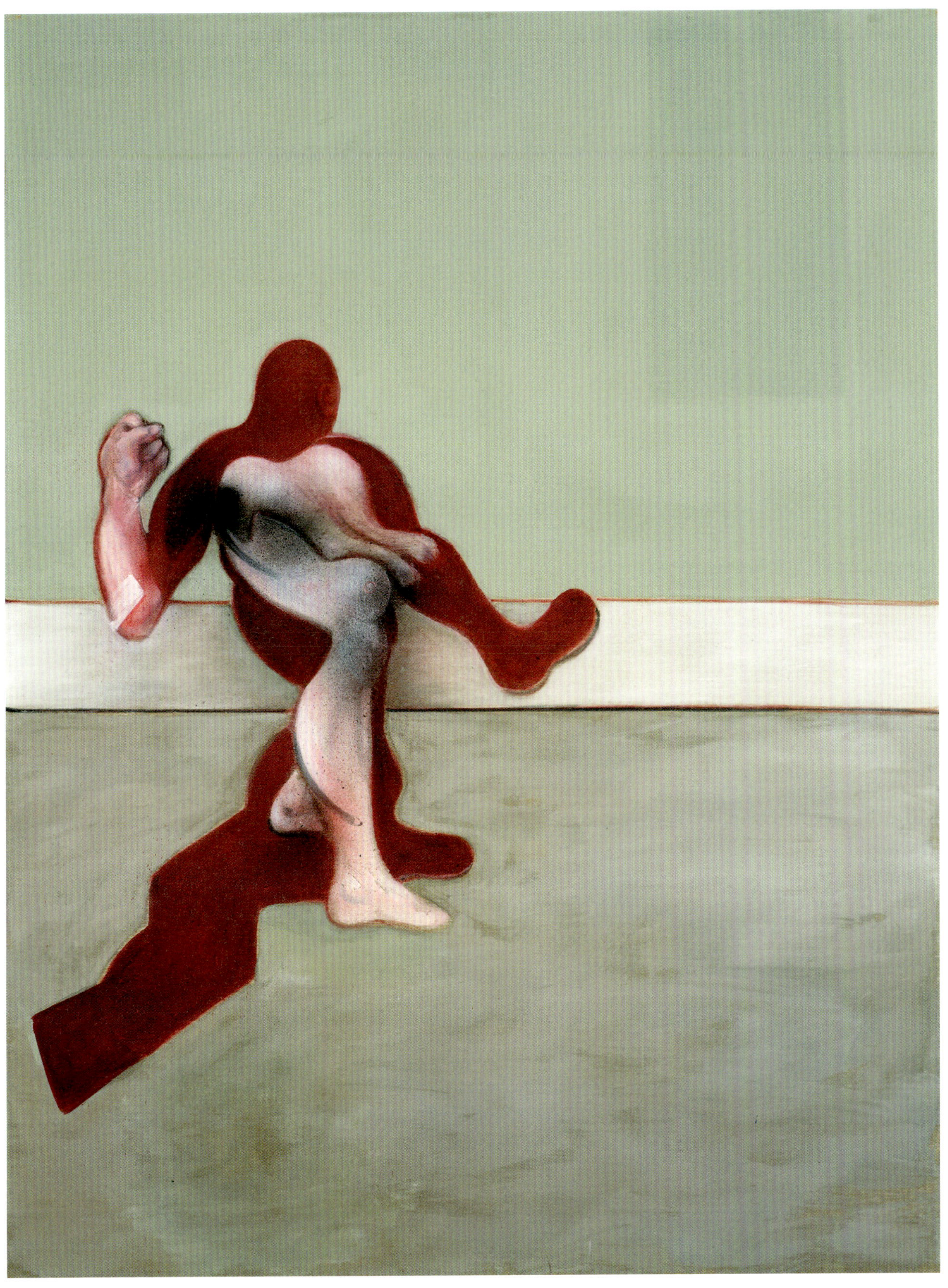

64. *Study of a Man and Woman Walking*, 1988–89

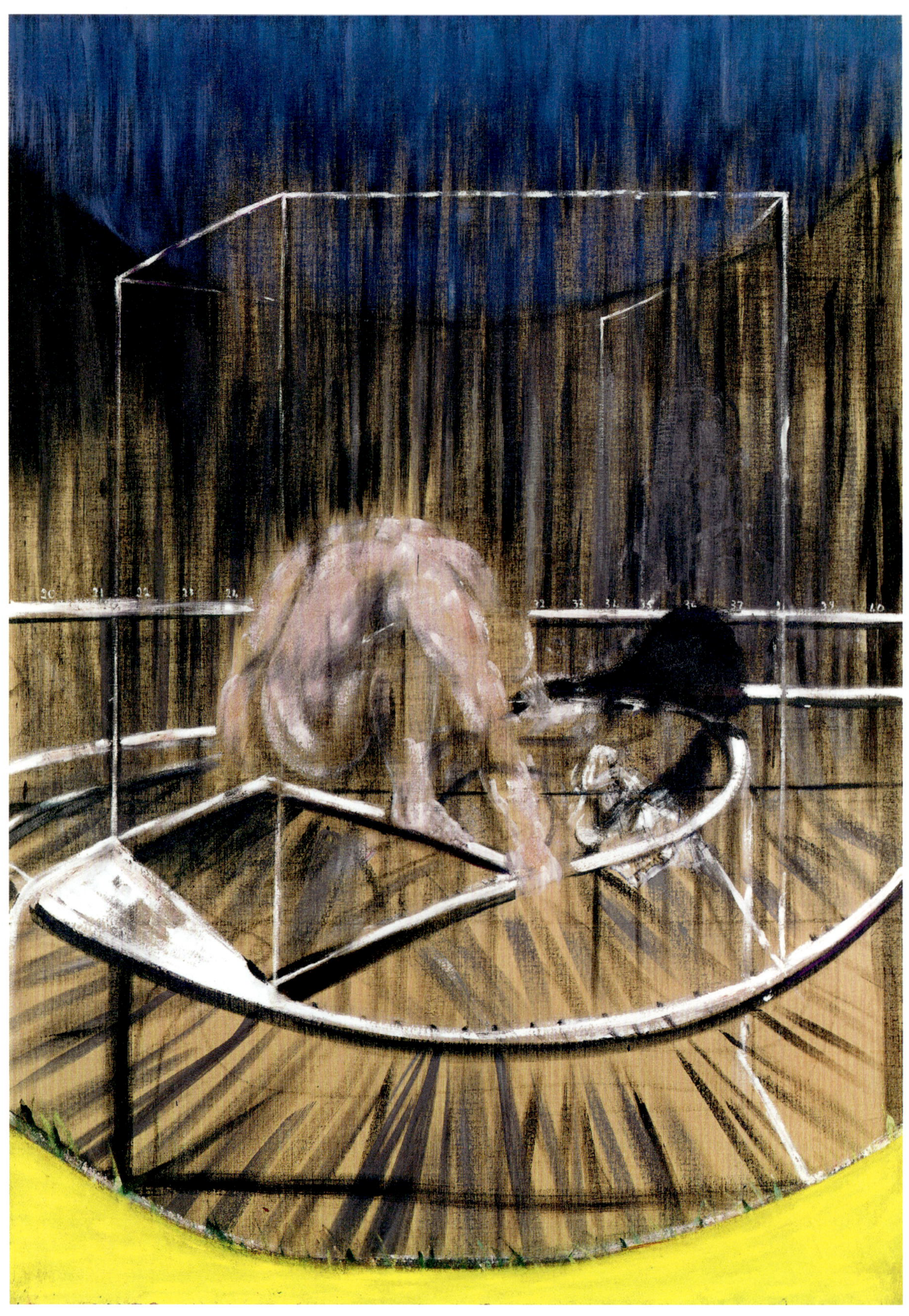

65. *Study for Crouching Nude*, 1952

Bacon's enduring attachment to *Study for Crouching Nude*, 1952, is confirmed in his illuminating comments: **It's one of the pictures that I'm going to repeat in another way. I think I can make it stronger than it is there, but perhaps the reason for me that it works is that it moves between solidity and … it's there and it's not there at the same time, and so if I make it stronger and more solid it may lose its mysterious quality that I feel it has. It's one of my favourite pictures actually, although it's done in 1952.** [1971] On another occasion he admitted: **I don't actually know how to talk about it because I just think it's an image crouching over its own shadow.** [1984]

Well this violence of my life that I talk about, when I say violence of my life, violence of which I've lived amongst, I do think it is very different to violence in painting because people can paint about violent acts but they're not very violent by the illustration of the act but by the *method*, by the technique and the invention of technique by which they can convey this violence. The violence itself is only a story, the violence would have to be *re-made* through technical, new technical means in the paint itself to bring over its violence, otherwise it would be an illustration of violence … It's a violence that has been exacerbated within the nervous system and comes out in the paint. [1971]

Because, if you take the single, for instance, the single portraits of Philip IV, they have a quite different thing, they are very specific portraits, deformed as many of them are but I'm certain – we haven't got a photograph of Philip IV – but I'm perfectly certain that if you look at those deformations he couldn't have been like that, I mean he would have been an absolute complete monster, if he was like those portraits. But in *Las Meninas* I think he got very, very close to what you are, or did bring off, what you are saying … I'm not trying to bring off that appearance. Firstly, I couldn't and secondly it's been done, perfectly, and there would be no point in doing it again. Pound or somebody said about something that if you can't do it better why try to do it again. No, it isn't that kind of appearance at all. Mine is to do, mine is to myself really to do … I sometimes find it difficult to analyse to myself what I do about this thing, for instance I think that the standing figure of Isabel that's now in Berlin, the very blue, glossy … I perhaps am wrong about this. I think it's very, very like Isabel and yet it's been made in a very peculiar way and I think it has a certain, by its technique, it has a certain shock of Isabel and, perhaps I'm flattering myself to say it has this, but it has certainly not come about in any way by really, if you analyse it, it's not brought about by copying Isabel's features. [1973]

15   The article by Gowing that offended Bacon, 'Positioning in Representation', was published in *Studio International*, January 1972, pp. 14–22. It is surprising, given Bacon's secrecy about his sources, that he was amenable to Gowing's article being published.

I think of course perhaps Lawrence Gowing has a bit over-emphasised, this is always the trouble of telling people about sources of things, is that they over-emphasise the sources, because for some reason they always find it difficult to write about my work, except disagreeably, when they want to be, they over-emphasise things that I have told them …[15] **But there was another side to the *Positioning in Radiography* that I actually liked, that interests me. I don't know how much I was ever able**

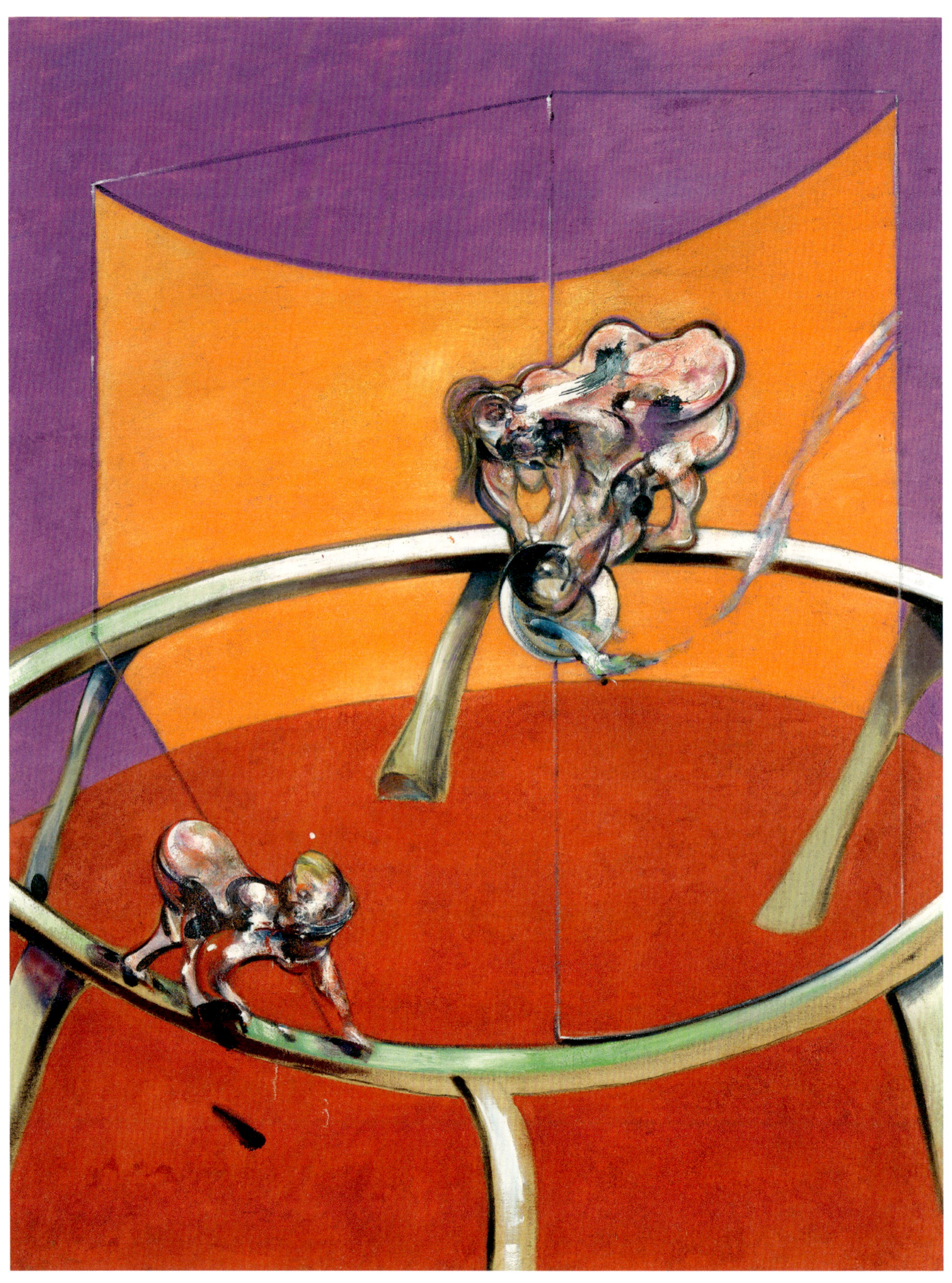

66. *From Muybridge 'The Human Figure in Motion': Woman Emptying a Bowl of Water / Paralytic Child Walking on All Fours*, 1965

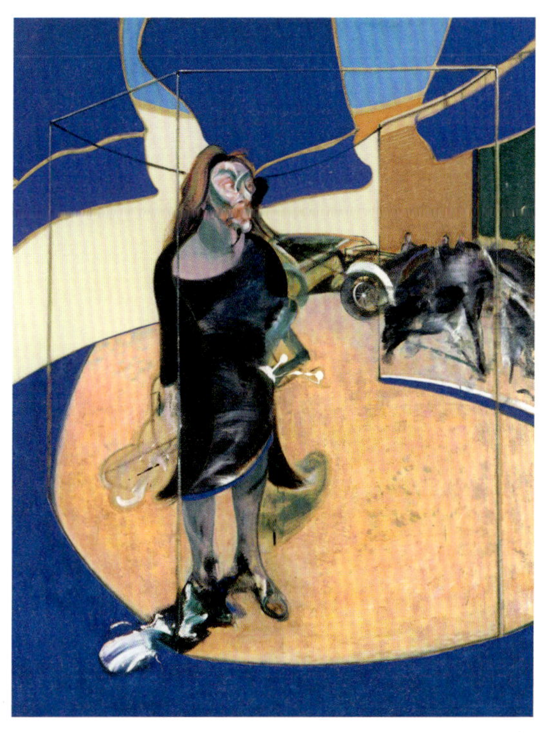

67. *Portrait of Isabel Rawsthorne
Standing in a Street in Soho*, 1967

to use it, but it interested me actually to see things like the vertebrae
and to see the teeth and the whole skeleton, as it were. [1973]

16   *Triptych Inspired by the
Oresteia of Aeschylus*, 1981.
(see p. 32)

This triptych I did from the Oresteia.[16] Well, now, I don't know that I
could talk about specific images that belong to the Oresteia, but it happens by reading it in translation that it suggests an enormous number
of images to me, and these are three of the images. I think of this one on
the left as the Eryinys. They really, when they are in their most vicious
mood, well, like our guilt haunt us with all this … We're always haunted
by our guilt, as you know. Well, they were well haunted by this image.
And Orestes was, well, haunted by this image. [1984]

[Commenting on his selections for the 1985 Tate Gallery retrospective]
That is a painting which I happen to like of a woman throwing a bowl
of water.[17] I very much want it for the exhibition, but it belongs to the
Stedelijk Museum. And they are making an exhibition of their own at
the same time as my exhibition at the Tate Gallery, and they don't want
to lend it. These ones are all of Isabel. I think the best one, at least the
one I like most of Isabel, is one where she's standing in a street in Soho,
which is in Berlin. [1984]

17   He is referring to *From
Muybridge 'The Human Figure
in Motion': Woman Emptying
a Bowl of Water / Paralytic Child
Walking on All Fours*, 1965

[About *Portrait of Isabel Rawsthorne Standing in a Street in Soho*, 1967]
Well this is the question, I actually believe that this, for instance, this
head looks very, very much like Isabel but it's very, it's gone a very long
way outside an illustration of Isabel. I think perhaps it's the best of
them … and I do remember when this picture was shown that Isabel told
me that several people came up to her in the street and spoke to her and
said I've seen a portrait of you. [1975]

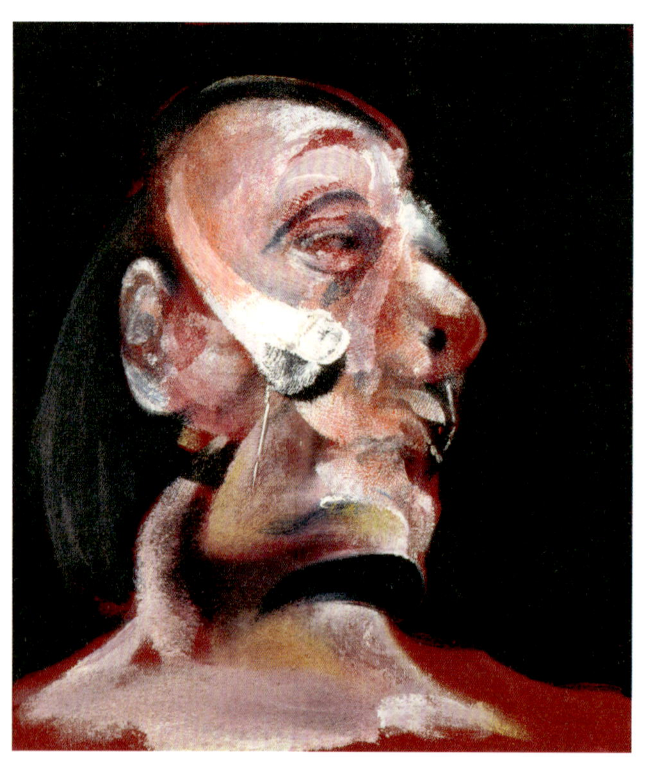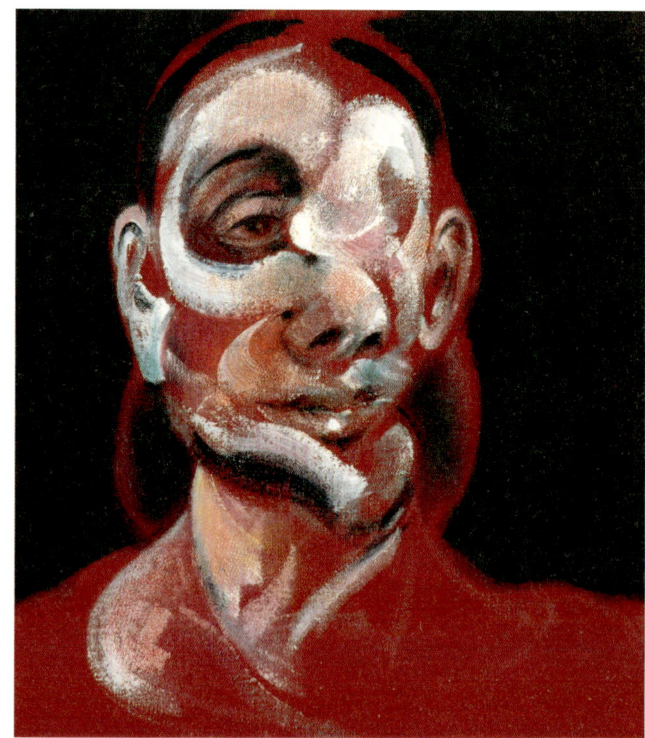

68. *Three Studies of Muriel Belcher,* 1966

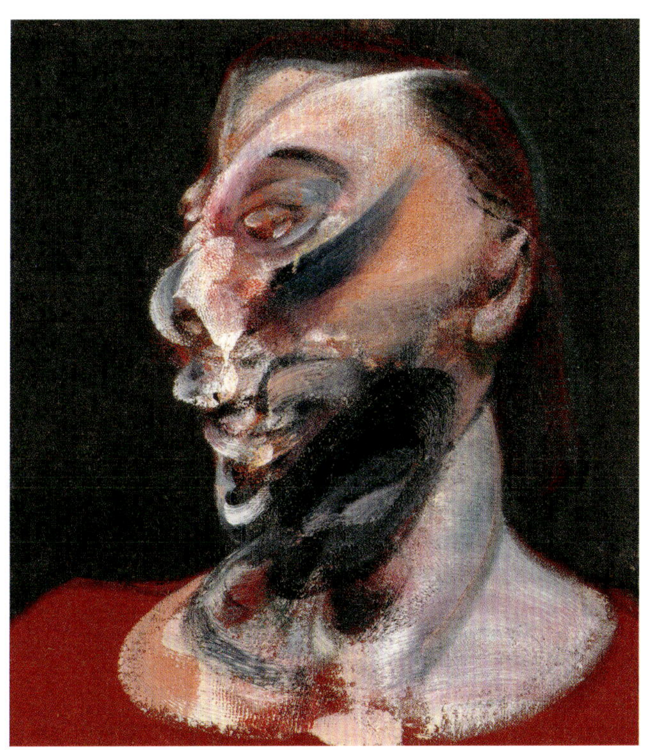

... I think, or hope, in a few portraits I have been able to make the irrational, bring the irrational marks back to the appearance ... I think, for instance, it happened by accident in the three heads I did of Muriel, of Muriel Belcher. [1975]

18   Bacon may be describing
Study of Isabel Rawsthorne, 1970

19   Bacon is again referring
back to his paintings of the
mid-1950s

I feel [my portrait of Isabel] is stark and refined, like I think Isabel
is. After all, she's a woman who seems to have come out of the ancient
world. I think that this will have to be terribly edited, because I think
I've said an awful lot of things that will sound horribly kind of vain, in a
way that I don't mean them to be.[18] [1973]

I think that in a triptych the images can be isolated and yet together.
It's perhaps, you may say … an easy way round the problem but it's the
way that I have found for myself where I want several layers of different
kinds of feeling to come in, the most satisfactory for me. But I'm not
suggesting it's at all a satisfactory solution, but for me it seems the kind
of best way. [1979]

Well, I think at the time that I was doing the dark colour things, I had
a feeling of, how can I give the impression with a minimum amount
of colour and the minimum amount of drawing? How could I bring
the image over with a minimum paint and the minimum work? Only
because I thought that one should be able to reduce things into reality. I
don't know if it worked, but there are not very many of them that I care
for, but they're just a very, very few have gone on.[19] [1984]

[discussing reproductions of his paintings that he pinned to his studio
walls] There are some of the pictures that I've done fairly recently, not
all of them, which I do prefer. And I keep that one up there that's in
the Museum of Modern Art [*Painting 1946*] because I always like the
reproductions of it, and I like the way it comes out in colour. [1984]

These are three that I did of Lucian Freud, and the old bastard who
bought it split them up. So, there it is. So, whether I'm going to be able
to get those, I don't really know. [1984]

And then these were the time when I did the popes. Unfortunately,
somebody called Peter Watson bought the best of these popes. He gave it
back to me because I wanted to alter it. And I altered so far that it completely disappeared. So, I had the rather inferior ones, unfortunately,
left. [1984]

[*Sand Dune*, 1983] … it's curious enough that lots of people say to me,
for some reason, that they think it has to do with the human body. But
I must say, I have never thought of it in that way. I just thought of it as
a sand dune. And when I was, last year I was in Brittany for a moment,
and I did see these dunes, and I had some photographs of them, and also
through memory of them. I thought in that for a moment I had created
something. I don't say it was very like, but a … I don't say the essence,
but at least a sand dune. [1984]

All the critics hate me. It's very interesting, the show in New York, nearly
all the critics have flung me down loathing the work. But the curious,
perhaps it is a curious thing, is that they say they've never had so many
people into an exhibition. So, one doesn't understand those things. [1975]

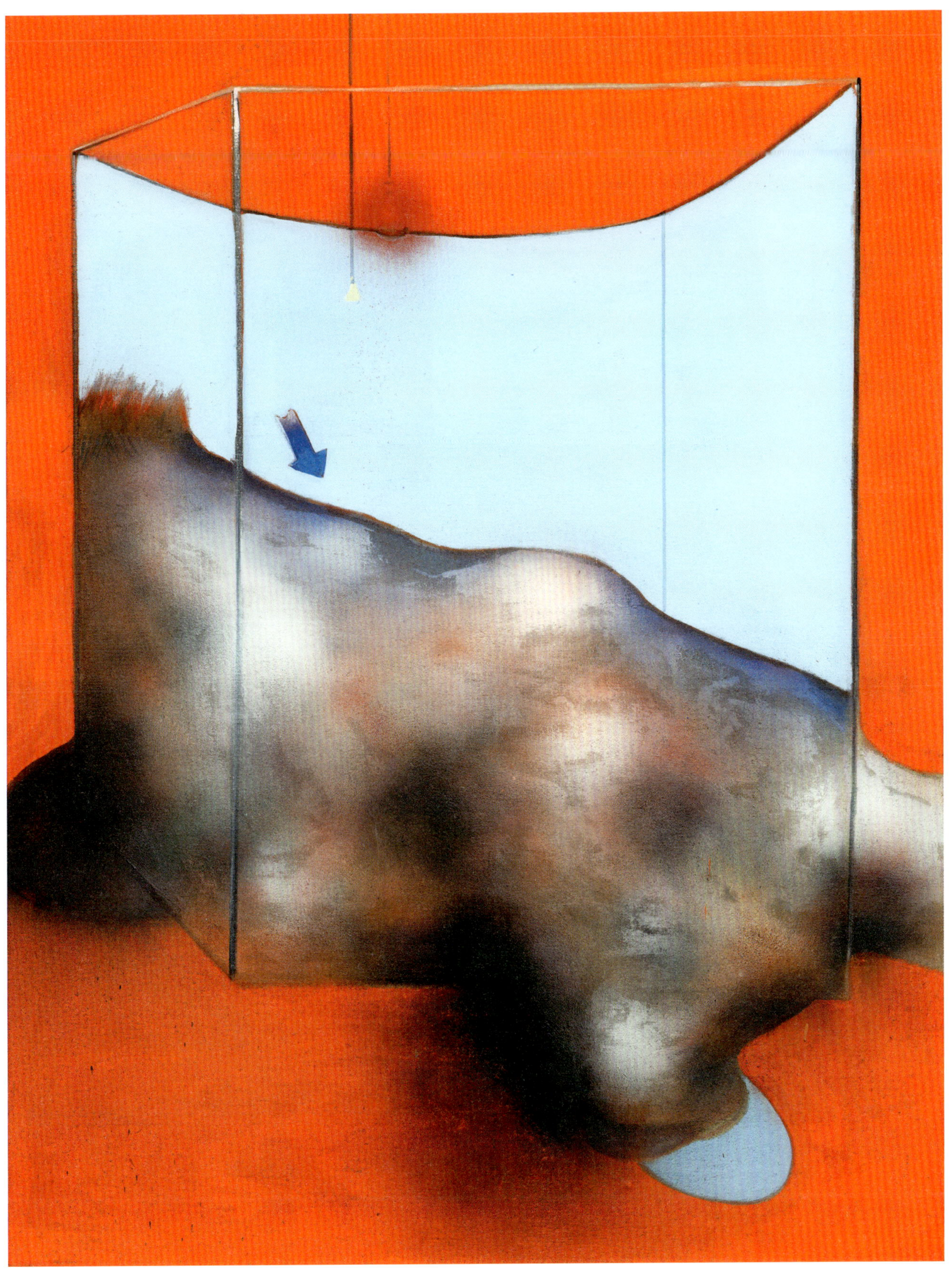

69. *Sand Dune*, 1983

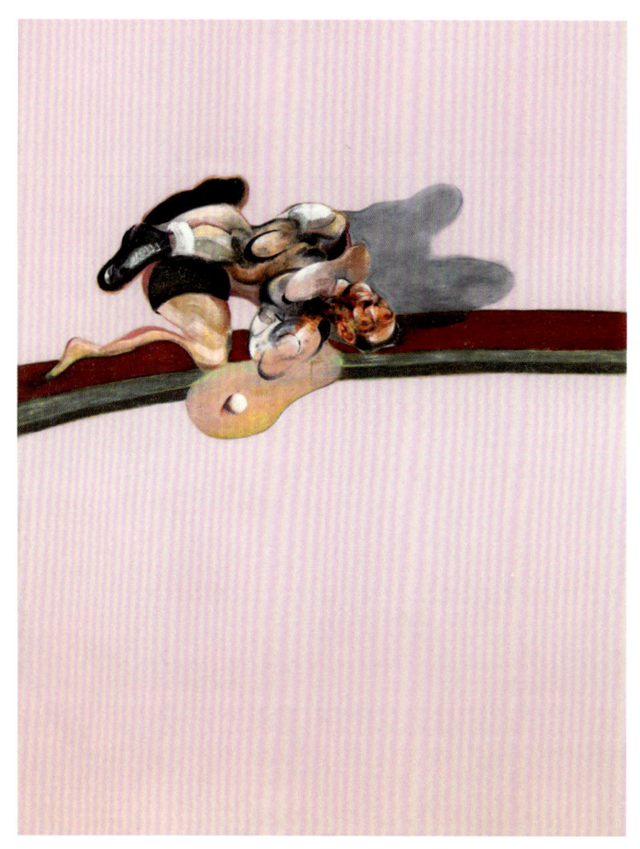

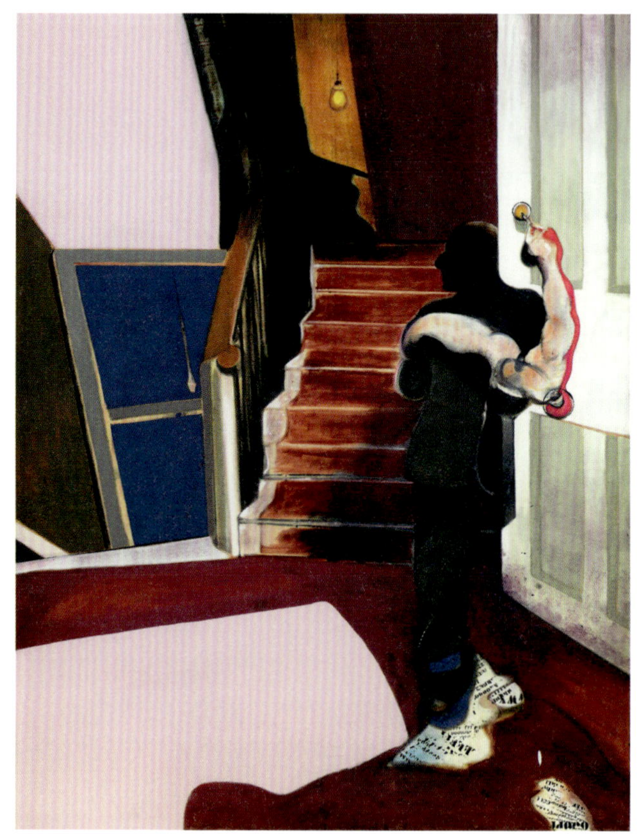

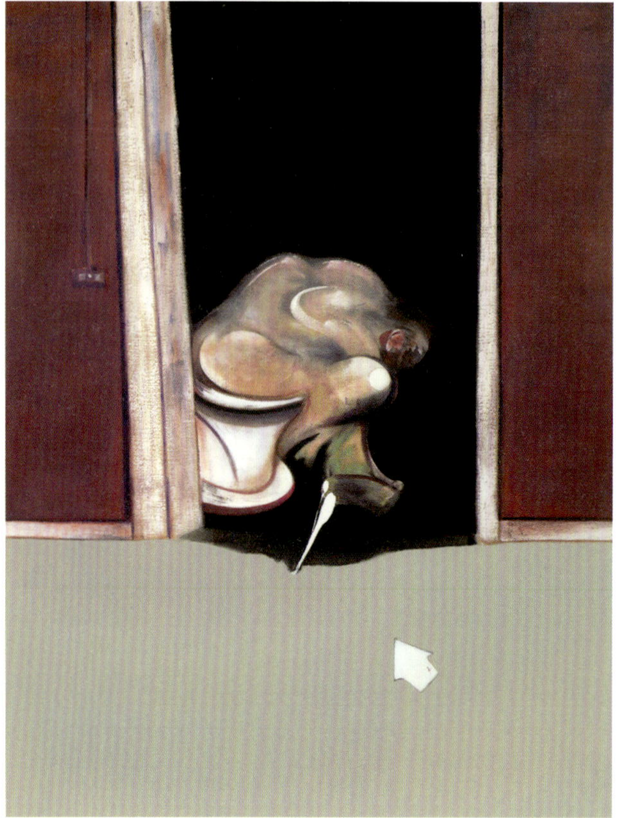

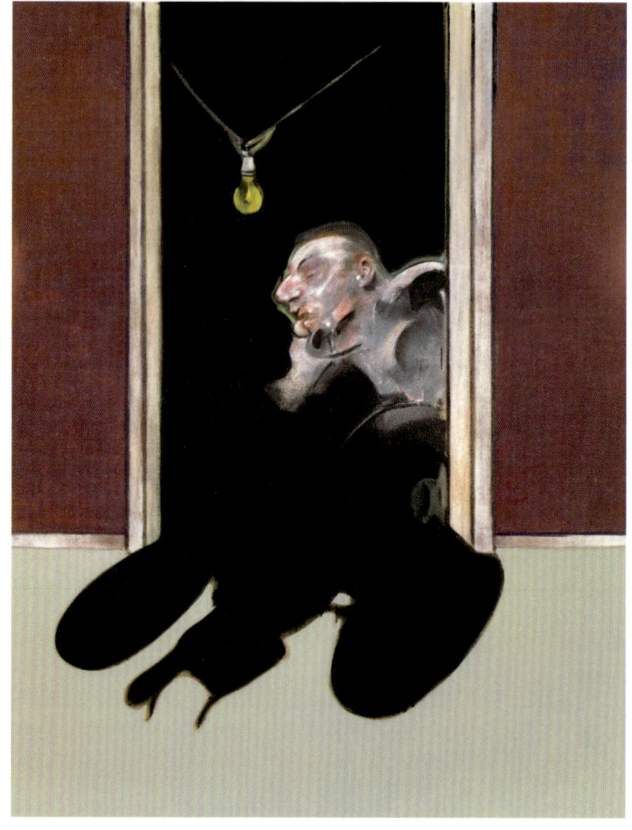

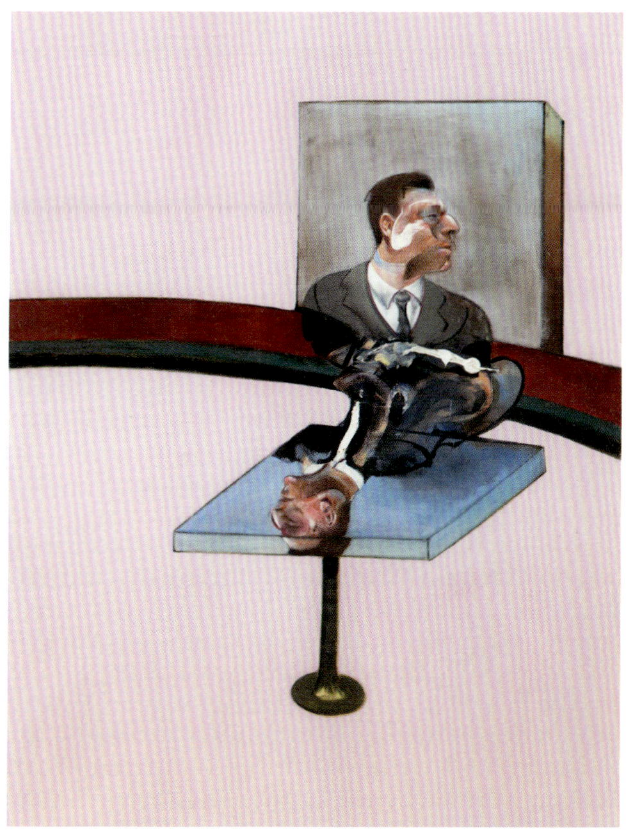

Well, the first one I did, which is this one done in 1971, '72, I can't remember which year it was. And it is, I mean the image in the centre is, very much a profile of George unlocking, unlocking the door. And this one, as he was very keen on games, is one of him, you know, sort of in the gestures of catching some ball or something like that. It's to do with that And then the other one is just somebody looking into the mirror. And in a sense, they were, they were done after the death of somebody. [1984]

70. *In Memory of George Dyer*, 1971

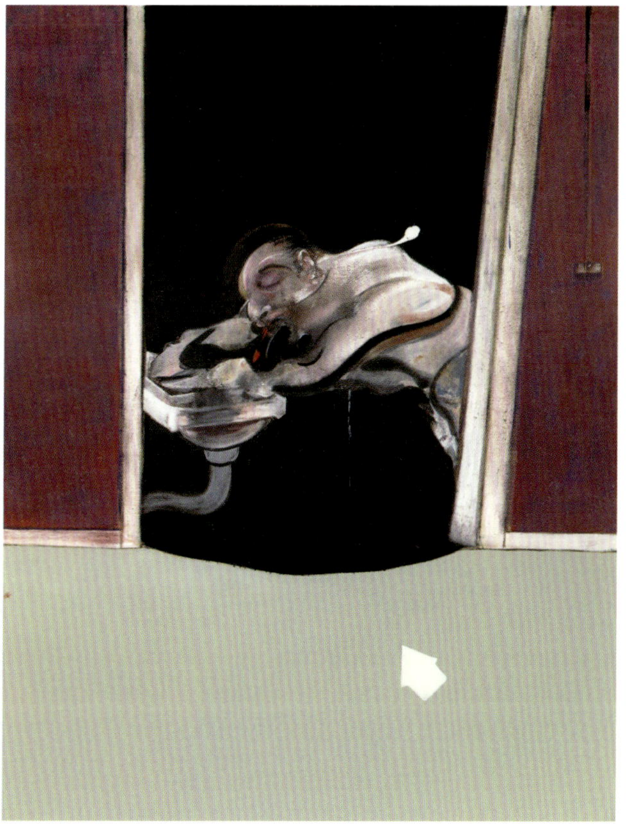

And I did do another one, which was after this one, where he is found sitting on the lavatory because that is where he was found. And so I used that. And they also found that he had been sick into the basin. And I used that. So, in a way, those are probably the two most descriptive triptychs I've done. And I thought of this, of somebody passing between one and the other, the centre panel. And that's about as far as I can give. I can tell you about it, but they are probably the two most descriptive ones I've done. [1984]

71. *Triptych May-June 1973*

It is worth reiterating that in these interviews Bacon seldom initiated discussions of other artists – he was mainly responding to Sylvester's questions. These were framed in a way that reflected Sylvester's opinions on, and grasp of, Bacon's artistic stimuli, and did not necessarily coincide with Bacon's preoccupations, hence the omission of Daumier. On the other hand, Sylvester referred fleetingly to Veronese and Tintoretto, but in neither case did Bacon react; it might, therefore, be assumed that Bacon was relatively indifferent to them. In 1984 Sylvester became involved in helping Bacon to choose masterpieces from the National Gallery, London, for his selection in the series 'The Artist's Eye'. Consequently, certain artists otherwise absent from the interviews made a brief appearance, such as Masaccio: **I would like to include the Masaccio 'Mother and Child', which has always been a marvellous … I think that the form in the Masaccio painting is superb.**[20] [1984] For the same exhibition he had considered including Raphael's painting of the same subject but changed his mind;[21] apart from mentioning that Raphael died young, his only other comment in the interviews was made in a different context: **I'm really trying to think of paintings of figures in action which I like. You see, what are the great paintings; what are the great figures in action, really? … Well, there are the very great cartoons of Raphael, of course.** [1973]

No, because I don't know what I'm doing. I mean after all, half the time although I like very controlled, and the older I get the more I like it to be highly controlled, it comes about by chance and when I, although I have an idea of what I want to do I don't know how I'm going to do it and that is where I'm hoping that chance will work in my favour and will bring up the way that the image can be made. For instance, one of the things where perhaps I feel myself to be perhaps outside what is called modern painting is in this. Is that I'm really haunted by how appearance can be remade, when I say remade how it can be made back onto what the appearance is but made in a totally non-illustrational way, or even that the appearance can suddenly be coagulated by the way the paint just works for you, and it happens. Why to me, for instance, that Chagall is so profoundly uninteresting is because, no matter what will there is, it can only be more or less beautiful aesthetic decoration because there's nothing else it can be. And whereas the excitement that I find in any painting that interests me is how has this image been made, how has this been remade? How has this thing been thrown together, as it were, without any illustration of the object and yet it throws it back onto what I choose to call the nervous system more strongly than any illustration of it could ever do. [1973]

I took a brush, a hard brush when I put it down, which you sweep the floors with, and ran it through all the things, the whole of the image, so you see this serration of the shadow run through as it were the image of the carpet as well which locks them both together.[22] [1971]

20 Masaccio, *Virgin and Child*, 1426, National Gallery, London. By 'form', Bacon presumably meant the figure of the Virgin Mary. Masaccio's sculptural qualities may well have resonated with Bacon.

21 This was presumably the 'Garvagh Madonna', c. 1510–11.

22 In *Portrait of George Dyer* æmay fit this description but not the rest of the painting.

I think as I want the paint to speak as strongly as it were, as it can, on its own account, not necessarily saying anything, but, as my, all my art is based on figuration. As I want the paint in itself to have a very strong quality, that may give it a feeling of. That I am also trying to say, saying something about people in extremities. But I think that would happen in my work if I just painted a person walking down the street, I think in the way I paint that side might, that could be read into it but then, only really because I want the physicalness of the paint to link to the physicalness of the image ... Perhaps that's not correct. [1971]

Scale is a difficult thing to do. I'm never very conscious of scale. [1962] These later statements appear to partly contradict this: I don't sketch ... I sort of do vague outlines, sort of outlines with the paint itself, sometimes ... Or I may make a very rough sort of thing, about the scale of it and everything. And on painting the body, he added: Well, I think that's – it's a sense of – it's a sense within yourself of the type of scale that you want. [1979]

[7 Reece Mews] This table used to be heaped, almost, it used to be heaped right up. But now it has become a bit tidier here because it just became you could hardly walk into the place, do you know? It was, it's like having a great dog in here [who] kept you out. There was so much of it in here. You see, most photographers love the walls here because I've used them as palettes. And so, because they like the different colours and things that go onto the walls and onto the door. That's the reason I really would be very sad if I have to leave this place. [1984]

Yes, I do. For instance, I very often look at the fragments from the Parthenon in the British Museum and they're profoundly moving to me and I'm never certain, true to say they're superb carvings, at least I believe them to be superb carvings, but whether they would be as deeply poignant and moving if one saw them complete rather than as it were reading in the fragments that have disappeared ... You know the very famous thing in the Cairo Museum, maybe in this book, of the man and his wife, painted, which is complete. Well, there's practically nothing in art as moving as that, and that's a complete thing, so it's an awfully complex thing this thing about when a thing has been damaged. I mean, it's very hard to know. There is one thing about it that it seems that it's only very grand things which will stand up to the damage and less things just look lesser by being damaged and so the certain grandeur, the fundamental grandeur of form seems to be able to support the distortion that has gone on obviously through the damaging, has happened through the damaging but I think they have to have started with very grand form. [1973]

... of course, I don't know what kind of sensibility painters have ... I can only say that I think of myself as having a very specialised grid that I was born at the moment of conception with a very specialised – everybody has a specialised one, but I happen to think that mine was very specialised. I have a very specialised nervous system. Because, I

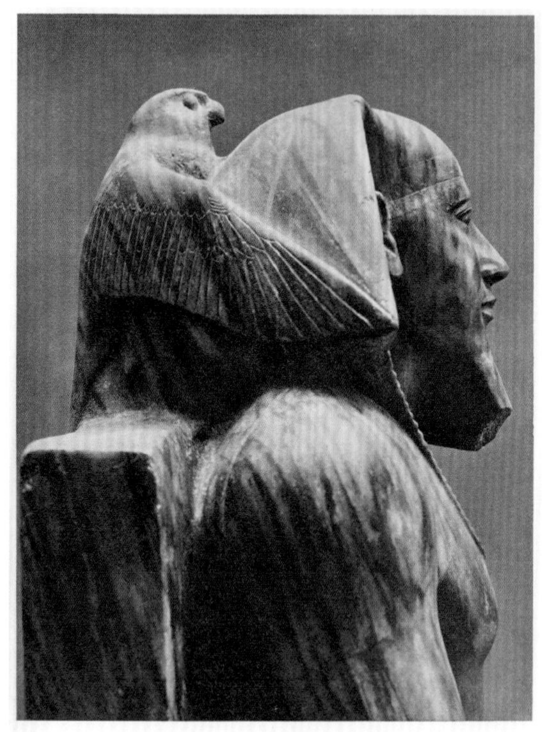

72. King Chefren with falcon
(which Bacon and Sylvester
misidentified as Sesostris); plate
from J.H. Breasted, *Geschichte
Ægyptens*, 1936. Bacon owned a
copy of this book.

think, you see, that one's formed at the very moment … one's whole
psychic, one's whole nervous system is formed at the moment of one's
conception and then you either develop it or you don't … I feel it's only
in a sense that I feel my work to be highly specialised and you may say
why is it highly specialised. Well, I can only say I don't know any work
really very like it … I'm not trying to suggest that I'm more unique than
another person, I'm only suggesting that my working, as it were, the
sensibility which I work by – I'm not saying it's more unique – but I
think it's very, very different to practically any artist, painter that I've
known of this generation … And I don't think, I'm not like what is called
the painters at all who say I'm just like the ordinary man, because I
know I'm not. I know my sensibility isn't like it and I know that's a false
kind of camaraderie that a lot of artists go in for because I know that
art's a very unique and very, very specialised and very rare thing. [1973]

I would find it very, very hard, for instance, to say what excites me
about this head of Sesostris. I mean, it's a very grand form, perhaps it's
that alone that excites one … Although you speak of the animality [of
Egyptian Middle Kingdom heads], I think myself would put it another
way; I think what they are to me is that they're both very stark, and very
refined, and … you feel that they are facing, as it were, facing their death,
but of course that is very much, I suppose, to do with their religion
… it's a romantic point of view and there's nothing against that, it's
a romantic point of view to believe, to think that way … On the other
hand, there is a superb, which I don't think is in this book, of Sesostris
with the falcon at the back of his head, and that is not damaged and
that is grander in a way even than this damaged head. [1973]

Subject matter is something one's obsessed by. There are many types of subject matter. For instance, there is a portrait which is one form of subject matter, and perhaps today one of the most absorbing and extraordinary. But then, there's the subject matter, which is one's whole psyche and that goes out, for instance, when I paint these triptychs they're mostly to do with my own psyche, with my own, finally, of course, although they're not about my life, they're to do with my own sensations about life, about existence. [1975]

Well in that Van Gogh, he escaped, I think, out of the illustration, the illustrational side, by what you call the striated way that he used to paint, and somehow you're both conscious of the appearance and I'm sure that the people he painted, and his self-portraits, were tremendously like but they were taken away from their literalness by the way he used the paint ... After all he, Van Gogh himself, used somewhere this expression that he wanted to take the thing as far away from appearance and yet bring it back more onto appearance. I can't remember exactly how it was put, in one of his letters, than any literal appearance could give. [1975]

I love other people's drawings, but I just don't think I'm gifted for it. I don't think I'm gifted in that way. I mean, I don't think of drawing and sculpture as being the same thing, at all. I know that people may do. But I don't even think, in people like Ingres the painting and the drawing [are] so totally different. People tend to say that because they've never thought about Ingres's coloured drawings, but I just don't think it is. [1984]

[On Manet's *Olympia*, 1863–65, as a re-imagining of Titian's *Venus of Urbino*, c. 1534] If you remember, in the Olympia, there's a bunch of flowers wrapped in paper, which wouldn't probably have been done at the time that the Titian was done. I mean, that, you may say, gives it a modern note. I think the Titian is much greater... there's quite an interesting thing that Michel Leiris wrote about, I think, about that picture, because ... the woman lying on the bed has a ribbon round her neck.[23] Well, that was a 19th-century fashion, and it wouldn't have been done, it wouldn't have been done earlier on in the same in the same way, probably. But I don't think that that is enough. I don't really think it compares. You see, I think when you take these great masterpieces, I think it's silly, really, in the end, to tamper with them, even with people with enormous gifts, in talents like Picasso, and genius, however you like to call it. I don't think it even worked with him. I don't think it worked with Manet, really. You see, I think that a wonderful bowl of flowers, or the peaches, or the ham, or things that Manet did were really greater than *Olympia*.[24] [1984]

But then that of course is why in our time Art Nouveau and I'm sure the Pre-Raphaelites and everything will become tremendously, it's why the young like them so much, because they have desperate stories. After all, practically nobody feels anything about painting they only think about the stories in painting. [1971]

23 Bacon was being disingenuous, for he owned a copy of Leiris's *Le Ruban au cou d'Olympia* in 1981.

24 Bacon's admonishing of Manet probably reflects his own avowed regrets about 'tampering' with masterpieces.

…no matter how much Surrealism may have influenced me, I don't want to be surrealist, in any rate what is called the known surrealist style… And I don't think Duchamp was surrealist in that style, really … I mean he remained with Dada didn't he, in a sense, although he made something else of it … what is so curious anyway from my point of view is that surrealists have been extremely bad painters … all their doctrines in a way have worked against them because they have been really illustrators, illustrators of mysterious states. [1973]

… that's the reason I tried to do the subject, because I really like very banal subjects: people just sitting on chairs. [1973]

Well of course that's one of the things that is so remarkable about Impressionism is that, in a curious way, it's one of the nearest things that great artists have come to happiness in art. It's a very extraordinary movement in that way. That they touched in some curious way on the, about the, joy of life. They're about the first and the last really. [1973]

… but then I never thought for instance that Constable's portraits … came near to the quality of his landscapes … And I thought that, I always have thought that Turner's figures were lamentable. [1973]

Of course, sometimes there are things like the *Descent from the Cross* of Rubens and the extraordinary crucifixion of the Christ in the centre with the two thieves on either side which of course is one of the most astonishing crucifixions. But, of course, I think … you see I think Rubens … obviously Rubens was one of the very, very greatest artists that have existed but that you can have that and still be out of sympathy with the majority of his work. [1973]

I think in this case, it certainly is; mind you, like all chance things it's luck in the quality of the damaging. Luck comes into the quality of the damaging; it could completely ruin this head. But you see, it so often happens in these heads to the nose, for instance, as it protrudes. Well, as you know, many people are improved in their looks when they've had their nose broken and pushed in. That's again a curious thing if you've ever looked at boxers' heads. Sometimes their good looks have been enormously improved by having their noses broken. I mean it's very strange that all these beauty parlours and things that go on making this hideous kind of pink crepey skin, that they don't have someone just bash their heads about a bit, and bash their noses in. After all, the Africans did remarkable things by cutting their face and very often made marvellous elongations of the face by the way they cut it. [1973]

The whole of my, all my work is chance. You see, everything I do in an odd way is, has come about by chance and if it has got any freshness for that very reason. And I don't sit down and paint like somebody drawing down a blind. [1974]

... I don't go on talking about accidents because it's been, you may say I've overplayed ... I've spoken too much about it. But the paintings that really worked for me are, in fact, very accidental. [1984]

The only thing I can say is those particular accidents you're suggesting haven't arrived for me. But sometimes when I've been working, I've been so disgusted with the thing, I'm so sick of it, that I just take the brush and put brush marks all over it thinking, oh, fuck this thing, I can't ... It's not going to work at all. And then suddenly, out of this chaos comes the possibility of making an image I hadn't thought of before. And that, I call accident. [1984]

I think that every artist or every plastic artist certainly, and I, no I would say every artist, hopes that the inevitability of the form that is given to him by chance will go on recurring for him. Because of course I always expect chance to work for me, even when I go into a casino expect to win and this doesn't by any means happen very often, as in painting, but I always expect, or each time I start painting I think a marvellously unresolved, unthought-out image will come out of, out of what you could call my hope in my despair. You could say that working with chance is working, in a way, with the despair of not being of not being able to logically make this image, because *if* I made it logically it would be an illustration of my idea. [1974]

You see, I know there's an idea of being just a simple recording machine, for instance, but then I'm not certain it's not even thickened if you're recording, if the whole attitude towards a person isn't recorded and not just the simple kind of descriptive side of a person, descriptive act. I don't know if I've got off the subject now, I don't know if I know quite what I'm saying, perhaps. You see, in my case, I really would like to find and always hope to find at certain times a technical way by which the whole thing both ... because any object is always sur-rounded in a curious way by one's whole attitude to things in general – everything one looks at in a way is conditioned by that. Of course, it's true to say that's what Duchamp tried to do away with and probably it's one of the few who succeeded in doing away with it; on the other hand he did also do something which was very odd – he recreated another myth which in a way you could say that that very myth was his person-ality which was coming through so strongly – if you take a thing like the Big Glass. And in fact, the ready-mades and things – the myth of the person is never really eliminated. It's a modern myth to believe of course that it is eliminated. It's a modern, as it were, stupidity, because it never is. I mean, I think lots of people have tried to, painters recently have tried to do this thing – I believe it's called keeping it cool – but of course the very act of keeping it cool is a judgment. [1973]

[Discussing Matisse cut-outs] The only thing is, of course, he was not doing portraits ... He was just doing the human, or very often the human body. Whether if he'd been younger when he started the cut-outs he would have attempted to see, of course there are the cut out

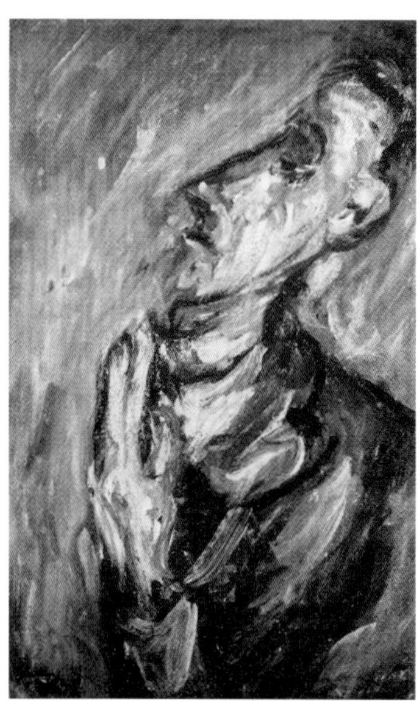

73. Chaim Soutine, *Man Praying*, c. 1921

25 Bacon wasn't specific about which of several versions of Praying Man he was critiquing. This reproduction is from the catalogue of the Tate Gallery's 'Chaim Soutine' exhibition, 1963, with its superb – introduction by David Sylvester; it is very likely Bacon saw it.

silhouette portraits of the 18th century, or 17th century, 19th century. [1975]

[On Soutine's *Praying Man*, 1921] On the other hand, I don't like, I don't like the expressionist form of doing it ... but that's very expressionistic. That is entirely ... I mean that's only brutalised El Greco ... when I say only, one knows what an extraordinary artist El Greco was. But it is brutalised El Greco and rather badly done, to me ... you see I always feel that Soutine was, I think there are one or two portraits where it's worked but I think generally he was in some curious, he was influenced by expressionism, or I feel it was, which is a side to it I don't like this, this, well, what expressionism means. I don't like this idea that one's expressing a specific state, as it were, of mind. I would like, myself, what I did to be very, very much more formal than anything Soutine did.[73] [1975]

You see, I don't think the layout of pictures in that sense, is to me that important; I mean, you can use the same layout for the whole of your life; it's the way they are painted; the method by which they are painted and the method in which they are presented; you can use the same layout ... why change the subject even? There's no point in it really. One just does this. [1979]

No, I think that they may look at [our period] as a very thin one, and partly the reason [fashionable artists] had the success is that people don't buy paintings because they like them now; they buy them as forms of stocks and shares. [1975]

I think it's in the air. Now this is ridiculous to talk in this way – that it's in the air. But I think that there are all kinds of experiments going on and I don't think, for instance, this art of digging trenches and conceptual art. But I think that out of conceptual art something marvellous, or somebody will come-up who will suddenly be able to synthesise this whole thing and make something remarkable. [1975]

I think the actual mark which you make or preserve has to do with one's sensations and one's sensations are being affected all the time. So, of course, in one sense, yes ... not consciously, unconsciously ... I wouldn't be thinking 'last night was a marvellous night'. Not at all. Those things are entirely unconscious and entirely instinctive... it's an extremely complex problem because one doesn't know how things that have happened between you and another person affect, as it were, the form which takes over, or by which you make the appearance of somebody. One doesn't know about – that's why painting is so that way – ambiguous. As you know, it's a famous thing – even the most literal portrait painters, they absolutely loathe them; people loathe their portraits ... [1975]

And in some curious way, this is not again quite the same thing, again if one thing is, for instance, if one thinks of a sculpture, of an old sculpture, where the nose has disappeared, of course one will not know what the appearance of that person *really* was, as strongly as if it was there. The thing I would like to do would be for this irrationality to *really* make the appearance. So that when somebody saw this thing, they would know exactly who it was. [1975]

[re Jasper Johns having said art is 'a hopeless statement'] I think it's a very good statement. I was just thinking of his work; it doesn't seem to happen a great deal in his work; I think the statement's very good. I'm not as they say 'tuned in' to his work. It's certainly a very good statement. [1979]

… the thing about it is, in painting, I certainly never, never think about my audience – how can I think about them, there's nothing to think about; it's just an unknown quantity, your audience. The only thing you can think about is really how it affects you, there's absolutely no other way. You can't think of an unknown audience. [1979]

What does one mean by realism? One thinks one knows what realism is. I think when I'm looking at you, I see you there. But it isn't, I can't just explain what you are. I see you there. And you could be photographed, but then after you'd been photographed, one still wouldn't know what your realism was. Then you would analyse, here is a human being. [1984]

… also series may possibly have come from looking a very great deal at those books of Muybridge where you will see, it's true to say they're not in threes, but they are in series … and I think that they may really have been how I originally started doing, as it were, triptychs. Because looking at these, of these figures in their movement in separate, as it were, in separate photographs but just slightly different movements, this may have been what really started the whole thing off, I can't remember really quite what started it off … I mean they're so haunting I wish I could ever get hold of the whole big series, which is almost impossible to come by now you know, there are about twelve volumes of them of very big ones, there's one in the Victoria and Albert and I have looked through all those and of course the books that I have are very diluted forms of, I mean they've only taken certain things from the ones which are much more comprehensive. [1973]

In the painting of Manet, of the execution of Maximilian, of course, the way that they've added little bits of raw canvas makes it look very much like an up-to-date pop art thing, and it adds an intensity to it in a curious way. Like those kinds of things often happen. [1984]

I don't particularly like Vermeer. But when you compare him to the other painters, Dutch painters of that period, of course he stands right out as being something very remarkable. [1984]

It just happens to be a very thin period. After all, at the early part of the century, we had the most remarkable people – almost three-quarters through the century. There were remarkable artists like Matisse, Picasso

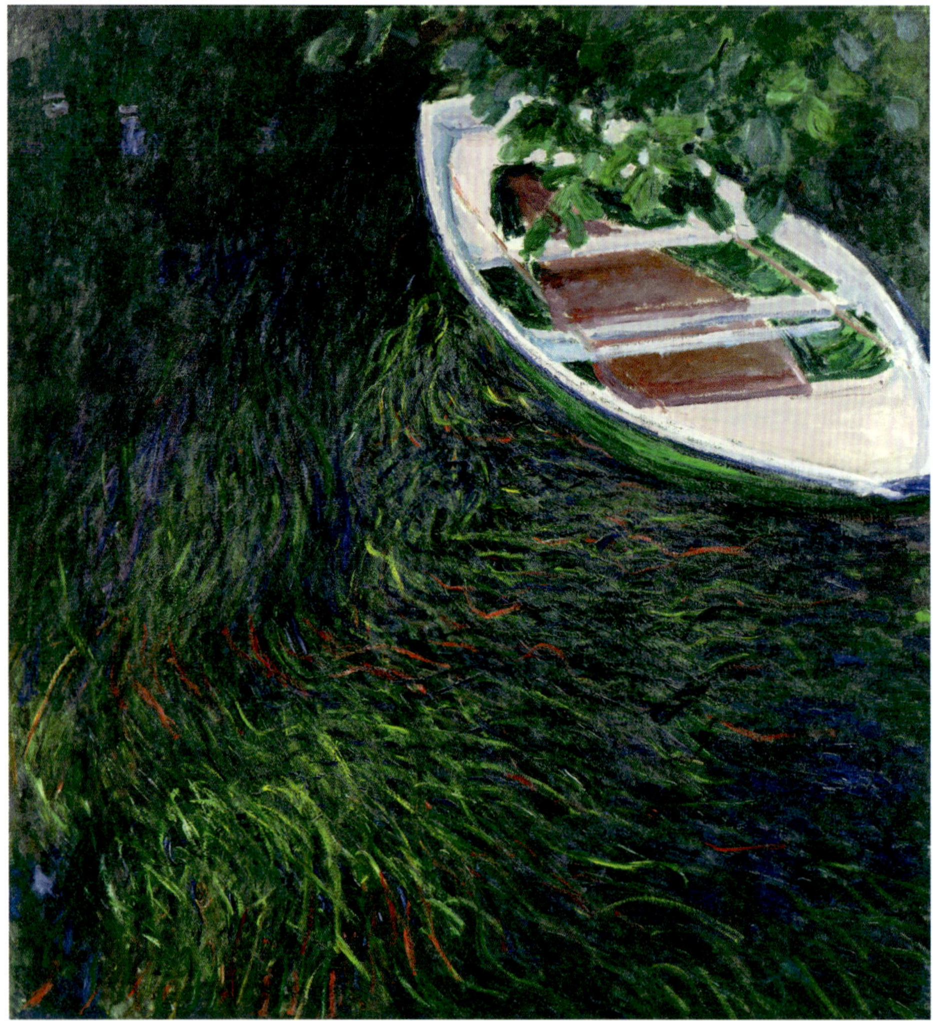

74. Claude Monet, *La Barque*, 1887

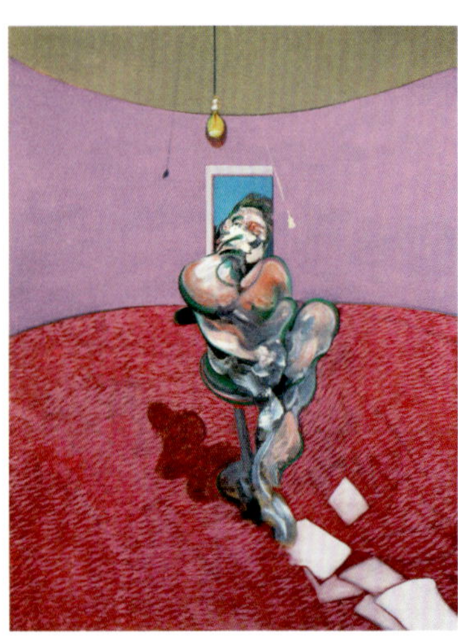

75. *Portrait of George Dyer Talking*, 1966

and many others – Modigliani, Soutine – so many remarkable people. Of course, there's no reason that there shouldn't be a lull in it. There always has been. There's been – after all, if you think of the great Elizabethan period in writing, the marvellous flow of extraordinary writers with Shakespeare, in a sense, at the core. But they were all around. But then there's a lull – it happens in everything. [1975]

I read a very interesting thing about Ingres the other day and I cannot remember if it was something of Valéry's, where apparently Ingres questioned how far logic could go in painting. Now, it's a nuisance that I can't (find) it because it was only a short time ago that I read this thing and he is certainly, one of the, I think probably Ingres and Chardin are Lucian's two very great, are two of the painters he admires probably most of all. Well, now, would you call Chardin a logical painter? I, myself, would. [1973]

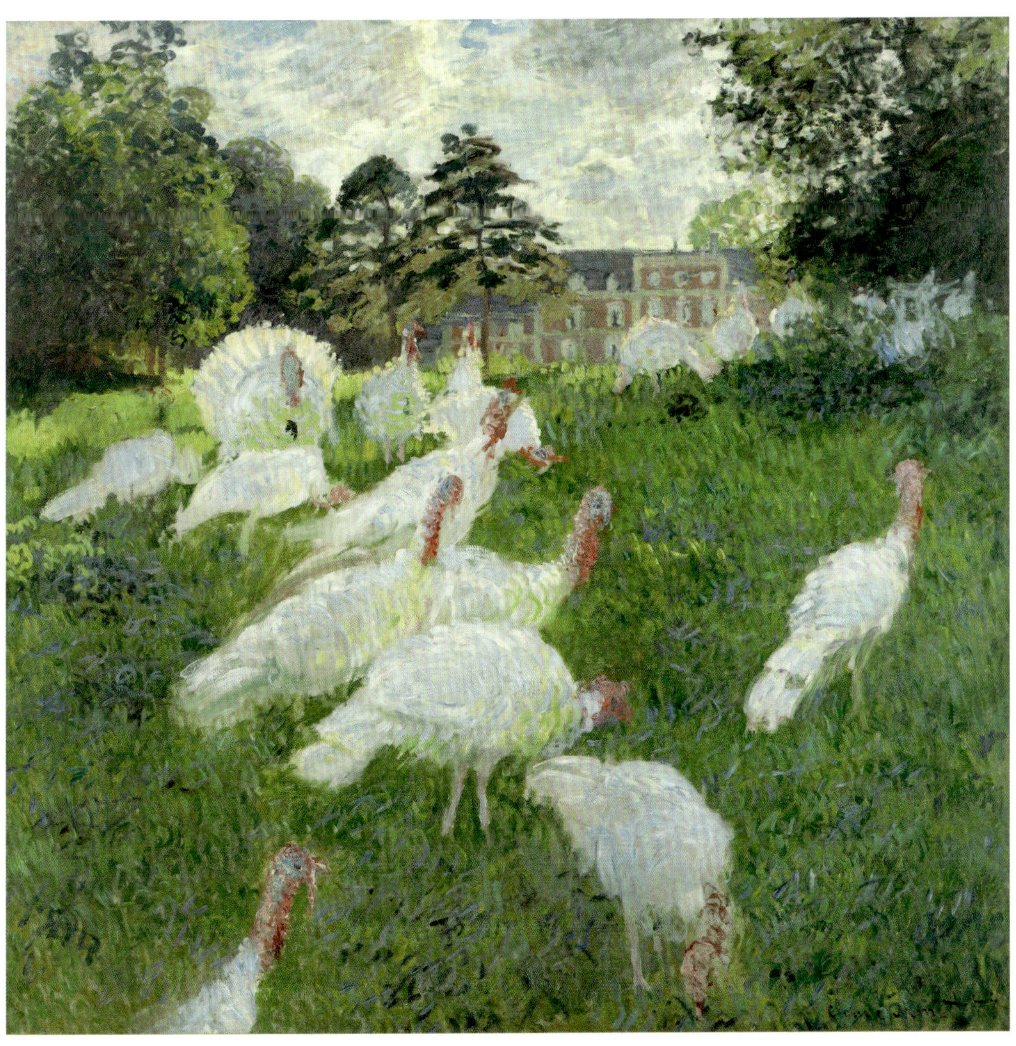

76. Claude Monet, *Les Dindons*, 1887

26 Monet made so many paintings of boats in rivers that it is impossible to be certain which one Bacon was referring to. A strong contender is *La Barque,* 1887, Musée Marmottan Monet, Paris. [74]

27 Claude Monet, *Les Dindons*, 1877; now in the collection of the Musée d'Orsay, Paris.

[Bacon diverts a question about violence in Monet's waterlilies to] **a much better example in some of the fronts of Chartres, [which is corrected to Rouen] … also this curious painting of, where's he going, a boat sailing down seen from a launch or something going down the river … It's their presence, I think violence is a bad word we keep using, it's the immediacy of the images that are brought back to me.[26] … take for instance Monet's *The Turkeys* in the Jeu de Paume.[27] You take the turkey, those white turkeys at the top of the stairs when you come up, with their white wings; there is an immediacy of these images of these birds suddenly brought back to you with a shock. And that's a – can one painter do it rather than another? Why does one painter do it rather than another, why, why? That is also a mysterious thing. And that's the reason why – of course I find I'm perhaps going on a diversion – abstract painting is never interesting: there is no real core to it. [1973]**

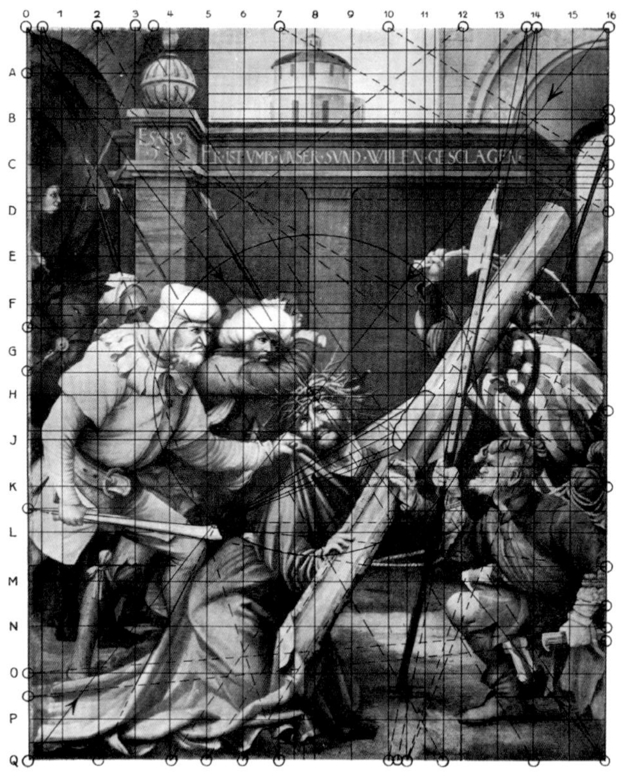

77. Page from Hans Heinrich Naumann, *Das Grünewald Problem*, 1930, with illustration of Grünewald, *Christ Bearing the Cross*, c. 1523–25. This page is visible in Sam Hunter's 1950 photograph of source material in Bacon's studio

[re painting a head 'of somebody'] ... and it'll go right out from abstraction and will have really nothing to do with it, although in a sense, of course these things have been influenced by abstract paintings. [1962]

It's why abstract painting is so popular today. Also, they don't think they have to have any story and they can just give themselves up to what they think is their aesthetic sense, whether it's there or not ... There's nothing complicated. It's so simple, abstract art, anyone can feel or not feel about it. It's so simple that you can't look at it. It just makes me yawn in two minutes. [1971]

[on painting copulating figures] Hard to do in abstraction isn't it. I mean it would be very hard for Rothko to actually paint the, as it were the sensation of the sexual act; I hardly think colour can, it's too diffused. [1973]

Of course, all art has tended towards abstraction, in a way. I mean, very often, I mean, what's more abstract in a way than Poussin. A lot of artists tended towards abstraction, but anyhow now we're talking about today, certainly Balthus is not one of the painters that interests me; he never has interested me. [1984]

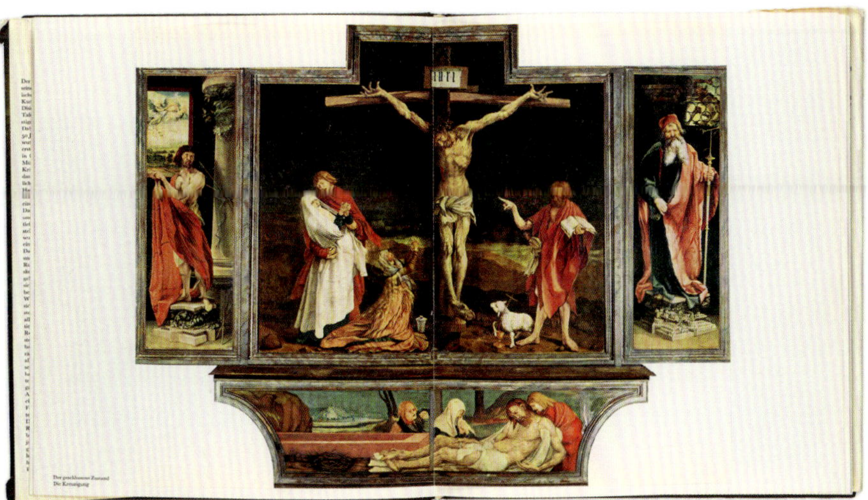

78. Grünewald, *Crucifixion*; pages from Georg Scheja, *Der Isenheimer Altar des Matthias*, 1969. Bacon owned a copy of this book

BACON ON ARTISTS

GRÜNEWALD

... would the Grünewald at Colmar be, I think it would be just as great without the other crucifixions ... [1971]

Well, I've always liked Grünewald until I saw it. And this year I went with some friends and we did a kind of tour, and we went up and saw the Isenheimer and I was actually disappointed, very disappointed in it. I didn't like the side panels really at all and the central crucifixion, in the images that I've seen of it, it seemed as though the image, although it's an extraordinary image of Christ on the cross, it seemed in the illustrations that I have seen of it, that it was a very, very much bigger image than it is. It is comparatively small, and it doesn't seem to have the same intensity when you actually see it than it does have in the, I have some very magnificent reproductions of it, as in the reproductions. [1979]

CIMABUE

Of course, I never saw it ... Except in reproductions and I believe it was destroyed in the flood in Florence wasn't it ... They've repainted it, re-made it. Well, why shouldn't they? Once somebody has given a great image to the world, now, with all the recordings of things there's no reason it shouldn't be re-made. Cimabue made it, he made this extraordinarily beautiful image, there's absolutely no reason, as it's left there and they have the recordings, I mean they have all, mean they had all the films and photographs and things of it, there's no reason once it has been conceived by him that it shouldn't be re-made. [1979]

I've had lots of influences. I mean, I've had the influence of Velázquez, of Goya, I've had the influence of that great early Cimabue crucifixion, and of course, Picasso. [1984]

79. Michelangelo, *Samson and Two Philistines*, c. 1540.
Leaf from Bacon's copy of Martin Weinberger, *Michelangelo: the Sculptor*, 1967.

28 *Three Studies for a Crucifixion*, 1962. The triptych was not in fact painted *for* the Solomon R. Guggenheim Museum, it was acquired by them in 1964. In 1971 Bacon had remarked that he thought the colour of this triptych too bright 'when I saw it'.

... now this is a painting that I did for the Guggenheim,[28] and I particularly like the right-hand panel of this. I did feel that this, in a way, was influenced by the Cimabue *Crucifixion*. It might be, it might be hard to identify it with that, but the Cimabue has always been a painting that I've admired enormously because it always looked like an extraordinary image sliding down the cross. [1984]

MICHELANGELO

... that's the reason if you take the Michelangelo drawings, why they're so astonishing in some way of course is that he may have poured out all his, his profound psychological difficulties and all sorts of things but they're so sort of profoundly, on a very grand scale, you can call them profoundly human, can't you, the things like the slaves and all his drawings in fact, practically. After all, the drawings perhaps of Michelangelo mean more to me than anything. [1973]

... going back to Michelangelo, I think he's a difficult subject to talk about because I think they are the most remarkable – his drawings are some of the most remarkable things that have ever been done and one knows that the Sistine Chapel is something absolutely extraordinary but

I can't say that it moves me in a way that some of the very great pieces of sculpture, especially 'The Slave' do. And, of course, that could be a homosexual side in me that I like the voluptuousness that Michelangelo gave to the male body. [1973]

[Medici Chapel] I have always been meaning to go to Florence. I'm certain from all the photographs, and I've looked at them continuously, that it is the greatest thing of Michelangelo. I don't like the late pietàs that people like; I hate the very last one [the Rondanini Pietà], where he turns into a horrible kind of ... there's a very unpleasant kind of pitying, almost rococo sense in those pietàs, something really horrible about them. [1973]

I've always thought about Michelangelo, he's always been deeply important ... in my way of thinking about form, and although I have this profound admiration for his work the work I like most of all is the drawings and for me he is one of the very greatest, perhaps, if not the greatest draughtsman. [1974]

Well, this is the thing with the drawings of Michelangelo. I think what they have certainly done for me is to give me a sense of the possibilities of volume within the human body. I think that is the thing that I've learned most from the Michelangelos, this wonderful sense of volume that he had. And, I feel, I think perhaps because they're not completely finished in the drawings, that they're more suggestive. And that is one of the reasons that they've always been a very, very strong, a marvellous thing to use, for me, from a formal point of view. I've used Muybridge, for instance, very often, and it's a very interesting work. But of course, it's not, from a formal point of view, nearly as great. The images are not nearly as great as what Michelangelo was able to do in his images. [1984]

[Michelangelo, *The Entombment*, c. 1500–01, National Gallery, London] Well, this, of course, again, we'd go on to another problem with that, with the unfinished part of the Michelangelo. But then that is rather like the broken fragments of sculpture, which one wonders if perhaps they are even more beautiful because they are broken fragments than if they were all in a piece. But I don't know. I think that somehow that the Michelangelo is enhanced by the fact that part of it has been unpainted.[29] [1984]

REMBRANDT

... one mustn't forget some of the greatest art, which I'm not trying to suggest this has anything to do with, but some of the greatest art has been a tightrope walk between caricature and appearance.
I would say, I would say particularly the great late Rembrandt self-por-traits probably were. Of course, you would know more now because one would be able to pin up the photograph of the people next to the

29 Although its status does not affect Bacon's comments on its unfinishedness, the attribution of this painting to Michelangelo has been challenged on many occasions and remains undecided.

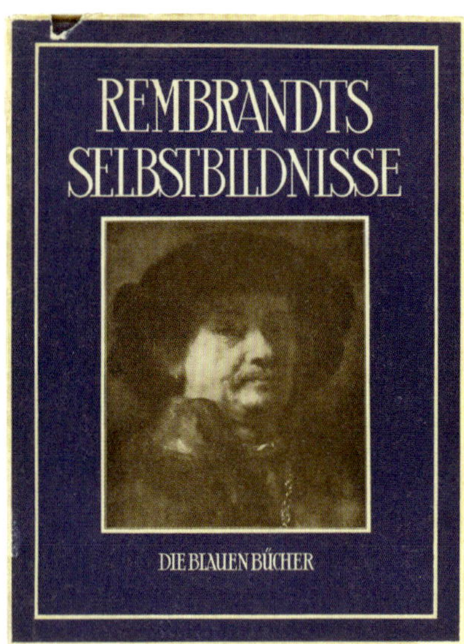

80. Cover of Wilhelm Pinder, *Rembrandts Selbstbildnisse*, 1945, in the *Die Blauen Bücher* series mentioned by Bacon

paintings of them which would be quite an interesting thing to do. Which of course you couldn't do at the time of Rembrandt. But from looking at a lot of Rembrandts and the early Rembrandts and the more literal Rembrandts I feel that in the great late self-portraits, what I think are the great late self-portraits, that he made this tightrope walk between, between appearance and caricature. [1971]

I believe the one in Aix-en-Provence is very much questioned … on whether it is a Rembrandt. But it certainly is in the style of the great late Rembrandts and is a remarkable, as it were, attempt to make a great Rembrandt, even if he didn't do it himself. But take the one in the Kenwood collection, I don't think there's any question about it, if it's a genuine Rembrandt. And you'll find in that also this very strong element of a tightrope walk … and a great number, you know that *Die BIauen Bücher* Rembrandt book which had all of the, that little book that had all the Rembrandt self-portraits in, given up only to Rembrandt self-portraits, and you do see this thing very strong, even in the ones where it isn't questioned at all as to whether they are Rembrandts or not. [1971]

I can't think what Rembrandt was trying to say. Or perhaps more Goya, sometimes. [1971]

I mean, if I look at a Rembrandt I don't think that he gives me any idea of what the person was like, the sitter, but he gives me a great insight into Rembrandt. [1973]

[re painting's inability to represent the sensations of erotic life] Well, I suppose there are certainly Rembrandts, I mean there are certainly Rembrandt etchings even or drawings. [1973]

I think he was doubling with two [mind and body]. I think he was using the changing of his appearance as an invention in his painting. He locked, after all, it is very difficult to unlock in the great Rembrandt paintings, to unlock. Because they're not illustrations, they are marvellous inventions of how appearance can be made by a brush stroke. [1975]

Well, I don't know; I don't know in Rembrandt's case. I never think of them as being a kind of autobiography; I just think he was … each one was very often very different. There was a generalised Rembrandt look. But they are often technically and everything about them – they were very, very different, one from another. But I never think … I don't know how he thought about them: I never think about them as an autobiographical series … I don't know, I haven't read enough … But I had a small German book which was entirely of self-portraits of himself from his youth to his old age and they were so … although there was a generalised look of Rembrandt, they were so different, that I never thought of them at all in an autobiographical sense, in the sense that he was wanting to say something different, as it were, about himself, but he was painting them in a different way. [1979]

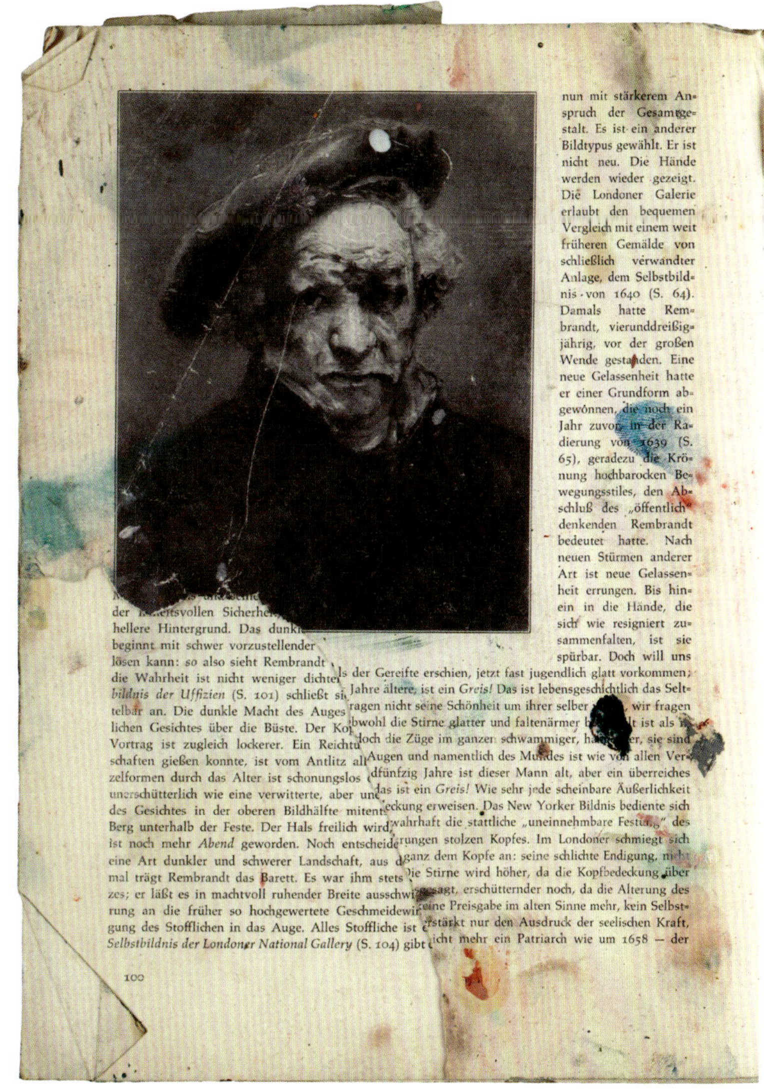

81. Torn pages from Bacon's copy of Wilhelm Pinder, *Rembrandts Selbstbildnisse*, 1945, with the Musée Granet self-portrait, c. 1660.

I think of it as, again, as realism, because after all, what makes a portrait, a great portrait, is what one can call the realism of the image, which, no matter how deformed it may be or how altered it may be, it returns you to the person that you are trying to catch. For instance, when you talked about these two portraits of Maria Trip, [he meant Margaretha De Geer] which were painted by Rembrandt when he was an old man, one doesn't really know how like they were of her. But nowadays, there will be this great difference because you will have the portraits of people done by photography, as well as the images of them that have been made in painting. So that it will now be quite an interesting thing, perhaps, to hang the portraits of them in photography beside the portraits of them that the artist has made, which would be quite an interesting thing to do. So you would see, perhaps, how the camera has recorded them and how the painter has recorded them. [1984]

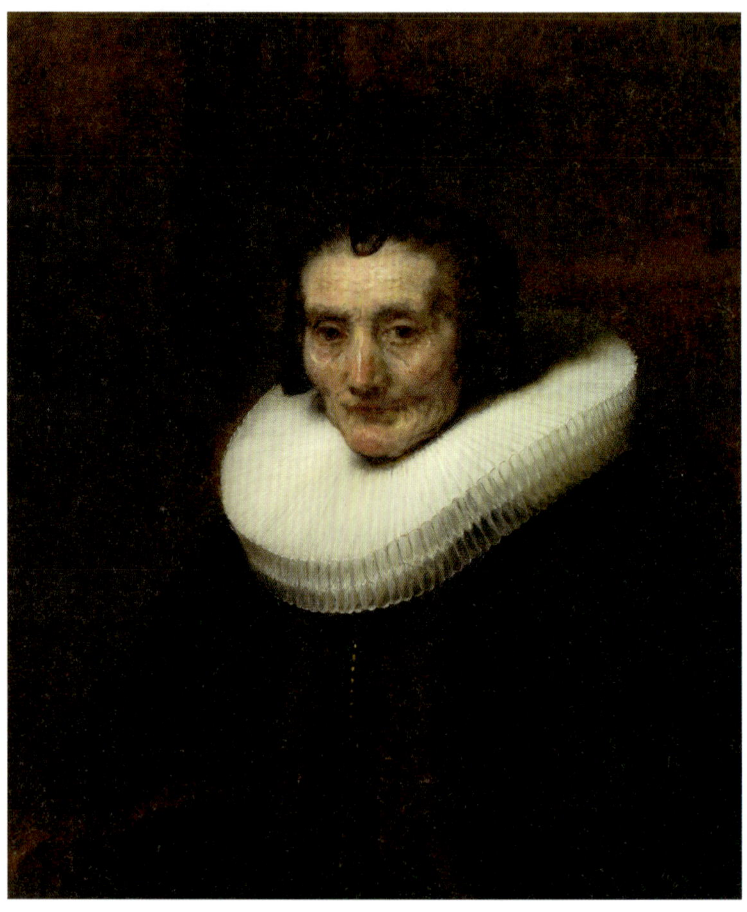

82. Rembrandt (?), *Portrait of Margaretha de Geer (wife of Jacob Trip)*, c. 1661

Well, I don't think that that is perhaps the greatness. When Rembrandt painted those portraits of Maria Trip [Margaretha De Geer], she was then an old woman. And one knows, that, I don't suppose he was naturally ... Perhaps he was not ... I don't know what Rembrandt was thinking of, but as she was an old woman, obviously she was nearer death. And after all, with age, death begins to project itself even more acutely. [1984]
[About Bacon's selections for *The Artist's Eye* at the National Gallery, London]

I've been thinking, really, I've been thinking of the choice I made ... And then I think we wandered through a lot of the National Gallery, and then came to the room with the Rembrandts and I thought I would like to put in those two that are, to me, wonderful portraits of Margaretha de Geer. I think perhaps the small one is the greatest one, but the large one is naturally, formally more remarkable than the very small one. The head of the very small one is perhaps painted in a more intense way. And what always interests me in this painting of Margaretha de Geer, the small one, is the way that in this painting the greys turn into blue, if you've noticed in the shadows of that painting. [1984]

[Bacon continued to misidentify the subject as Maria Trip; the authorship of the smaller painting remains undecided]

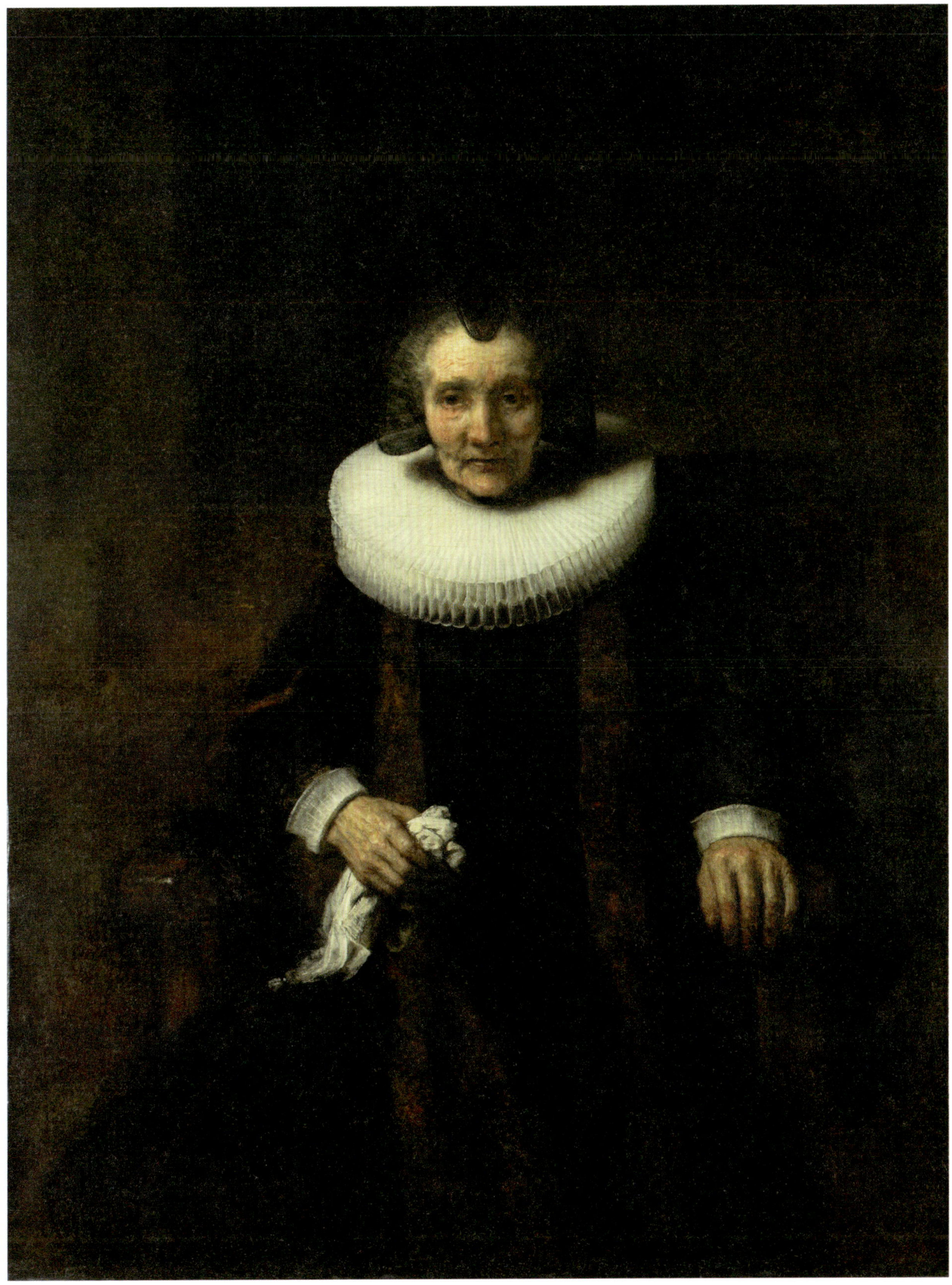

83. Rembrandt, *Portrait of Margaretha de Geer (wife of Jacob Trip)*, c. 1661

... when almost forget about the type of form because of course the form of a very young child's face is, has got the kind of pulpy look which [Velázquez] gave it so one is not really very conscious of the form, in a sense, of the little boy. [1975]

No I don't; no, I think it's marvellous the way it works in *Las Meninas*, but generally speaking I don't like paintings with a great number of figures – I don't like very much the Velázquez of *The Spinners*.
Nor do I like very much the one of the soldiers standing with the tall lances ...[30] Apart from the *Las Meninas* it's the portraits I really love. [1979]

There are no drawings of Velázquez. [I don't think there are]. I don't know. I know that I've certainly never seen any ... Perhaps he just put it straight down. [1979]

Well, one knows very well that work is very, very much on the edge. Some of the greatest things of the past have been on the edge of caricature. Now, if you take Velázquez, for instance, you take all those portraits that he did of Philip IV. If you analyse them, it would be almost impossible to have that structure of the face that you find in those portraits of Philip IV, unless Philip IV himself was already born a caricature. I don't really know ... Well, you see, there weren't any photographs, so we can't really tell. But one only knows him through Velázquez's portraits of him. [1984]

That is, I think, why he [Philip IV] invited Velázquez. He wanted Velázquez around him. That's the reason he painted him so often and painted his own entourage. And I think it could easily be that Velázquez was the least boring person that Philip IV had around him. Mind you, I don't know that. It's supposition, of course. [1984]

There's the Philip IV, and then there was the Rokeby Venus, which I think both of them, to me, are marvellous paintings. [1984]

But of course, the thing with Velázquez is that he was ... they do appear. I mean, if you take *Las Meninas*, they do altogether appear slightly ... they seem more real, even than Goya, and yet they do seem to be drifting, in a way, on the edge of caricature. [1984]

GOYA

Of course, another painting I feel that is so supremely, and I think much more than any of the black paintings for instance of Goya, is the great Goya, I think the big one in Castres, of the, I think it's called the *Junta* or the *Sessions of the Junta* ... and there of course you find something other that is also a miracle, is where you feel these figures that are seated in the town are just woven out of the air.[31] [1971]

30   He means *The Surrender of Breda*, 1634–35, Prado Museum, Madrid.

31   Francisco de Goya, *The Junta of the Philippines*, (*La Junta de Filipinas*), c. 1815, Goya Museum, Castres.

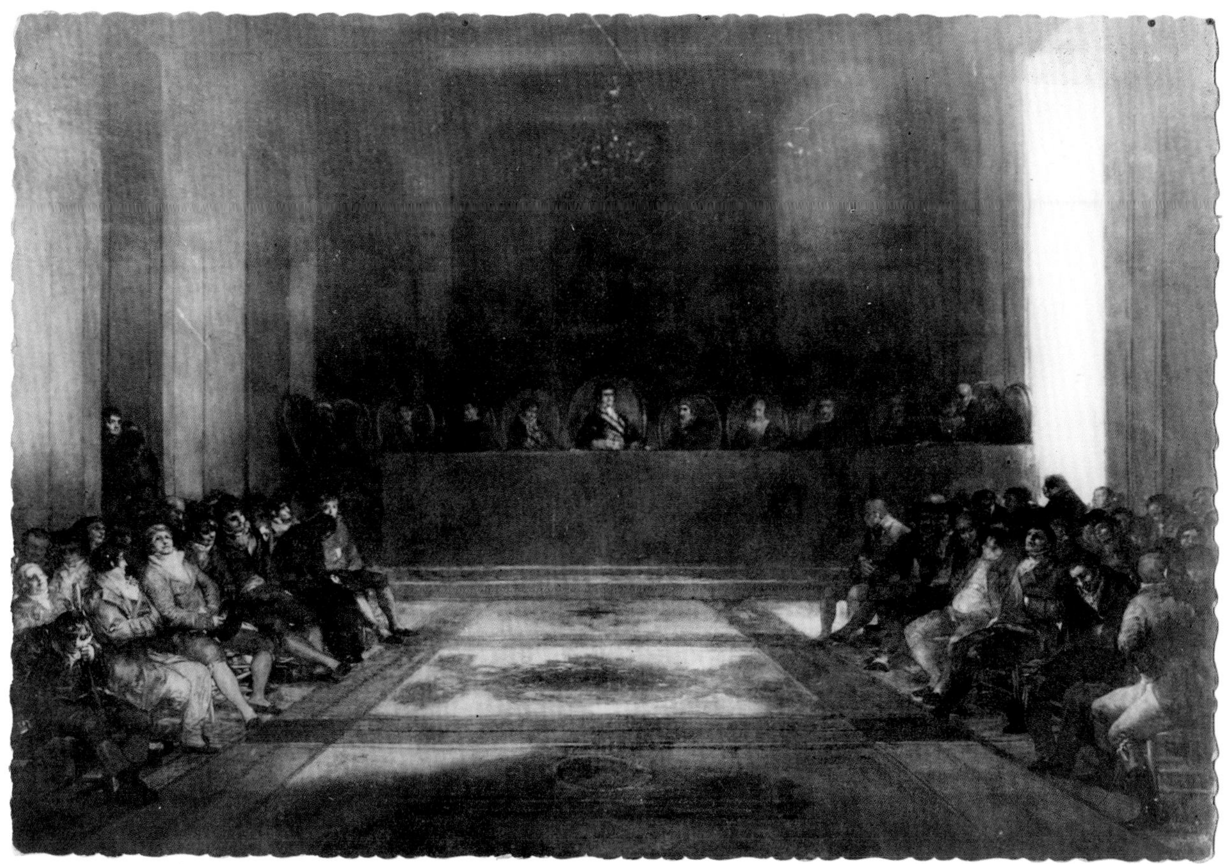

84. Postcard from the collection of Denis Wirth Miller of Francisco de Goya, *The Junta of the Philippines, (La Junta de Filipinas),* c. 1815, Goya Museum, Castres,

The great Goyas, they aren't consciously trying to say anything at all. But what is called the black Goyas have never worked for me … [1971] I don't like the grotesque side of Goya. [1973]

Yes, but the *Junta* is a very special painting because … I don't know in that painting so much as the portrait the figures seem to have been woven out of the air in such a mysterious way, as though the air actually entered into the being of each image of each person. [1973]

I think that if you are able to really bring over the intensity of somebody's appearance, you very often are drifting on the edge of caricature. I mean, you can think of some of the great Goya portraits, which are so remarkable. [1984]

… to go over the general influence that Goya had, I would say it was something that is extremely difficult to analyse which is the general tone or atmosphere of his work. And that has been always very, you may say, the fastidiousness, in a way, of his work has been always very important. [1984]

DELACROIX

I've never had this great feeling for Delacroix ... I like the sketches of Delacroix so much better than anything else. The small sketches – oil sketches. [1979]

[On Delacroix's illustrations of Shakespeare] I think it's Delacroix at his worst, or nearly always, when he does these things ... Well, I suppose it's a conscious ... a conscience of our time that won't go on at all; but a thing belongs to its own – absolutely belongs to its own technique and not translated, as it were, the ideas of Shakespeare. Delacroix attempted to translate scenes of Shakespeare into painting; and that's why it's nothing to do with modern art, what Delacroix was trying to do. I think the only way you could do it was if you were able to transpose the sensation that you might get from a play or poem or something like that into your painting, but it would be a transposition – perhaps would be very difficult to even know that it had anything to do with ... or it might for certain people who had a very strong feeling about, well, this is in the same atmosphere, in the same vein, as this thing – belongs to the same range of feeling. [1979]

DEGAS

I think Degas made marvellous forms and he may have made marvellous portraits, but I never think of the bodies as portraits of specific people. [1974]

Well, I think they're the very greatest things, the late Degas pastels ... but then I'm not thinking of the portraits I'm thinking of the nudes ... where you're not conscious so much of the body but of the formal qualities, I mean of the head and the formal qualities of the body. [1975]

Yes, but many things have happened since Degas. I mean, I know that Degas was interested very much in the photographs of Muybridge. But there's a great many things. The cinema, the film hadn't developed as far in Degas's life as it has now. Another thing is that when we talk of Degas, the very great Degas are the pastels. And don't forget, that in his in his pastels, he always serrated the form by these lines which were drawn through the image, which in a certain sense, both intensified and diversified its reality, the reality of the form he was making. Because I believe, at any rate, from my point of view, he was very, very much greater in his pastels where he did this than he was in his oil paintings. So I think that is one of the reasons that I think that as the techniques of the cinema and of all forms of recording have become better and better. So, from the point of view of the painter, it's made it more exciting, but yet, in a way, more curtailed, or the painter has to be more inventive to be able to put over the realism. [1984]

I don't think that Degas's horses really worked. I think the very great things of Degas are the pastels of the nudes … They were generally out in the bath, or they'd come out of the bath, they were towelling themselves or sponging themselves. And I think those are the very for me, at least, of the very great Degas. You know the one we looked at the other day in the National Gallery, that magnificent one of a woman seen from the back with the towel where she's wiping herself, drying herself. And I think that is one of the types of Degas, where Degas is at his greatest. [1984]

[Regarding the colour Degas put in the striations in the bodies] … which he probably wouldn't have been able to have added to the flesh, not at his moment. It would have to have come later with the fauves and the whole expressionist movement. [1984]

SEURAT

And, I think that you find that in some of the late Rembrandt self-portraits and you find it in some of the oil sketches of Seurat, of the figures; they're just brushed in and if you analyse them they're quite unillustrational but they bring over the appearance of the body either moving or sitting in a way that, or to me in a much stronger way than if it had been carefully delineated, as it is, for instance, in Durer, but I, you see, there is this question – to me the mystery of painting, today, is how can appearance be made? … I'm only talking about the oil sketches of Seurat. [1973]

I think in fact [Seurat] was a very much more logical painter in what is called a curious way than Cézanne. [1973]

If one thinks perhaps one of the most interesting of his are where the, the oil sketches that Seurat made, where when you look into them it's very hard to take away the irrationality of the brushstroke and what it conveys in the formal image. [1975]

Much, because he was, he was a generalised effect, much more, you wouldn't be able to distinguish probably one person from the other in the, perhaps if one had known the clothes they wore and everything one might possibly have been able make out, but certainly from the faces one wouldn't have been able to make out one person from another. They were not really portraits but they were generalised statements. [1975] … they were done on these cigarette, on these cigar boxes, on the backs of the, most of them were done, where the luminosity of the wood came through, quite apart from the colour he used … you almost feel that those sketches are flecked with gold. … he was always trying to sidestep the, in those sketches, the illustration of the appearance. Even in the portraits of his mother, and I believe, I'm not certain there's one of his father or not, he puts them in a fog rather than approach the problem of illustrating them.[32] Then there was, of course, the Seurat painting, the *Baignade*,[33] which I always think is one of the … I think that grass,

32   Evidently, Seurat's 'irradiation' technique in the remarkable portrait, *Madame Seurat*, 1882–83, Getty Museum Collection, failed to impress Bacon.

33   *Une baignade à Asnières,* 1884, National Gallery, London. [85]

that type of grass, has never been as beautifully painted as it is in that particular painting of Seurat's, of clipped, not carefully clipped grass, but grass that is just growing roughly on the edge of the bank of a river. [1984]

I think that Seurat might have done even greater things if he'd gone on. [1971]

CÉZANNE

… supposing Cézanne had died young. We'd probably never have had, it might be no loss, but we would probably have never had Cubism … if you take a man like Cézanne, if you'd only seen his early paintings, they might have been remarkable but not nearly as remarkable as his great late paintings and especially the great late watercolours. [1971]

I'm not certain that I find it in the apples as much as in the landscapes of Cézanne but, or in the watercolours of Cézanne, but I'm talking about, we brought up this thing about violence. I think appearance or so-called reality is in itself is violent. And that of course it's a technical thing. How are things made? After all it's a re-making of the technique to bring over the sensation of the image. [1971]

… well you see, Cézanne in a sense to me was a more complete painter because he wanted not only to paint as it were the things his apples tilted as you say, a penny or something like that, but he wanted to paint, he wanted to bring in himself painting, and I don't know about that. [1973]

I feel that there he is at his, generally, in the fragments of landscapes or fragments of things, rather than in the fully composed ones, that he's at his most incisive or precise … I think the fugitiveness of appearance perhaps is what forces one to try and trap it in a more formal way. You see I think that for me … those late watercolours of Cézanne are much more what I think of as real than what would be called realistic paint-ings … but it's not the clearness, as it were, of definition, which gives, which traps reality, it's trapped by, by … appearance can only be trapped by methods which one doesn't have any control about, and I wonder how much control, for instance, Cézanne had over his late watercolours. [1974] … there's been a very long period in the art in France, for instance you had the impressionists and then you had the Cubists. You could say that Cubism was a decoration on Cézanne, that Cézanne really in a way had done the whole of Cubism … [1975]

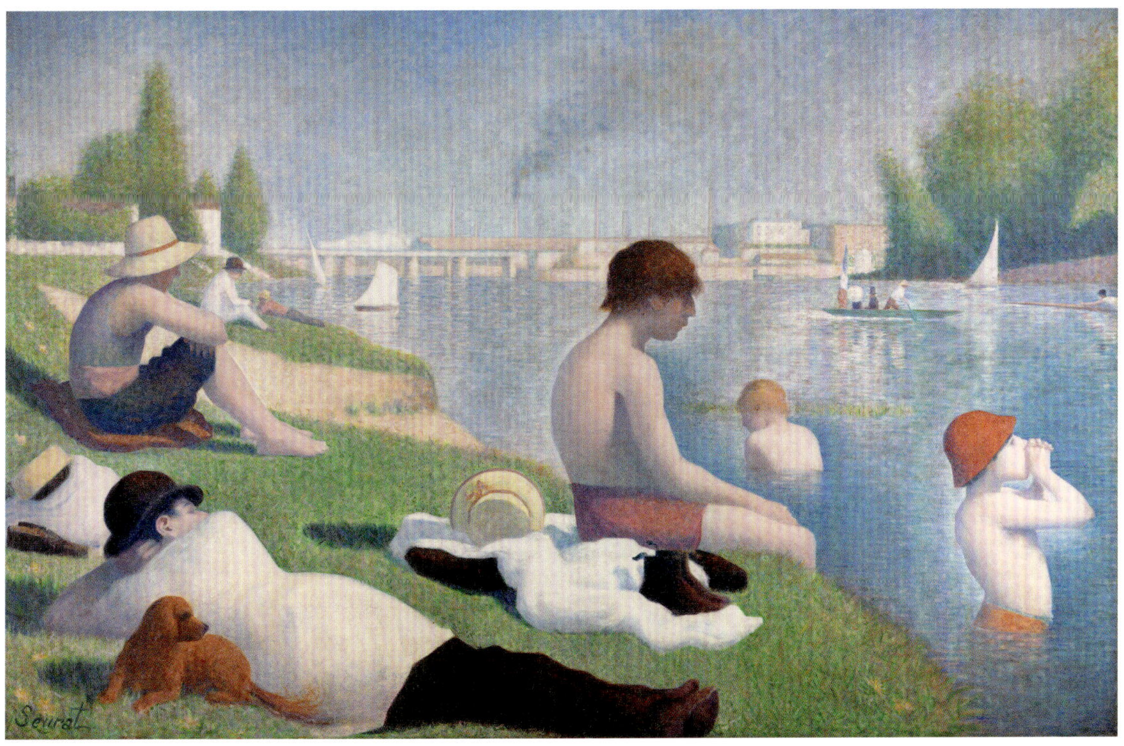

85. Georges Seurat, *Bathers at Asnières,* 1884

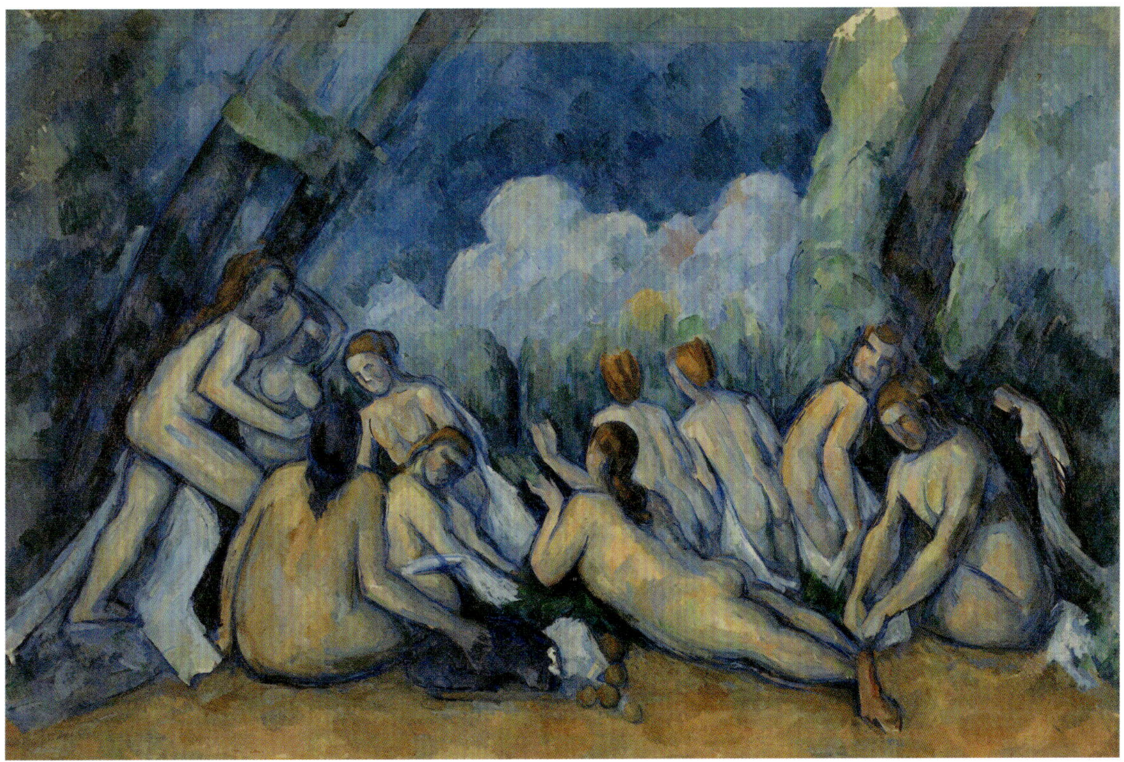

86. Paul Cézanne, *Bathers (Les Grandes Baigneuses),* c. 1894–1905

Perhaps in the portrait of Kahnweiler, Picasso knew what he wanted to do but didn't know how to bring it about. And I don't know about that. [1971]

(Copulation): It's an extremely difficult subject to do, oddly enough, I think. I don't think the Picasso ones worked because they always looked like toys you pull along the floor. I never saw one that looked, of Picasso's, that ever looked erotic. [1973] Of course, Picasso did very much at the end of his life. [1973]

I don't think people like Picasso tried to change the technique in quite that way. [1973]

I very much admire a lot of Picasso's sculpture, and I don't think that those particular painted sculptures would have been better in sculpture than in painting … but I think that many of his sculptures, especially the large heads with the large noses and a lot of the sculpture was extremely beautiful and amongst the most beautiful things that Picasso did. And I don't see my own sculpture in quite that way. I see it as a much more organic human image but departing a long way from exactitude. I know that Picasso departed a very long way, but I don't say that mine would depart further, but depart, as I see them, depart differently. You see all the best so called modern sculpture, except for Picasso, has really been abstract, and I'm not, when I'm talking of modern sculpture I'm not going back to Rodin, I'm talking of the work that's been done since Rodin, and I think that, and of course the early Matisse sculpture of the heads of Jeanette and the backs … and then I don't know whether Picasso was influenced in his big heads by the heads of Matisse but Matisse's were done I think about 1910 and Picasso's were done in 1930 and something and there does seem to be a remarkable relationship between them. [1974]

Well, of course, as I'm old, well, I'm 65, and I often did live through a period when Picasso and Matisse were working. After all that was a tremendous stimulus, and I can still look back on that with – it's difficult to say – they still can give me a marvellous enrichment by looking back on what they did during their time and if I don't specially like what's going on now, or find most of it fairly boring, I nevertheless look at it and I think, of course, that something marvellously exciting will come up again very soon. [1975]

I don't feel it about certain things at the end of his career; I think the difficulty with Matisse was, although there are a few things I admire enormously, I think he had a profoundly decorative concept, and I think his things so easily lost their drive and became decoration … I think there are one or two magnificent ones, but I think it does apply to some of them because he had this kind of innate kind of decorative sense, which is not the side of Matisse which I like … But certainly, Picasso

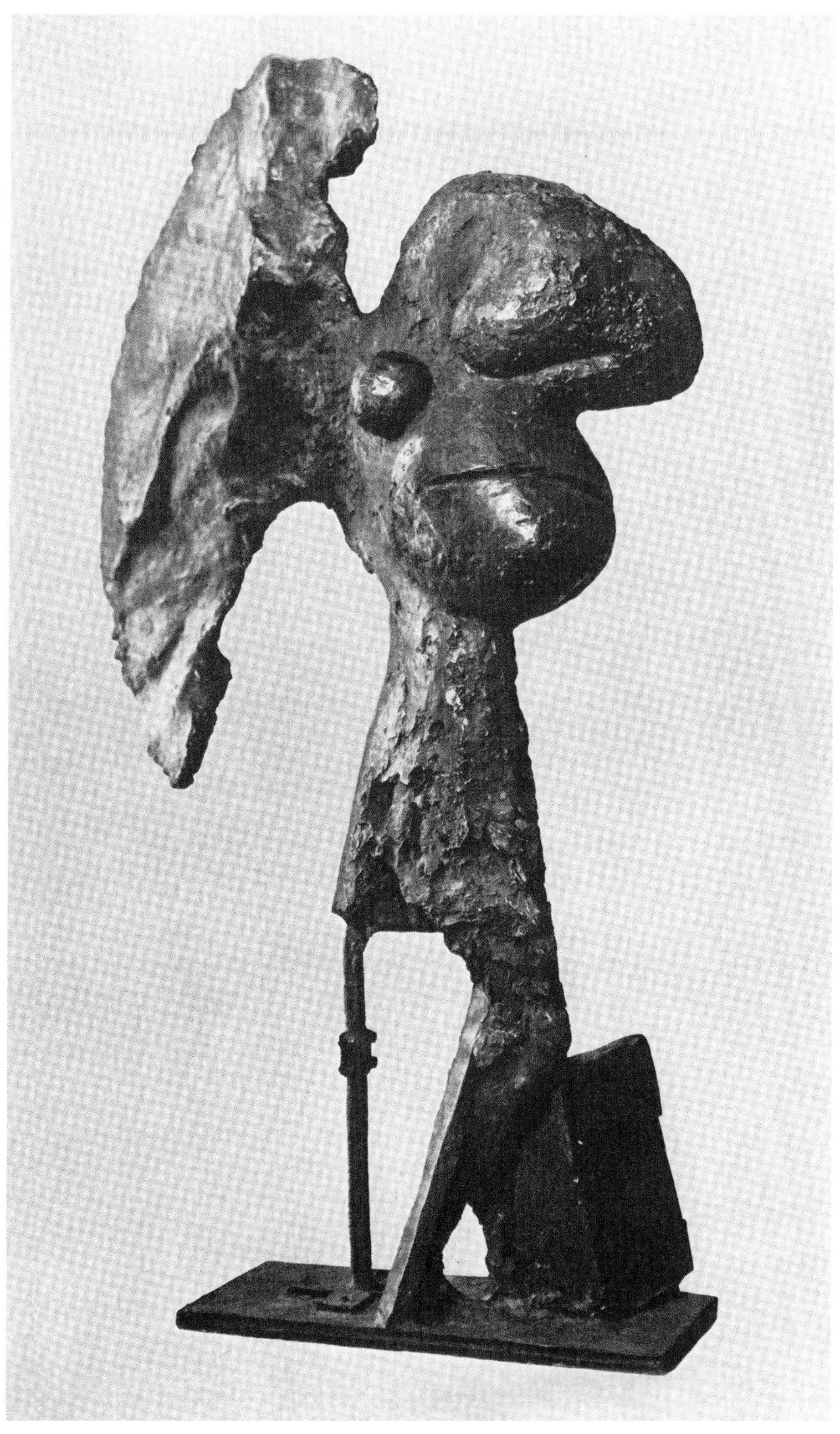

87. Picasso, *Tête casquée*, 1933, bronze; plate from Werner Spies, *Picasso, Das Plastische Werk*; Bacon owned a copy of this book.

interests me very much more than Matisse. Whether one or two things –
where one thinks of the greatest Matisses and the greatest Picassos, one
set against the other, I don't really know … Certainly as a source for my
own work, but primarily now I just find his ideas much more interesting
– his attack upon a subject much more interesting than Matisse's … I
think fundamentally I believe he was a greater artist at his very best. I
hate his work towards the end of his life, most of it, but he was such a
very surprising artist, nevertheless; I don't know if he was so surprising
at the end of his life, as some great artists have been, but nevertheless
he did, in the last twenty years of his life he's not so interesting. [1979]

I think that Picasso is much nearer what I feel about the psyche of our
time, than Matisse. I think that he tried to make what one calls the
psychic side of one's experience to find a visual equivalent in it – to try
to find a visual equivalent for the whole psychic side of one's sense of
reality in a much more positive way than Matisse. [1979]

I remember once talking to Michel Leiris about this thing, about
Picasso, and he said, as he was a great friend of Picasso's, and I said to
him, he said you realise that Picasso was never surrealist. But then I
always think that Picasso was the man who absorbed everything, and
he absorbed surrealism, too. Michel Leiris doesn't quite accept that,
but I don't know. I don't know about that. I don't say that I like it the
most, I do like it enormously certain things that Picasso did, especially
those figures that he did in Dinard and the things down at Cannes. But
also, when you saw the Cubist exhibition here, the interesting thing
about it was that the Picassos came out as the most strong, as the
strongest Cubist paintings. There's so much of Picasso. I admire Picasso
so enormously. And I do, of course, often think about Picasso sculpture.
And I do think perhaps … I often think Picasso was one of the greatest
sculptors of our period. And I often think that he said almost everything
in his sculpture, but there it was. As he was a man with these prodigious
gifts, he was able to move from painting to sculpture. [1984]

Picasso always practically remained in the thing of realism. I think just
in that aspect, he pushed this problem even further. You see, I mean,
to start again, we're talking about something very, very difficult. We're
talking about the extreme points of realism. But in a way, it's only the
extreme points that are interesting. And so this is why perhaps we seem
or I seem, very dumb in talking about it, because it's something which
can't be really formed. It's almost impossible to form into words. Well,
it's because we're talking about this very extreme difficulty. It's an
extremely difficult thing to talk about. It would have to be done before.
It would have to be painted or created before you could really talk about
it. Because then after it's been done, you could talk about and analyse it
and all that sort of thing. But before it's got, in fact, to be done, before
you can really talk about it. And I think this is one of the reasons that
figurative art, practically always, is so boring, because there's … There
isn't anybody who is really able to reinvent the technique by which
realism can be caught. [1984]

It's stupid to take a subject matter that has already been perfectly achieved. I know that many, even very great painters, like Picasso, have, of course, used it, like his versions of *Las Meninas*. He did an enormous number of *Las Meninas*, but even with, it's such a very great painting that even with Picasso's enormous genius, I don't think he ever did anything Velázquez hadn't already done. I don't think he added to the painting at all. [1984]

DUCHAMP

I'm not meaning to make the form more extreme, but the technique of trapping reality by, you may say, these inventions that have been made by which it can be recorded, to record it as a painter makes it more the problem more difficult, unless you're just going for sheer naturalism, which for me doesn't mean today anything at all. I mean, the person who I think got in some ways the nearest to it was Marcel Duchamp. If you take the Big Glass, which in a sense looks abstract, but if one knows that, for instance, those nine malic forms in the Big Glass, they were taken, for instance, he took the uniforms of nine different people, which he reduced down to very small images. So he was never abstract. I mean, he was many things, Duchamp, but in this famous great glass, Big Glass, he was never abstract. But he perhaps took to the limits this problem of abstraction and realism. [1984]

GIACOMETTI

But I think what Giacometti says is, in fact, a very limited way of putting it. I don't think it's just the gaze after all. There's all your flesh, your skin. When I say this, I don't mean it in any other way than the emanation of somebody … I don't think Giacometti is right in just saying it's the gaze … then it's a very limited thing. I mean, you don't just look at the gaze. You're not in a person, you're not just conscious of their gaze. You're conscious of the whole structure of a person. I mean, one knows Giacometti is quite right that a skull is more abstract because it hasn't got eyes, but then you've got your nose, your mouth, your teeth, your tongue, your everything, your lips. You've got all those things, too. So he's limiting it very much when he said it's just the gaze. [1984]

[re existentialism] It may be political theories – it got into Sartre's hair as it were – it got into his way; after all he never had very good sight I believe, and it may have been political – the political actions of Giacometti which coincide with Sartre … Did he isolate man as it were in his absurdity any more than any other artist? I don't feel that. I know that people used to always talk about that, but it always was to me nonsense. I know that the things that touched me very much – it's the drawings of Giacometti that really touched me – much more than anything else he ever did, that I know of. When I saw his big … I know that his drawings, for instance, when I went to the Fondation Maeght, touched me much more than the big sculpture. [1979]

[On the notion of violence in Giacometti's bronzes] They were becoming more violent at the end of his life, curiously.

I've never cared much for Giacometti's painting; I just feel that somehow he said nothing more than he said in his drawing; it has nothing really to do with painting. [1979]

BACON, AESTHETICS AND PHILOSOPHY

Although you say I have moral judgment, I may when we discuss, but I don't really hold moral judgments very much about people. I think there are certain ways that if one could behave well towards a person it's better than behaving badly, but that's not much more than that. [1973]

Do you ever say about painting what particularly pleases you? I can't. [1973]

I think you can have the psychological ideas without them having the aesthetic rightness but I'm not certain that you can have an aesthetic rightness without them having a psychological rightness. [1973]

Well, I think it's easier than calculating about the bill, it is just dead boring, that's all, probably it was only that. When I know many people are in the situation where each person who is together … have to calculate the different parts of the bill from one another but, that oddly enough it's not, I absolutely understand his way of life is necessary, but I have never had to live that life or never lived it because it is inhibiting to me. I feel the freedom is menaced, my freedom is menaced, and I suppose that's the reason that if I had the money I'll pay it out of, I wouldn't pay it out of generosity but out of well, if you've got the money you might as well pay for what you're doing. [1974]

I think the fate of a person is their whole metabolism whereas I think their, which nothing really can protect them, nothing can protect them against their, the *weaving* of their, the way their metabolism works, you could say it's that *psyche* and their *instinct* works, but can't in any way be protected. [1974]

I think it is very possible. I think that also the few criminals that I have known through my life have got very often, or had, a very much great imagination. And it may have been this thing that turns them into criminals, I don't know. Or perhaps they were criminals because they found the cat and mouse play between themselves and the law and added excitement their lives. I don't quite know about that but certainly in the method that they've used to try and defeat the law they had, it gives them, it has given them an impetus to their imagination. [1974]

My sister said to me the other day, 'Shall we both go and have a face-lift together?'. I said, 'Yes as soon as possible'. When I see myself in this bloody thing … [1975]

Of course, because art is the great life-giver. I mean, art is the greatest life-giver. I mean this doesn't, when I say all this, this doesn't invalidate, because what we're talking about is something much in a way is different about that when I say all is futile, but within the futility in which we exist, art is far the greatest life-giver. Sport is the next one and sport touches more people than art, many, many more people, but there's art, there's sport, I don't know what comes after that, you can say there's love, but love of course is such, or the sexual obsession; I don't know where you, how you grade them, sexual obsession, art, sport. One can grade them anyway one likes, like the calendar. [1979]

I think it's because I have been labelled with this, as certain people are, as being a painter of horror. I don't think it's horror at all. I think if you are able to give over as directly as you possibly can your feeling about the excitement of life, they have labelled that as being a horrific side. You can say that life is horrific. If you think about being born and the short interval between birth and death, it is in a sense, horrific. I mean, after all, religion was really, all the religions have been, in a sense, invented to try and take this away from the people because religion, in a way, is an antibiotic to death. People have tried to use … I mean, this is what religions of all types have cashed in on, because people don't want to feel that they're mortal. They long to feel there's a possibility of life not just ending. That is one of the things. I am not capable of any form of religion whatsoever. And I know, here I am, gone tomorrow, as they say. [1984]

But then, after all, that is, that is of course, that is the real, that in a sense, is what is called, is the tragedy of life, is to be born and know that every second that this thing, this, once you've got as it were consciousness, after the age of, I don't know what age I'd say, it alters in people's things, but to know that this thing is falling away from you. [1973]

Well, it is, because I certainly don't believe in equality. Some people are born with greater gifts than others. Some people are born better-looking than others. Certain women are born more beautiful than others, and they're going to have greater chances just for those very reasons. And so, I have no belief in equality. I do believe in one thing, that people should, when it's possible, be given equal opportunity. But even when they're given equal opportunity, very few people will be able to avail themselves of it. I absolutely have no belief in equality. One just knows some people are born with more gifts than others, as we said before, and that's all it is. [1984]

When I was young, I thought of nothing except enjoying myself. But I didn't really think about that. I suppose that later you could say my philosophy; you wouldn't call it a philosophy. I think life, in a way, is so difficult that you may as well be as decent as you possibly can be, or as indulgent as you possibly can towards other people, hoping they'll behave in the same way to you. It doesn't necessarily work out that way, but that's how it comes about. I haven't got a very coherent philosophy of life. [1984]

Yes but the id, is just, doesn't really tell us any more. I was just reading that book of J.Z. Young's. Well, it's a very long book … he is a biologist, and I used to remember him at the Gargoyle. And it's very brilliant, but he leaves so much of it with a question mark. They don't really know. I always found him so interesting. I haven't seen him for years. I saw him one day with that same girlfriend who used to be about him, in that pub in the middle of Beauchamp Place.[34] [1973]

I think because, although I was born in Dublin I have lived most of my life in London and I think I became accustomed to London and so I didn't think about it, as it were. I just knew that I walked from one place to another, and I saw the crowds moving along the pavements. But I didn't sort of worry or think about anything and that made it easier to work in. Because I've known Paris – since I had an exhibition there in 1971 I've known Paris for some reason much, much better and I've also made, in so far as we can ever talk of making friends, I've made a lot of friends in Paris and there's another side of it. I like the clarity of thought of the French. After all there's something that's no doubt – the French education is very much better than the English education because it just has produced through every – firstly it's a more classless society than England, and also the people are much more aware and intelligent. You can talk to anybody in France whereas it's very difficult in England to talk to anybody. [1975]

LITERATURE

Well, you know, I read generally the same thing over and over again. I very often read those translations of Aeschylus. I read Proust, I read anything, anything that comes to my hand or any rubbish as well … The rubbish. Well, most things are rubbish. So I can't tell you exactly what rubbish is, but there is very little, after all, there's piles of rubbish and very little stuff that's any good. [1984]

I think it's urgent also because I don't think I have got any musical sense but the thing is, is that poetry has always meant a very great deal to me and the poetry that moves me most is always the poetry that returns, returns me to life with, even if it's very tragic poetry, with a kind of vitality, and almost makes you, brings life back to you more violently. I mean what more ghastly play, from the point of view of its subject or something, than Macbeth, and yet seen or read Macbeth, or seen a great performance of Macbeth, you're absolutely reinvigorated. [1973]

34   Beauchamp Place is in Knightsbridge, London; the pub was then called Grove Tavern. Young's book was *An Introduction to the Study of Man*, 1971.

I think – it was the imagery of [Pound and Eliot] that I like; not only, you may say, the actual imagery and what one could call the psychic imagery as well. [1979]

... But then I think Eliot has talked very well about that in some of his essays, where he has spoken about some of the Elizabethan plays, not necessarily of Shakespeare, but he may have included Shakespeare as well, but where he says that his portraits of people, I mean, portraits in words of people, are very often drifting absolutely on the edge of caricature. [1984]

I've read both Freud and Nietzsche. I can't say that either of them brings up images in the same way that the poems or the plays of Aeschylus or Shakespeare or the poems of Eliot have brought up images to me. I think of Freud and Nietzsche as both having a much more analytical ... They have much more analytical minds, and they don't happen to bring up images in the same way as the other people we were talking about ... Well, of course, I've been influenced by Nietzsche. And of course, I mean, if you read Shakespeare, it's a thousand different philosophies in the different plays. I mean, probably Shakespeare never ... I don't know if he ever held a philosophy as we don't really know who Shakespeare was. One doesn't really know if he had a coherent philosophy. He probably hasn't. He was just a marvellous artist who could use anything for his own ends. And of course, in a very small and minor way, I would always hope that I will be able to use anything to work by. [1984]

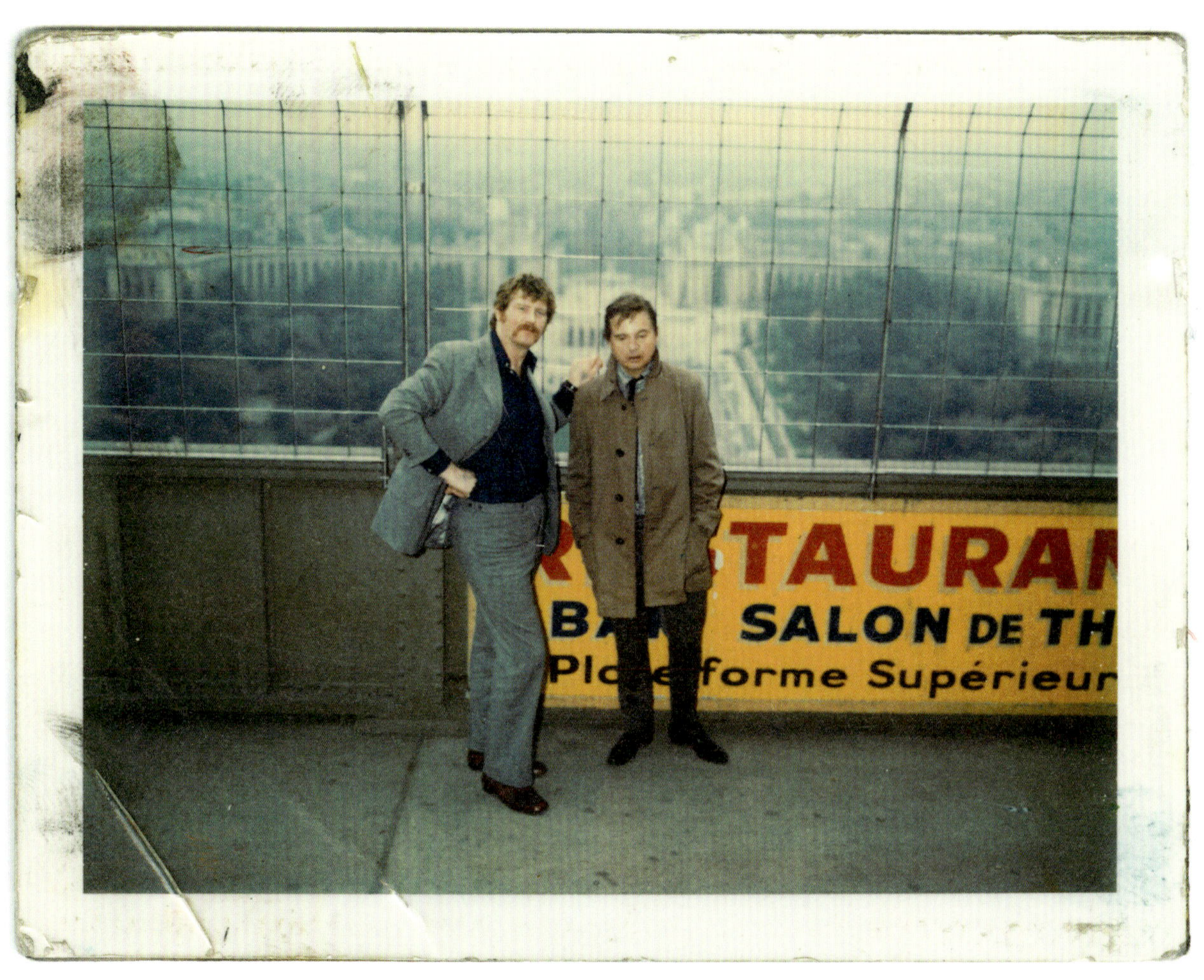

88. Ted Westfallen (Onsloe) and Francis Bacon on the second stage of the Eiffel Tower, Paris, October 1969; Polaroid by Photo-Express

Afterwords

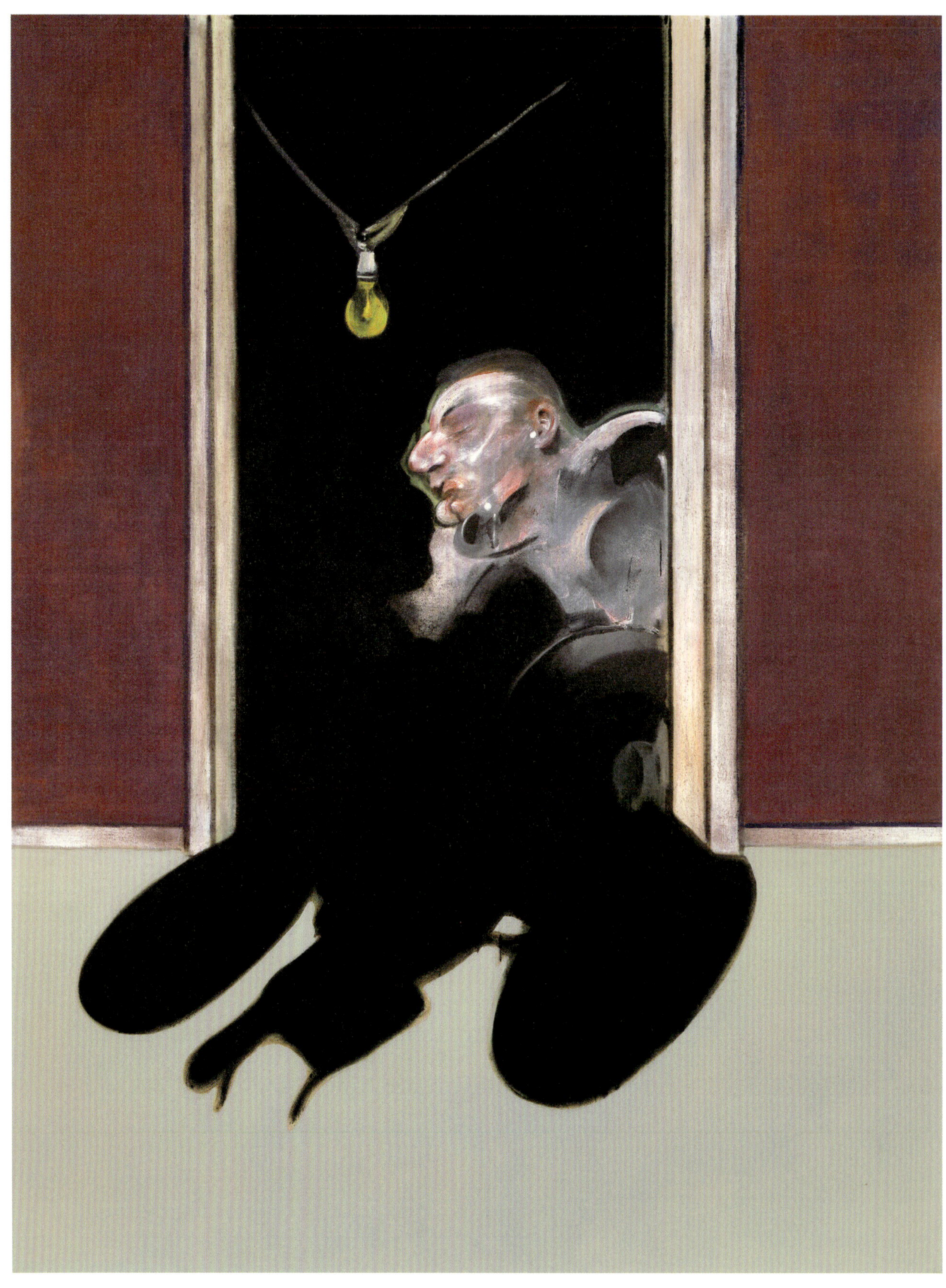

89. *Triptych May-June 1973* (centre panel)

Notes on *Triptych May–June 1973*

Amanda J. Harrison

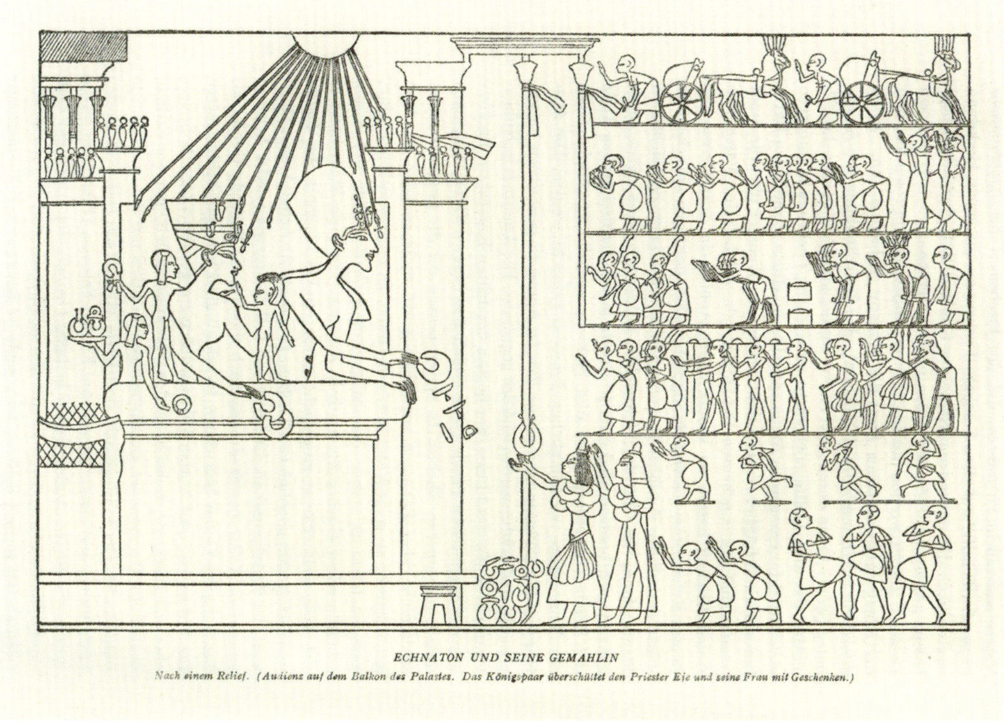

90. Akhenaten and Nefertiti, plate from J.H. Breasted, *Geschichte Ægyptens*, 1936; Bacon owned a copy of this book

Triptych May–June 1973 was Bacon's most avowedly narrative painting [see pp. 94–95]. In the outer panels Bacon addresses directly the circumstances of George Dyer's death, while in the centre panel Dyer inhabits a sepulchral space and in an ambiguous state. The top half of his naked, dissolving body has limbs that seem to revert to foetal buds. Uniquely in Bacon's oeuvre, the light bulb suspended above Dyer's body does not hang from a vertical flex. Instead, Bacon painted the bulb touched by a diagonal ray (or two rays), invoking the ancient Egyptian wall reliefs of Akhetaten (now Tell el-Armana), the capital city founded by pharaoh Akhenaten.

Bacon kept a large collection of books on Egyptian art in his studio and would have been familiar with illustrations of Akhenaten receiving the blessing of life from the god Aten. In the Egyptian reliefs, rays emanating from Aten's sun disc each terminate in a stylised hand; those directed at Akhenaten and his queen Nefertiti hold an ankh, the symbol of life. The affinity between the ankh's shape (and its connections with light and the blessing of life) and an incandescent light bulb, was deployed by Bacon to convey his thoughts on the cessation of life.

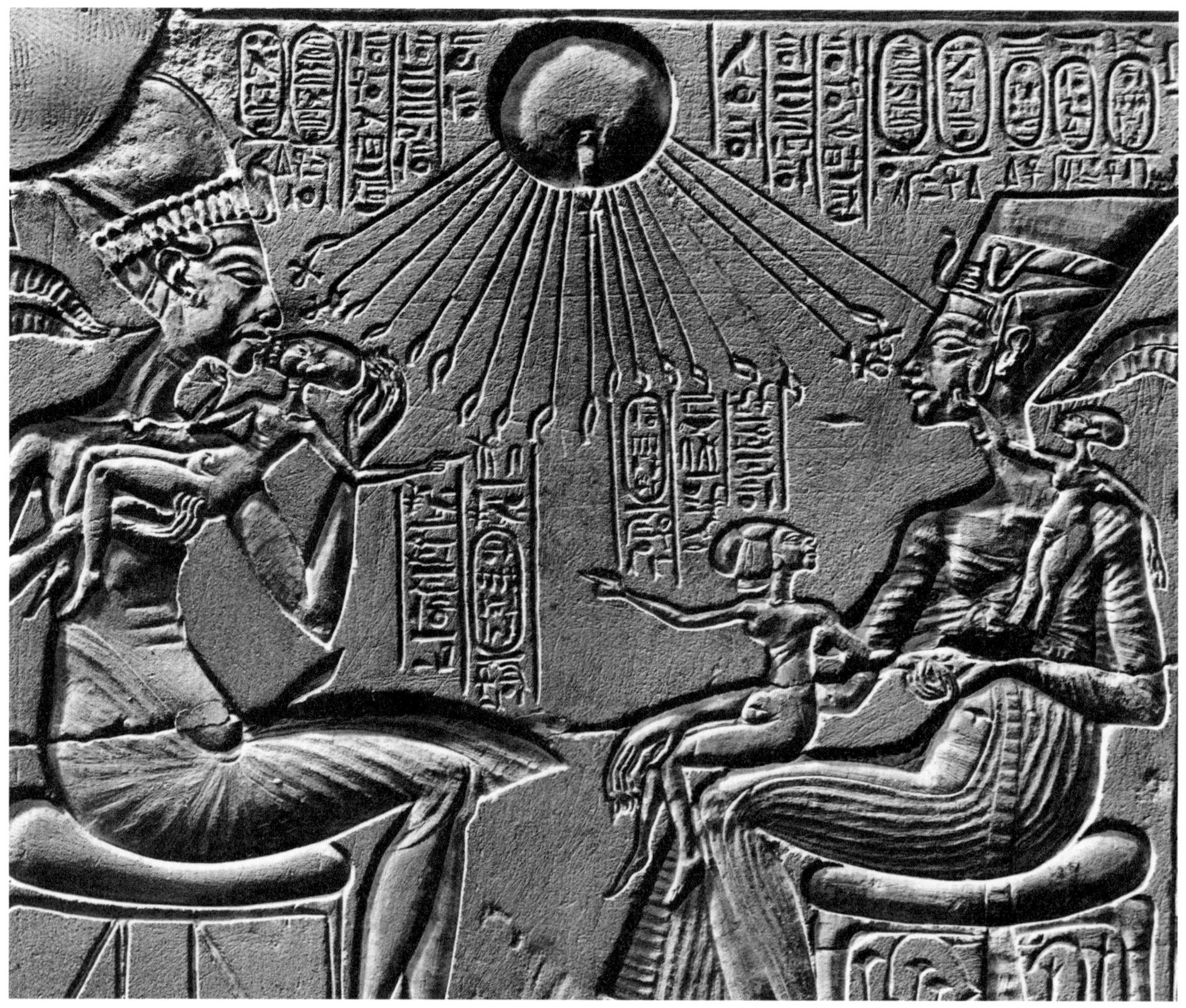

91. *Stele of the Amarna dogma,* plate from C.D. Noblecourt, *Ancient Egypt, The New Kingdom and the Amarna Period*, 1960 (detail); Bacon owned a copy of this book

The stylised hand with which the sunray terminates touches the lamp holder in Bacon's painting, implying the power to switch it on or off. Bacon was also alluding to the tradition of *memento mori*, in which a portrait is accompanied by a guttering or extinguished candle: he grafted onto a three-thousand-year-old religious concept a seventeenth century trope and combined them with a contemporary light-source.

The soft yellow glow of the light bulb contrasts with the menacing black shadow below and the triptych's funereal atmosphere. The three panels are painted in the colours of half mourning, the stage of formal mourning following deep mourning. Historically, fifteen months after their husbands' death, widows exchanged their black garments for sombre greys, mauves, black and white for a further three months. The triptych was the last produced in Bacon's 'period of mourning' and was begun at the time the designated period of mourning ended.

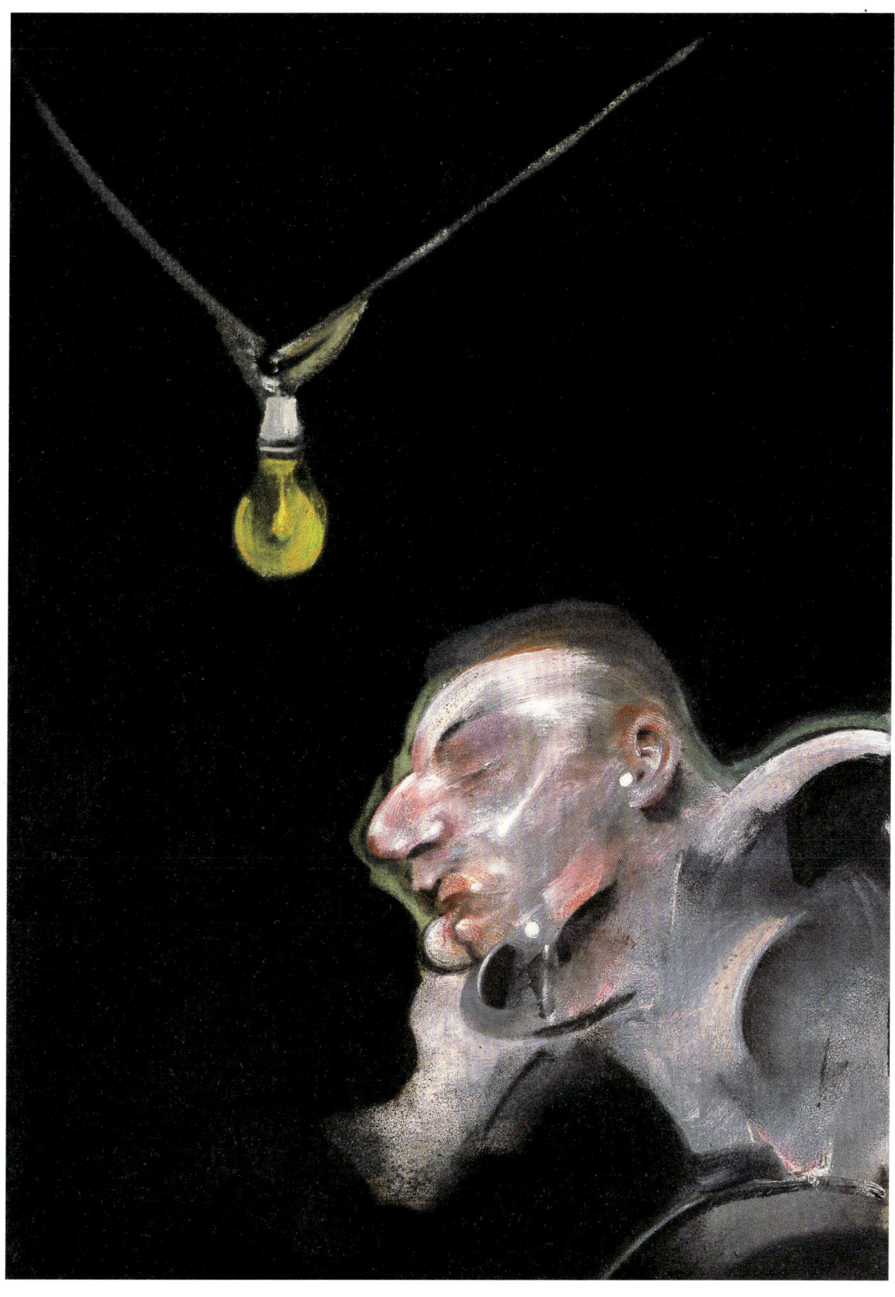

92. *Triptych May-June 1973* (detail)

The washbasin waste pipe in the right panel emerges at the bottom right of the
centre panel to drain out into a black main sewer pipe. It is as though effluent
discharges into the shadow/pool that flows from the black space behind the entrance
onto the floor of the triptych's foreground. This draining away of waste intensifies
the sense of grief (and guilt?) over Dyer's death, as the past actively persists and
infiltrates into the present. Not normally given to sentimental gestures of this kind,
Bacon had remembered and noted the anniversary of Dyer's death in his otherwise
sparse diary for 1972.

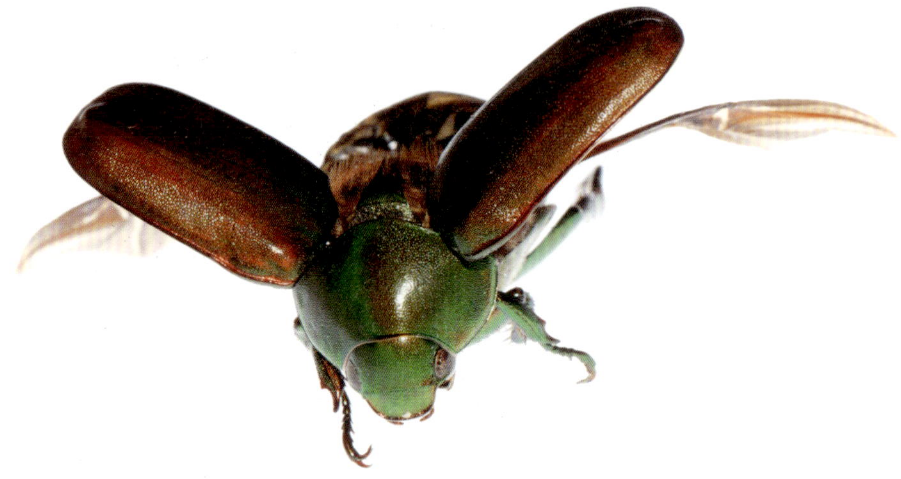

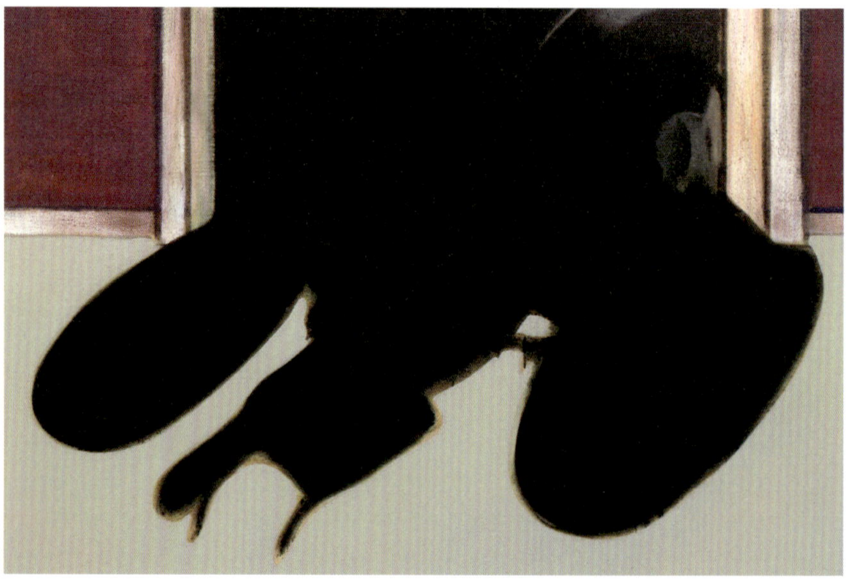

93. (above) Green Scarab Beetle in flight
(below) *Triptych May–June 1973* (detail of centre panel)

The shape of the louring shadow is cast by a winged being. Clearly, in the context of this triptych, Bacon was referencing a (modified) scarab beetle, an animal sacred to the ancient Egyptians. The scarab beetle's wing cases, antennae and palps are transfigured by Bacon to powerfully graphic, intimidating effect. Bearing in mind that the black pool/shadow flows from a sewer fed by the waste pipe draining Dyer's vomit from the right panel, and the left panel shows a lavatory pan, the connection is relevant because scarab beetles collect dung. In the Ancient Egyptian pantheon, the scarab-headed deity Khepri was understood as an aspect of the sun god Ra/Aten. Khepri and scarab beetles were both believed to create themselves 'out of nothing'. The beetles were thought to be solely male, and to reproduce by depositing semen into a dung ball from which the next generation emerged fully formed; Khepri regenerated nightly in readiness to move the sun across the sky each day. The balls rolled by the scarab were considered analogous to the orb of the sun travelling its daily course. Khepri and his symbol, the scarab, signified the hope of transformation and rebirth.

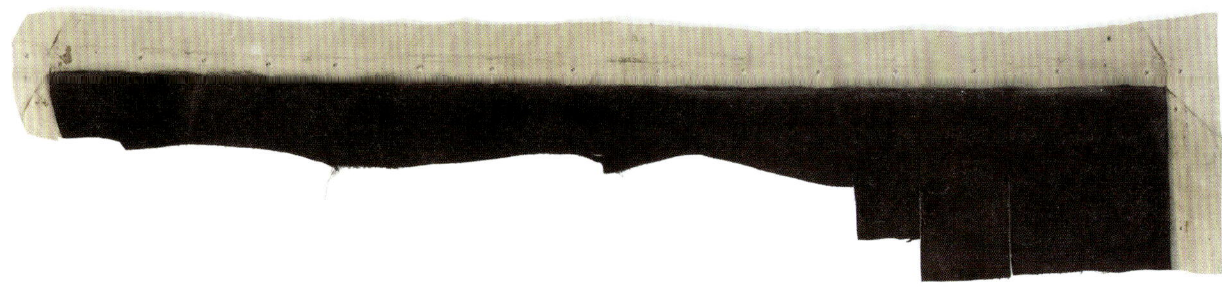

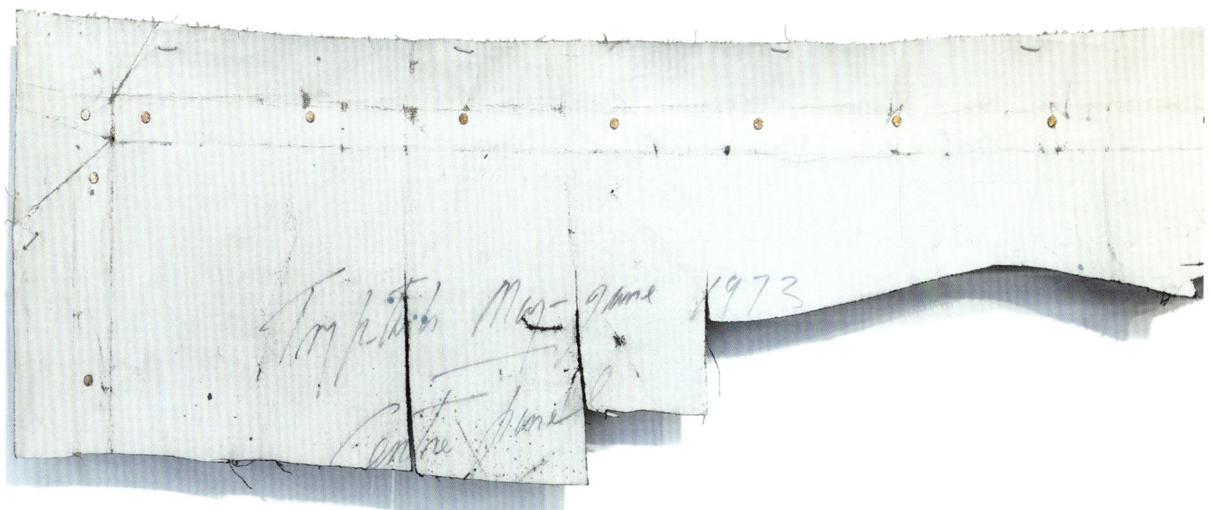

94. Fragment of early version of *Triptych May–June 1973*, recto (above) and detail of verso (below)

Among the remnants of destroyed canvases found in 7 Reece Mews after Bacon's death was an uneven strip cut from the top of what had been a large, finished canvas. The front of the strip is painted black and on the back Bacon wrote *Tryptich (*sic) *May-June 1973 Centre panel*. In the extant panel which replaced it the black central area is flanked by vertical sections of purplish maroon divided by two door jambs in cream. Why Bacon completely reconceived this panel is not recorded, but that he did so points to the triptych's exceptional importance for him. It is consistent with Bacon's veneration of Ancient Egyptian sculpture that the formal structure of the triptych suggests three tomb entrances and that for this exceptionally emotive and personal response to mortality he had recourse to the potent symbolic meanings of Egyptian art.

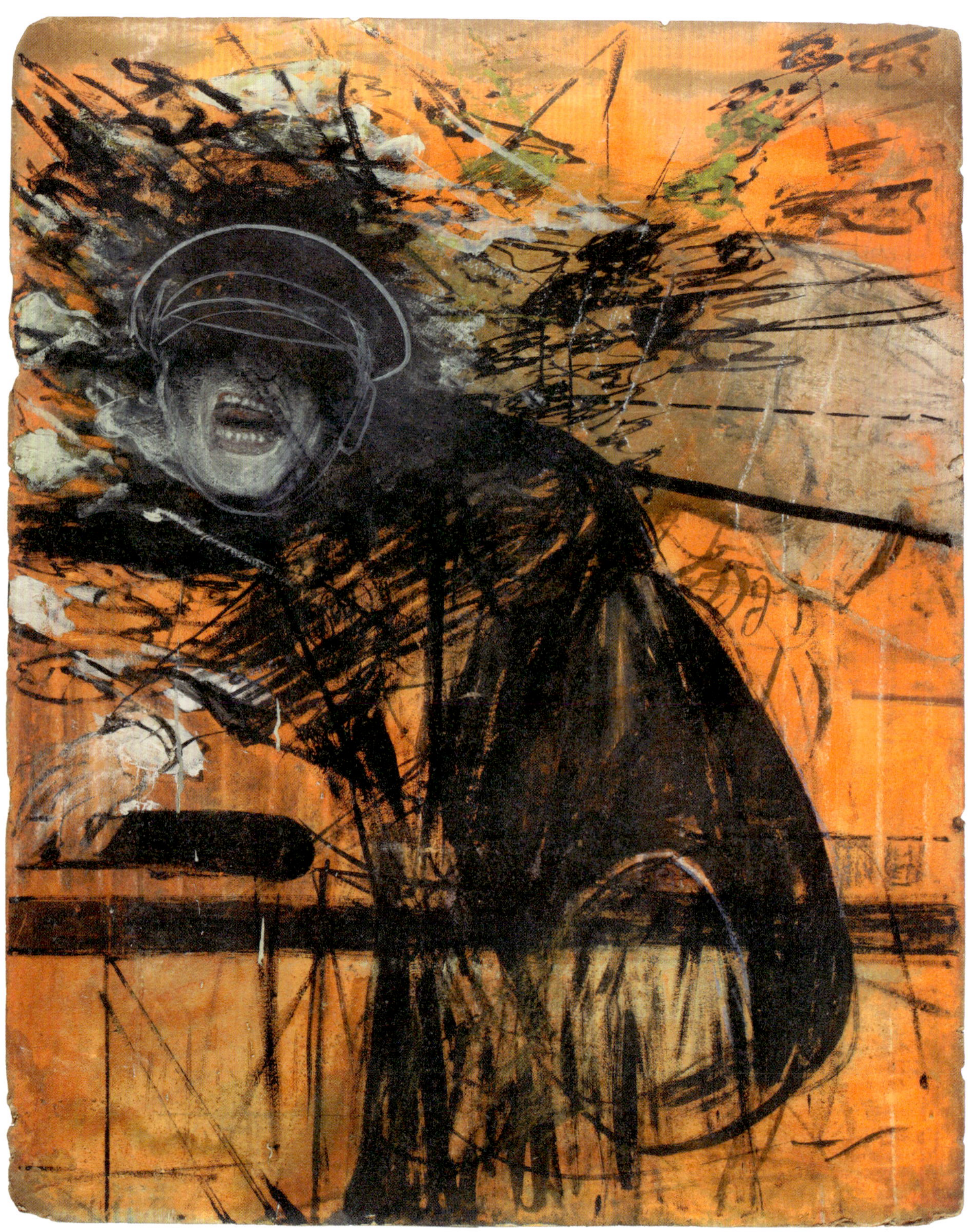

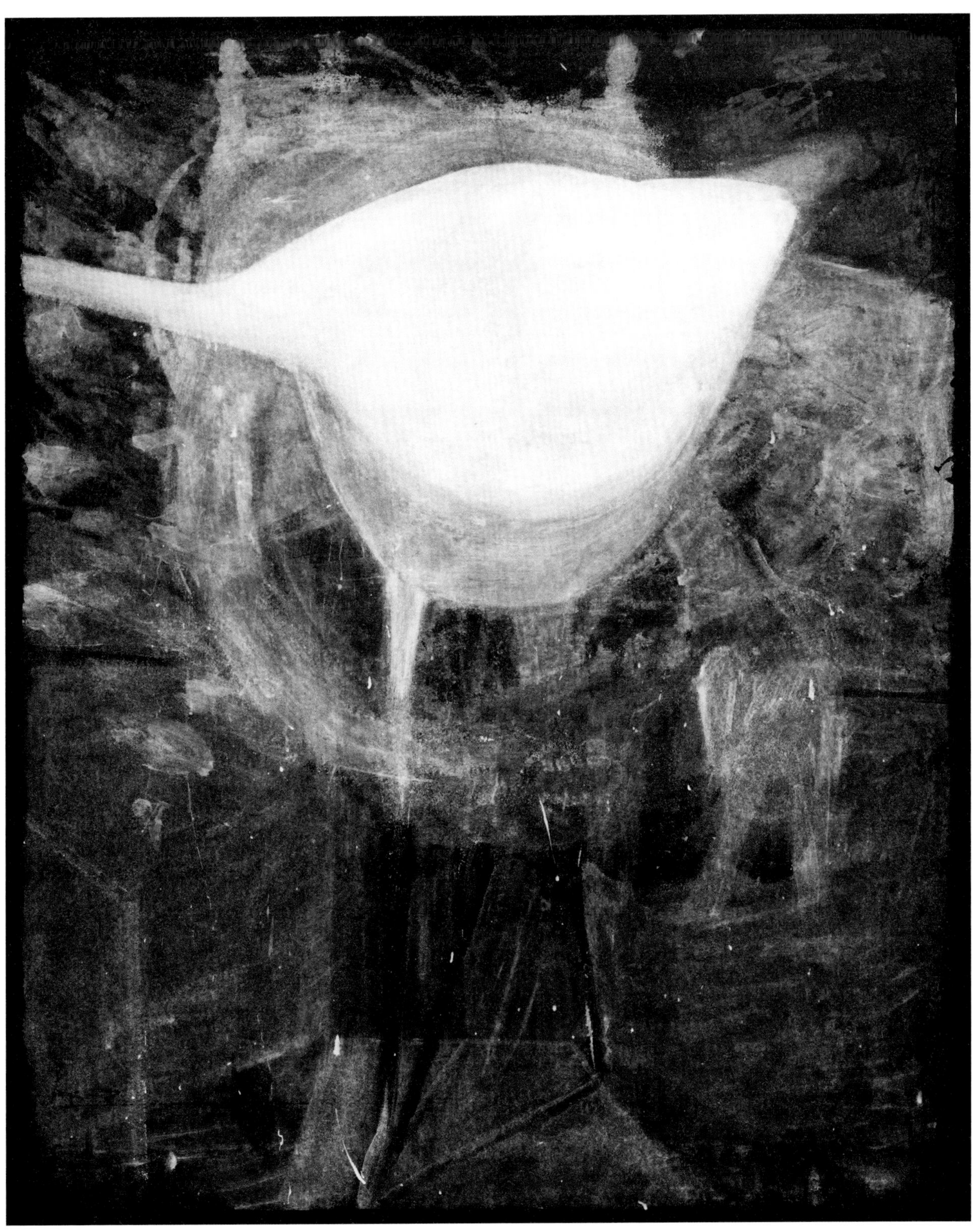

96. **Man in a Cap, c. 1945, X-ray**

Man in a Cap, c.1945

Martin Harrison

It may not have been evident to many readers that in *Francis Bacon: Catalogue Raisonné* (2016) the illustration of *Man in a Cap* was made not from a high resolution scan but stitched together from two rather poor images. The then owner had refused to allow a new photograph to be commissioned unless I misrepresented its title and date. *Man in a Cap* was among the paintings that Bacon abandoned when he left his Cromwell Place studio in May 1951. Robert Buhler, who took over the lease, sold on most of the paintings to the Piccadilly Gallery, London, in 1953; many of them, including *Man in a Cap*, were bought by Luca Scacchi Gracco, in Milan.

In 1963, Scacchi Gracco exhibited the painting in Milan as 'Peaked Cap', but when it was included in 'Da Bacon ai Beatles', at the Museo della Permanente, Milan, in 2011–12, it was retitled 'The Man of Military Cap' and dated 1947. These were the errors that the previous owner refused to reconsider. It was a principle in the catalogue raisonné that the information published by John Rothenstein and Ronald Alley in the 1964 catalogue raisonné was sacrosanct, on the grounds that it had Bacon's approval or acquiescence; accordingly, we retained Alley's simply descriptive title, *Man in a Cap*. Since 2016 I had continued to hope that circumstances might permit a high quality image of the painting to be published; fortunately, it passed to new owners, who were entirely sympathetic and arranged for a professional photographer to make a high resolution digital scan of it.

The opportunity this afforded to closely scrutinise a technically excellent image led me to speculate about imagery that may have been hidden under the final layer of paint. Again, the owners readily agreed to have an X-ray made of the painting. The result was revelatory, not only in respect of *Man in a Cap* but also about Bacon's practice around 1944–45 and the origins of what he considered his 'Opus 1', *Three Studies for Figures at the Base of a Crucifixion*, 1944.

The most startling new fact manifested by the X-ray is the bird-like form in the upper centre. Its affinity with the 'biomorph' in the centre panel of *Three Studies for Figures at the Base of a Crucifixion* strongly suggests that 'layer 2' was an early version of the panel in the triptych. Below the 'bird's' spindly legs the geometrical lines are comparable with those in *Abstraction*, c. 1936, testifying to the prolonged gestation of this image. Unfortunately, Bacon destroyed *Abstraction*, preventing any further comparisons. It is highly improbable that the chair/throne finials visible in the X-ray above the biomorph related to either the biomorph or the man in the cap on the front surface, which suggests there was yet another painting underneath *Man in a Cap*. Given the earliest finials in Bacon's extant oeuvre are those in *Head VI*, 1949, their appearance in c. 1943 is as unexpected as it is prescient.

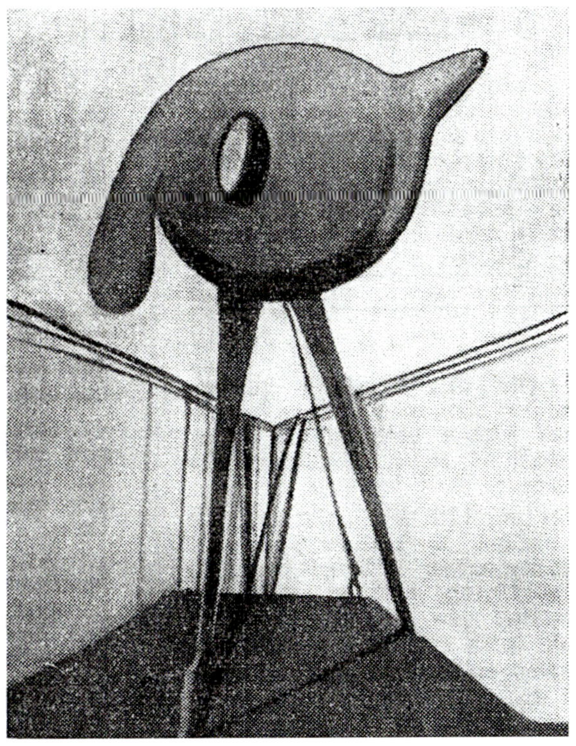

97. *Abstraction*, 1936

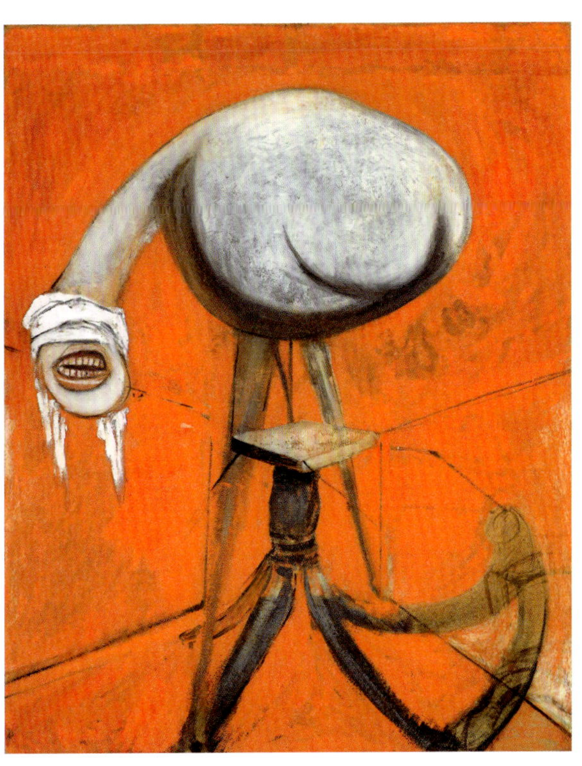

98. *Three Studies for Figures at the Base of a Crucifixion* (centre panel), 1944

Canvas was very scarce during the Second World War, and *Man in a Cap* is one of seven paintings Bacon made on fibreboard supports. On the reverse of *Man in a Cap* is written 'F Bacon Petersfield'; this relates to the cottage at Steep, about two miles (3.2 km.) distant, where Bacon sometimes stayed with Eric Hall, c. 1940–43. One other fibreboard support that Bacon used is marked 'Petersfield' – the right panel of *Three Studies for Figures at the Base of a Crucifixion*. X-rays of this panel revealed that it was originally orientated in a landscape format. Its imagery was entirely distinct from what we see today, and is dominated by a head of a man, who I have speculated is Eric Hall.

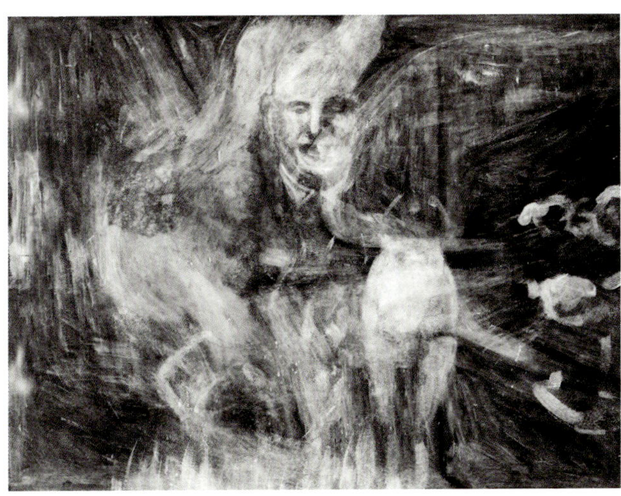

99. X-ray of *Three Studies for Figures at the Base of a Crucifixion* (right panel), rotated 90° clockwise

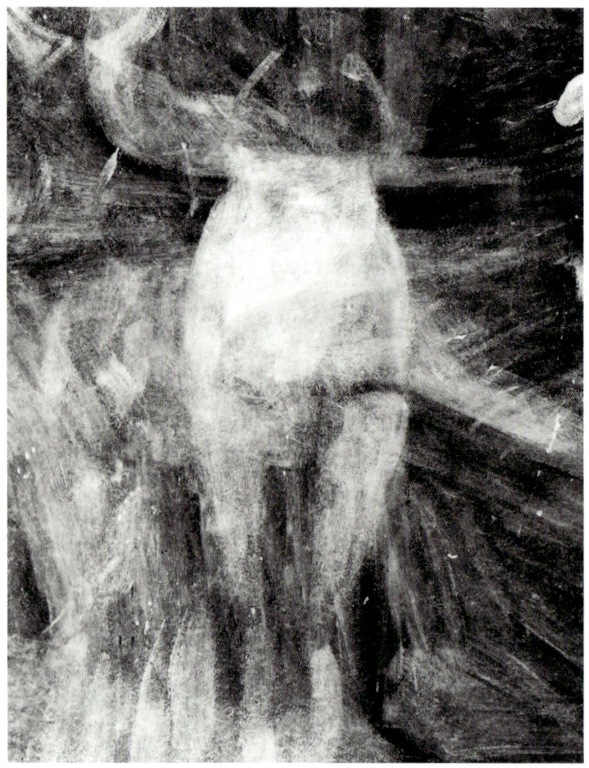 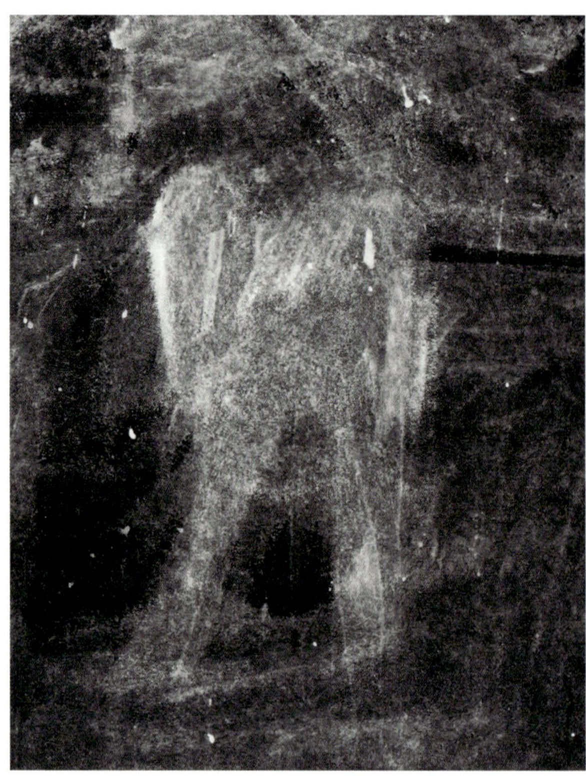

100. Detail of X-ray, *Three Studies for Figures at the Base of a Crucifixion*, (right panel)

101. Detail of X-ray, *Man in a Cap*

Owl-like forms are present underneath several of Bacon's paintings in this period, as are avian creatures in general, but they did not figure overtly in his iconography until the 1950s. The owl-like form to the right of the man in [99; 100] is similar to that visible in the X-ray of *Man in a Cap*. In the panels under discussion we seem to be witnessing Bacon over-painting images that may be regarded as preliminary studies in his formulation of *Three Studies for Figures at the Base of a Crucifixion*.

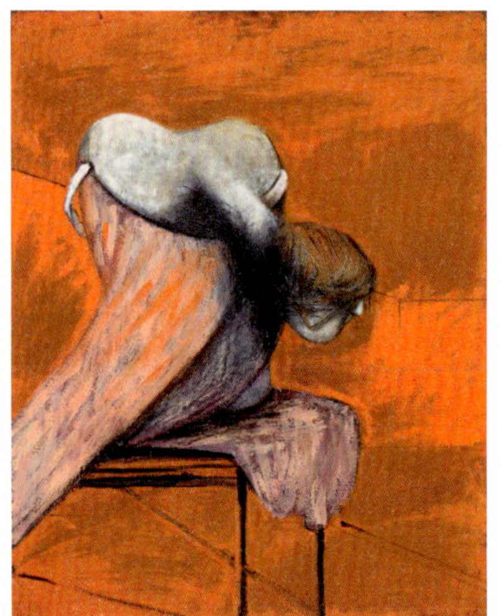 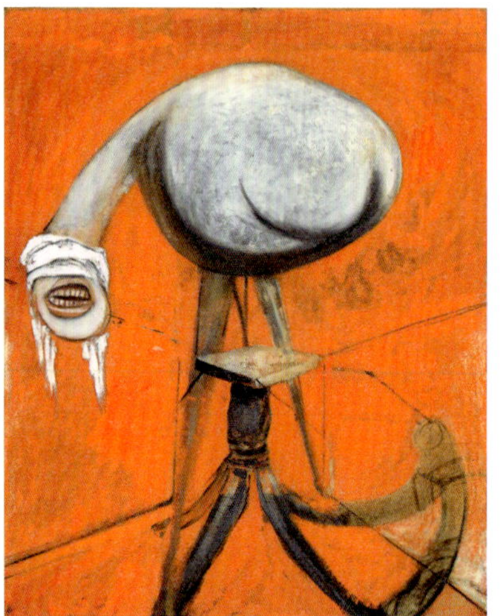 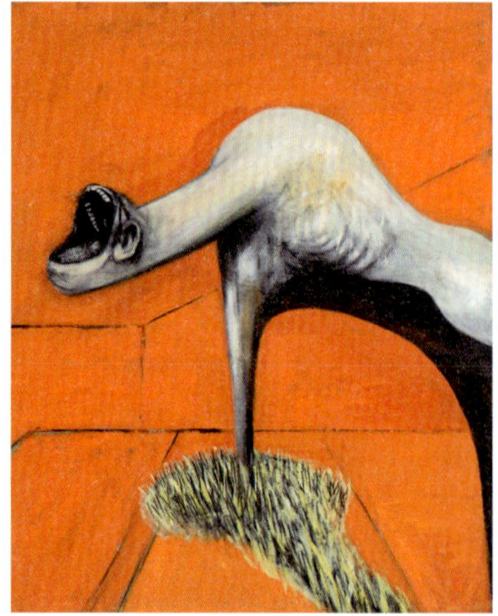

102. *Three Studies for Figures at the Base of a Crucifixion*, 1944

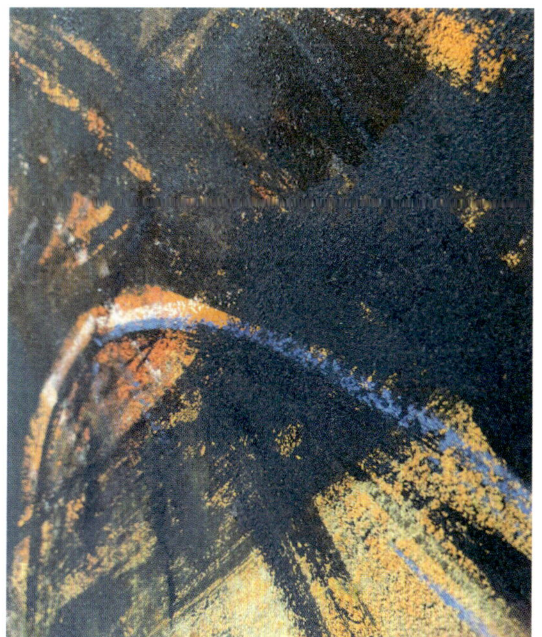

103.

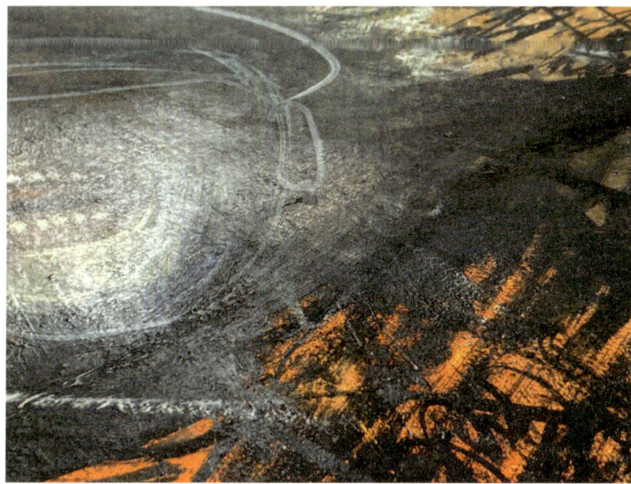

104.

The three photographs of *Man in a Cap* on this page were taken by conservator Brian McLaughlin while he was obtaining paint samples for future analysis. Photographed at an acute angle and in raking light, in [103] several strokes of bright blue are revealed that are difficult to discern in the 'normal' scan. As usual with Bacon, the paint application is at its densest on the head. [104] The pigments Bacon employed in this painting await scientific analysis, but the shiny black area may indicate the admixture of linseed oil. [105]

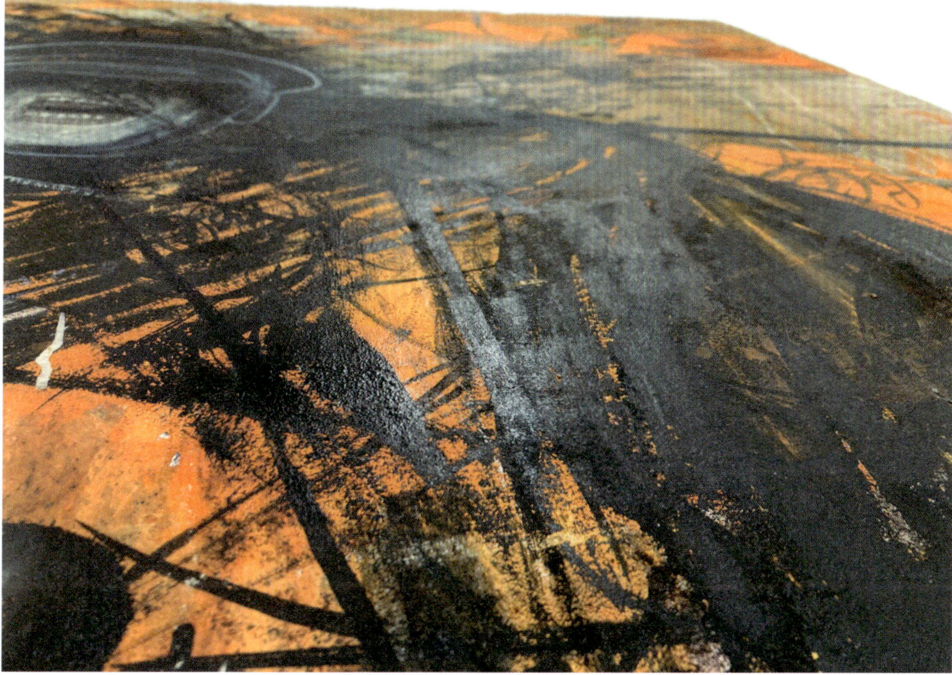

105.

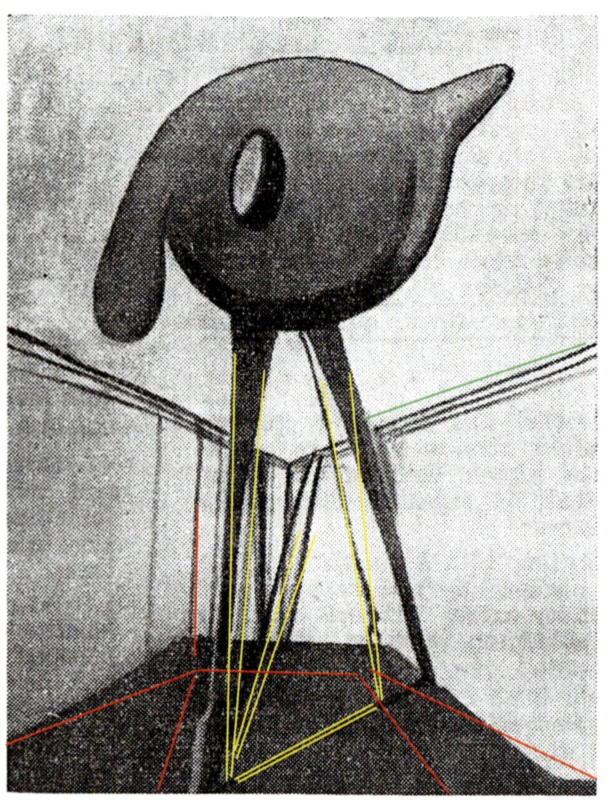

106. *Abstraction*, 1936

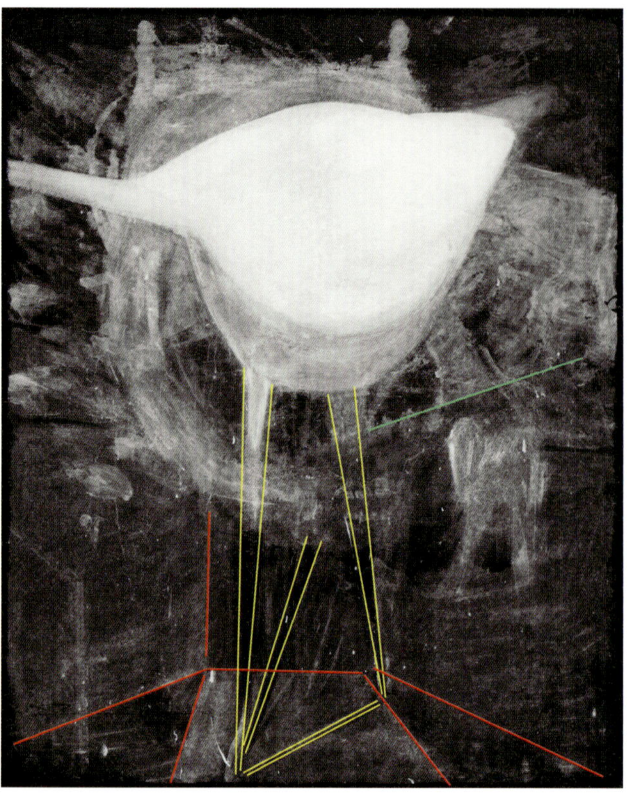

107. X-ray of *Man in a Cap*, c. 1945

The affinities between the biomorphic forms on their bipod
supports, as well as the delineation of the room spaces, led us
to hypothesise that *Man in a Cap* may have been painted over
Abstraction, despite the suggestion Bacon destroyed it. However,
the coloured lines superimposed on the images show that
while the two are very similar, they do not exactly correspond.
The comparison is further problematised in that there is no
contemporary record of either the dimensions of *Abstraction*, or
its support; Ronald Alley speculated it may have been hardboard.

The two finials above the biomorph present an intriguing
puzzle, for neither thrones nor finials featured in any of
Bacon's extant paintings until dimly in *Head VI*, 1949, and more
prominently in all three Popes of 1951. Bacon may have been
quoting from G.F. Watts's *Mammon* (1884–85; Tate Gallery),
possibly intrigued by the skull finials, or foreshadowing his
later borrowings from the throne in Velázquez's *Portrait of Pope
Innocent X*.

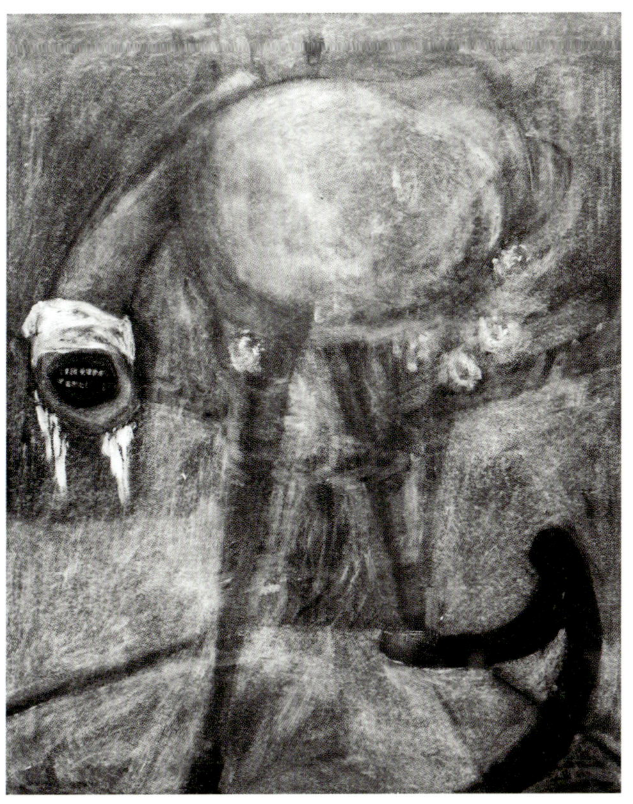

108. X-ray of *Three Studies for Figures at the Base of a Crucifixion*, 1944 (centre panel)

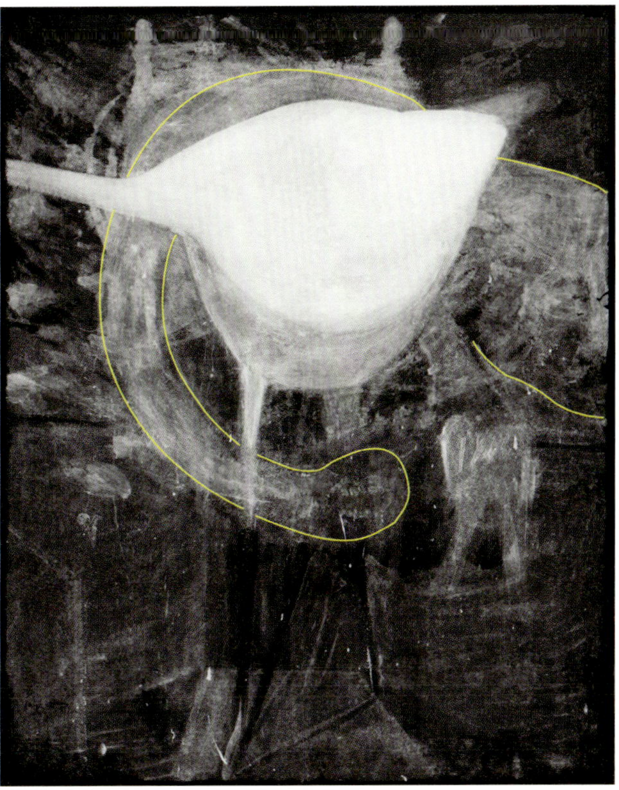

109. X-ray of *Man in a Cap*, c. 1945, with superimposed lines to indicate long-necked form

Rachel Billinge, senior conservator at the National Gallery, London, kindly helped unravel certain elements of Bacon's composition(s). She identified specifically the long-necked form that terminates in a grimacing mouth, the closest parallel to which is the figure in the centre panel of *Three Studies for Figures at the Base of a Crucifixion*, 1944. [102]

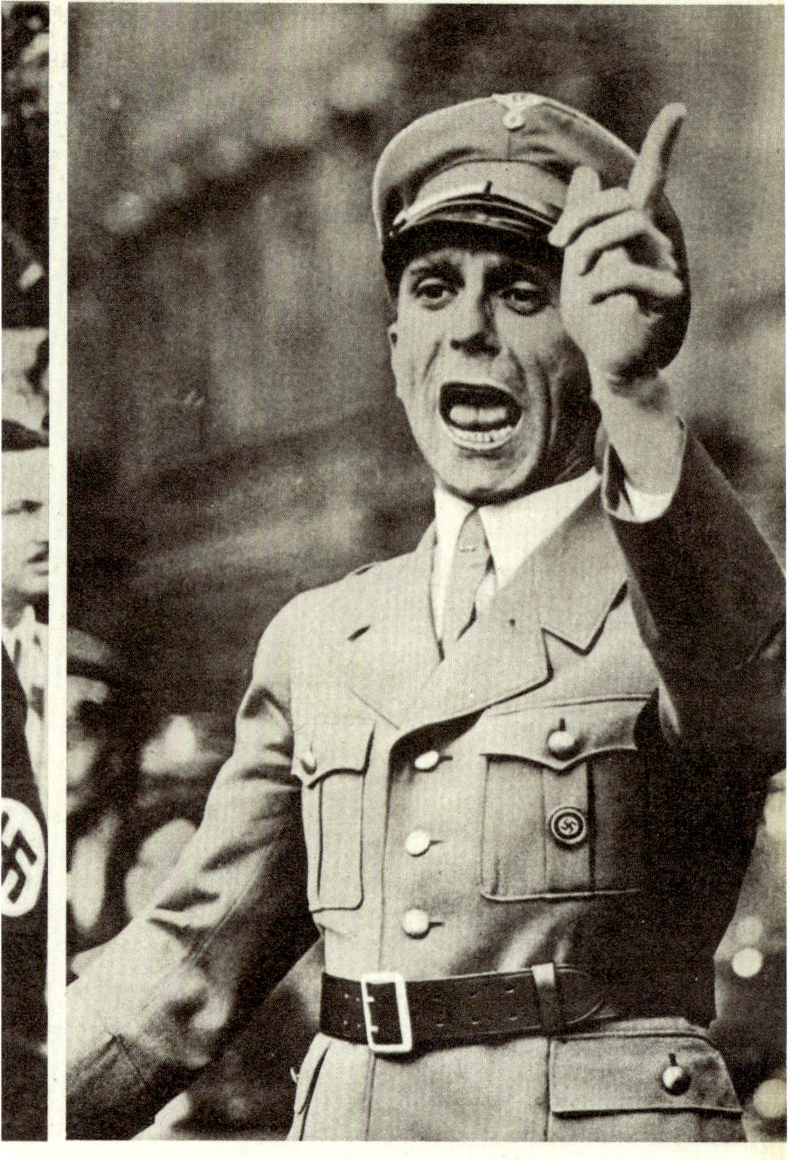

110. Joseph Goebbels, image from *Picture Post*, 13 July 1940

This was another image that was recorded by Sam Hunter in his photographs of Bacon's pictoral sources, taken in Bacon's studio in 1950.

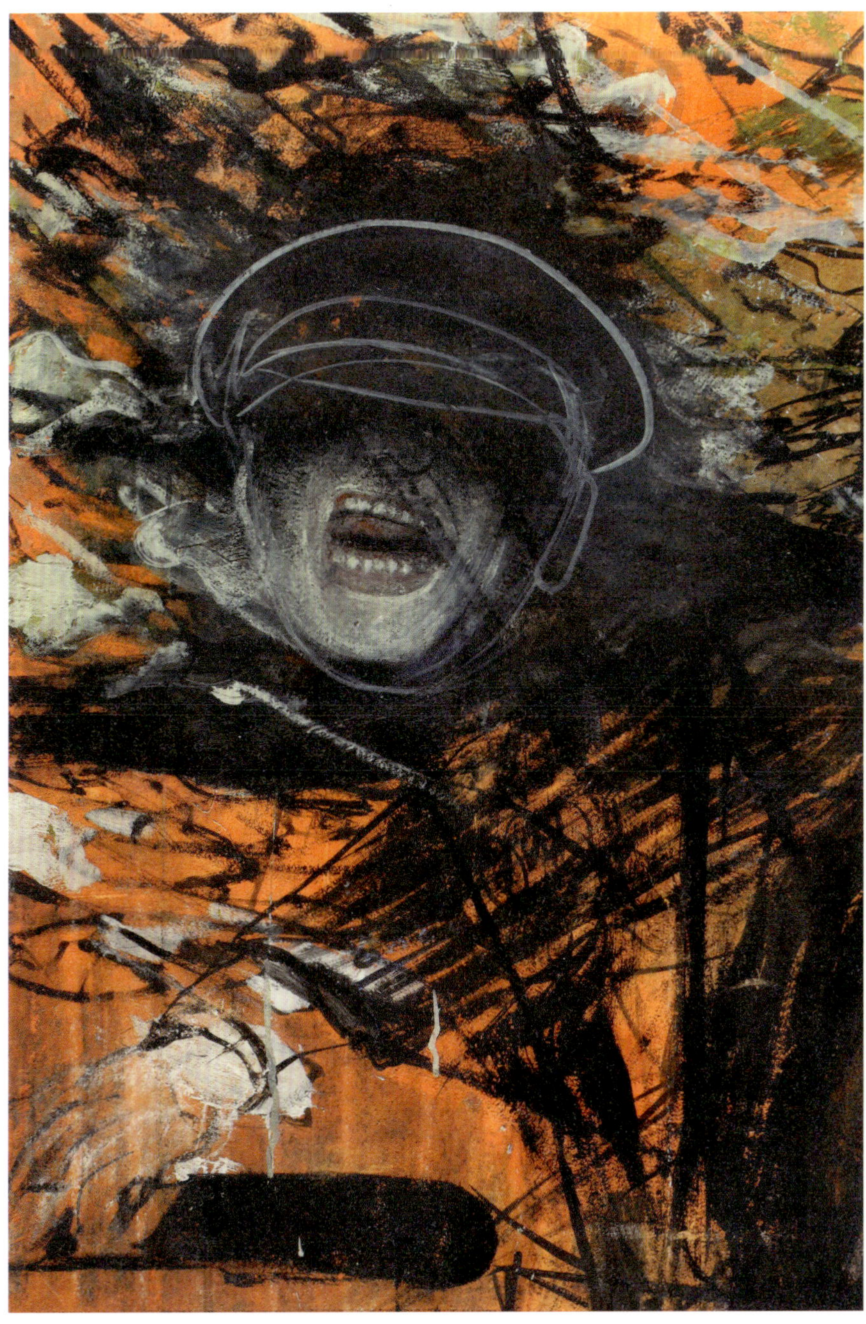

111. *Man in a Cap*, c 1945 (detail)

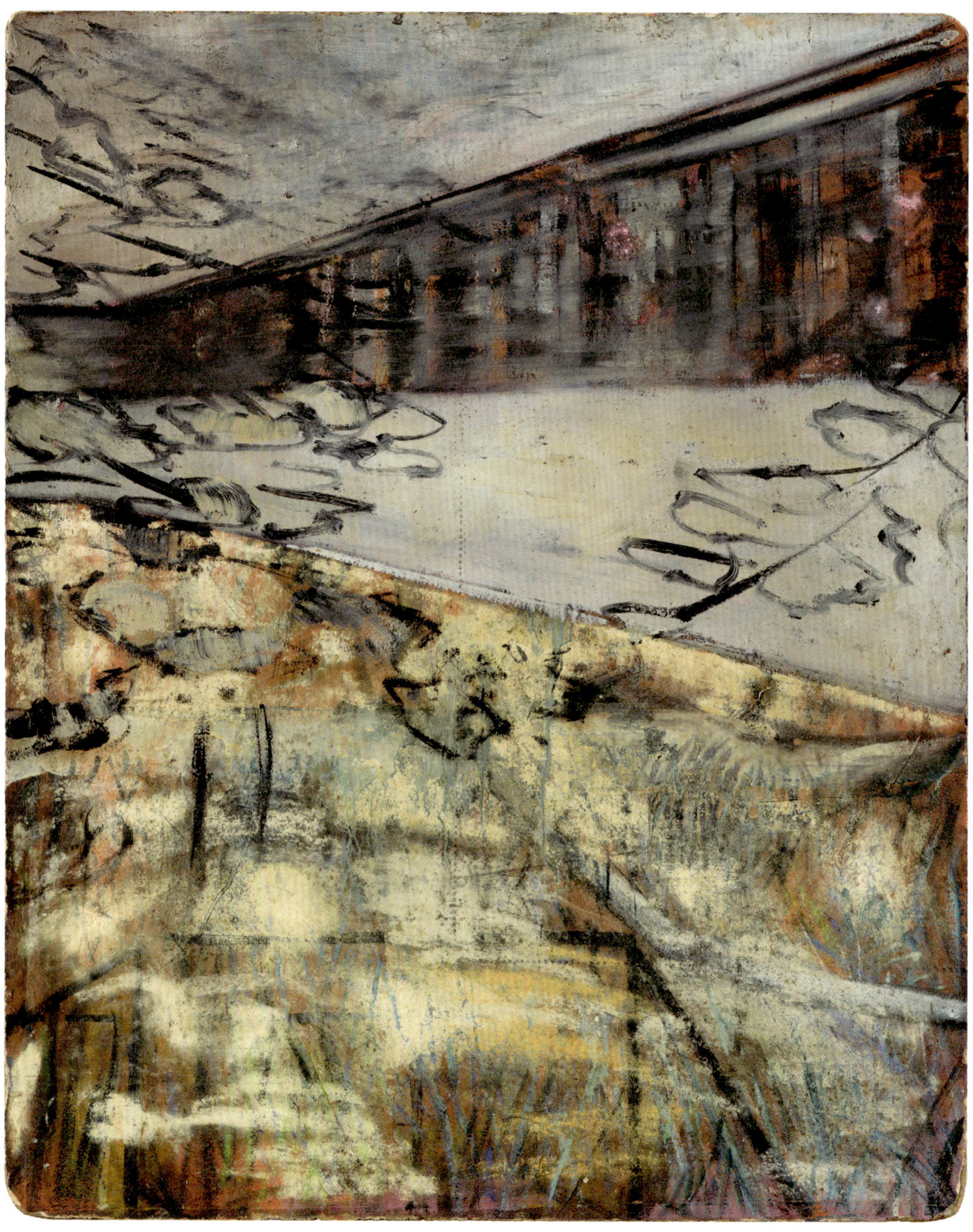

112. 'Landscape with Colonnade', c. 1945

113. 'Landscape with Colonnade', c. 1945, X-ray

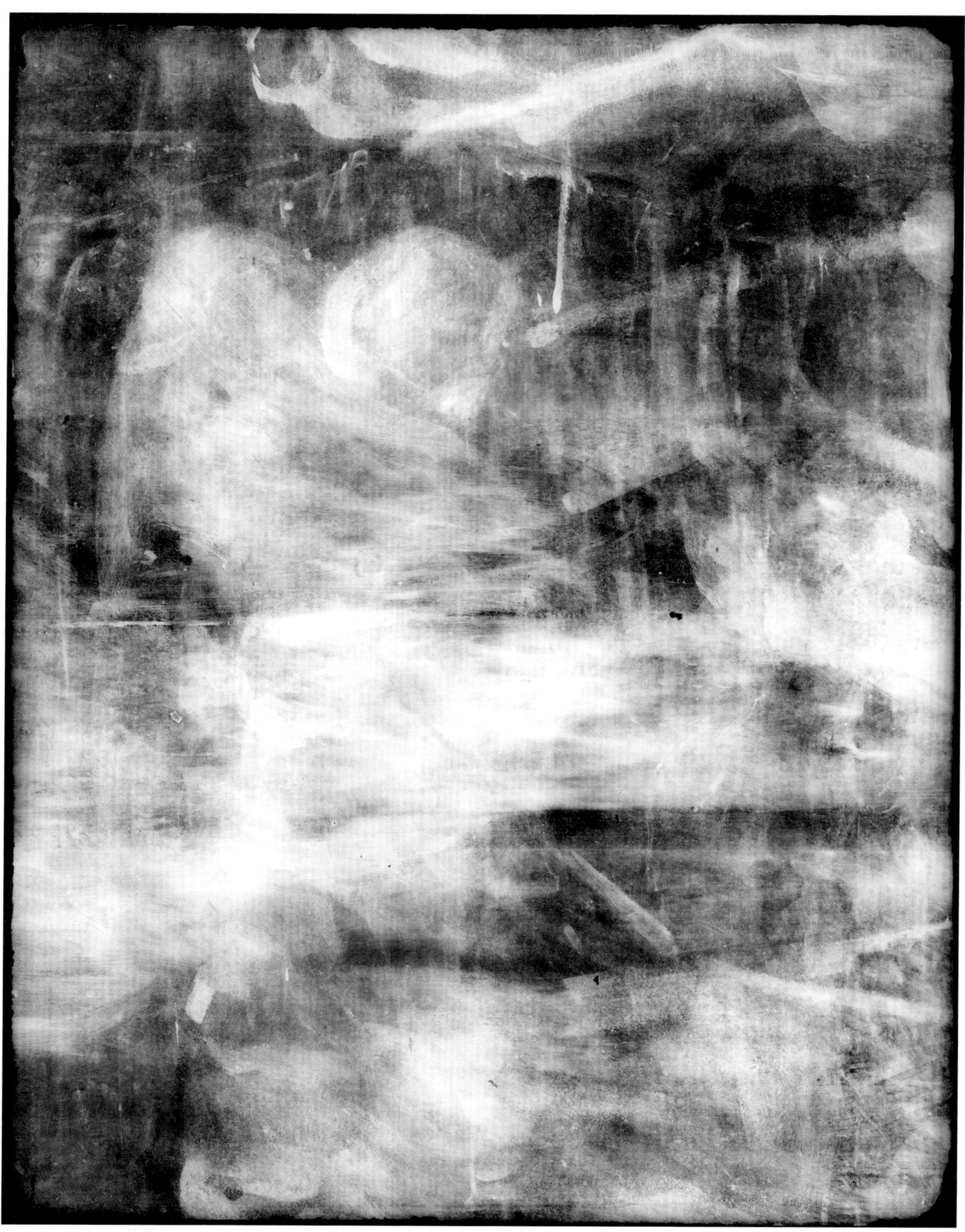

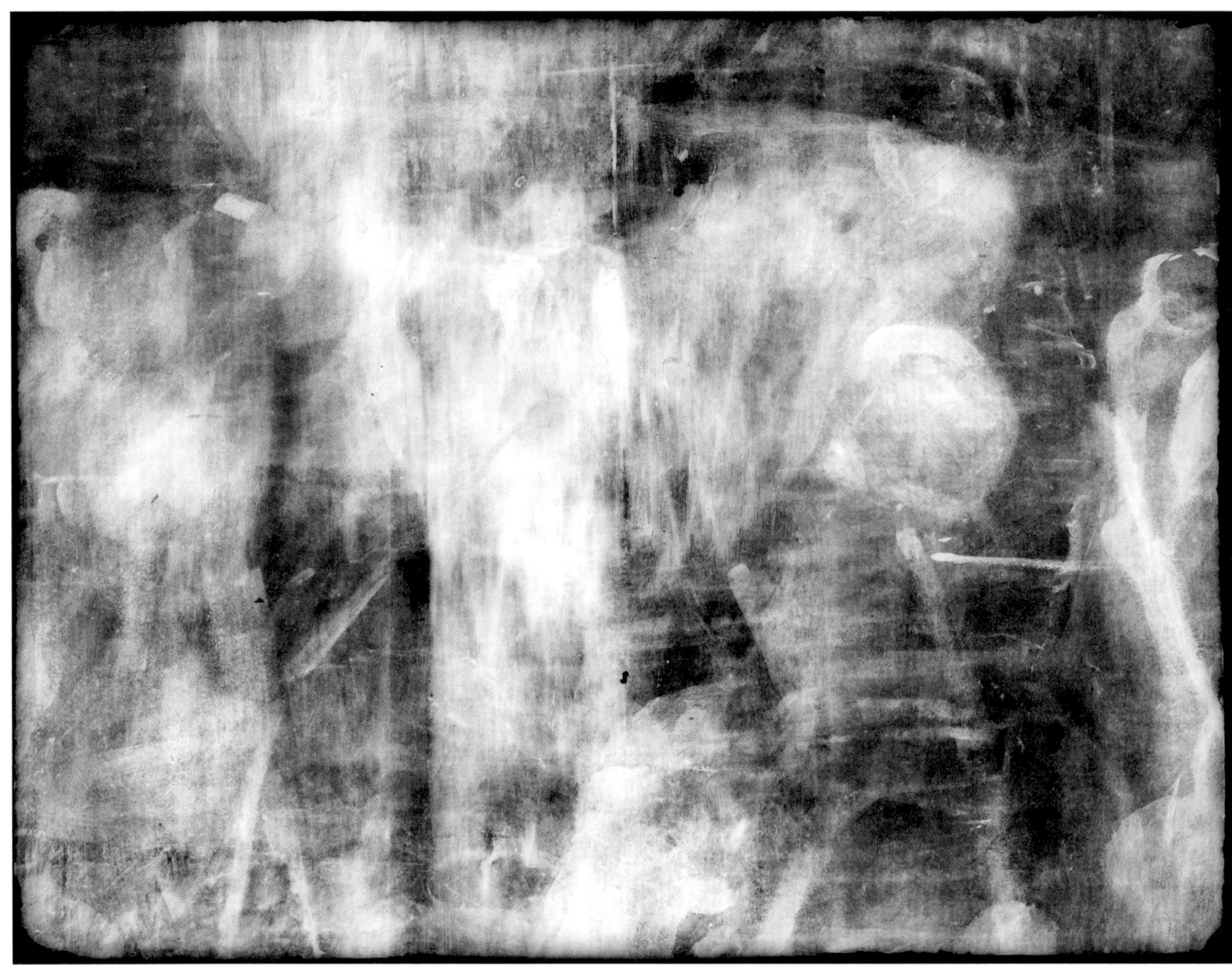

114. X-ray of 'Landscape with Colonnade', c. 1945; rotated 90° clockwise

This painting was X-rayed at the Courtauld Institute of Art, London, in October 2024, under the direction of Prof. Aviva Burnstock and Dr Nathan Daly. For various reasons it has proved more difficult to interpret than the X-ray of *Man in a Cap*; this was due partly to a full examination not being feasible because the fibreboard is glued to the backing board. It was noted in *Francis Bacon: Catalogue Raisonné* (2016) that it was painted on a layer of paper adhered to the fibreboard support, but Prof. Burnstock suggests that two, and possibly even three layers of paper are present. This alternative method of overpainting on fibreboard supports may indicate that Bacon had tired of the laborious painting out of pentimenti that had been necessitated in earlier wartime renditions.

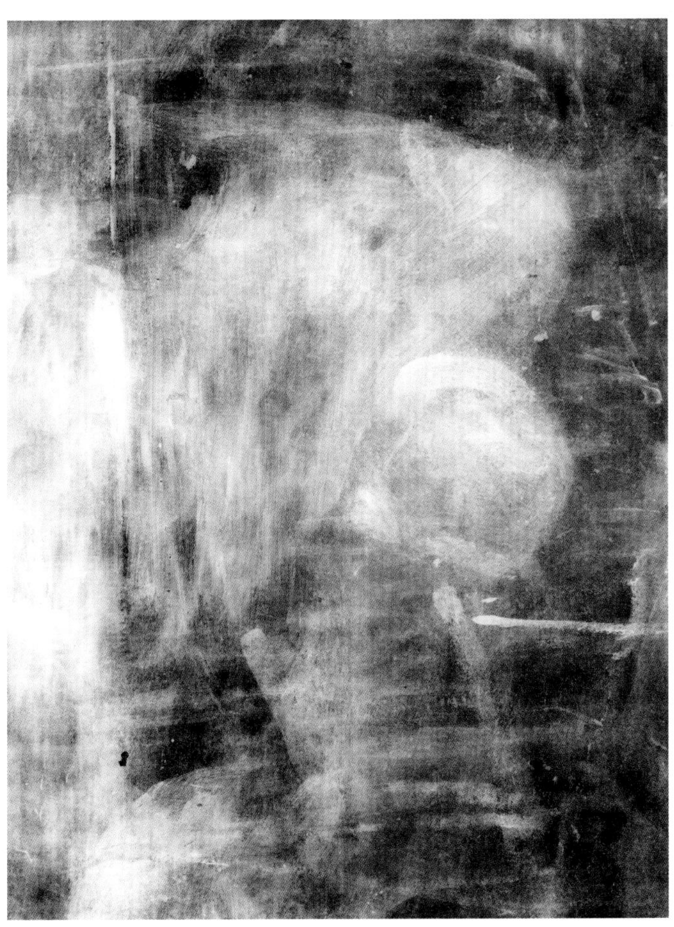

115. Detail of X-ray of 'Landscape with Colonnade', c. 1945

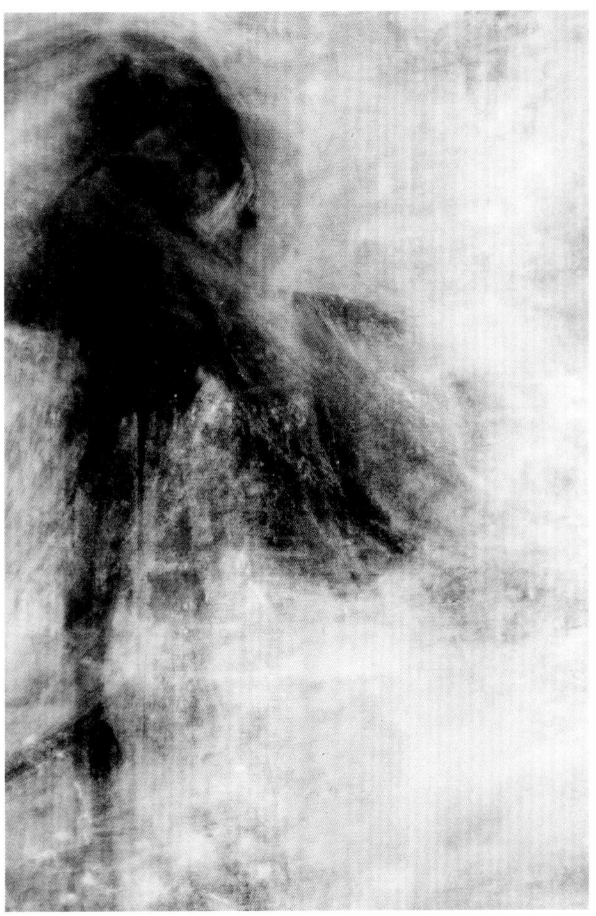

116. Detail of X-ray of *Three Studies for Figures at the Base of a Crucifixion*, 1944 (left panel)

These X-rays may reveal the heads of stooping forms, although in the case of 'Landscape with Colonnade' the identification can only be regarded as tentative.

Edward Onsloe: the man in *Study for Portrait*, 1969

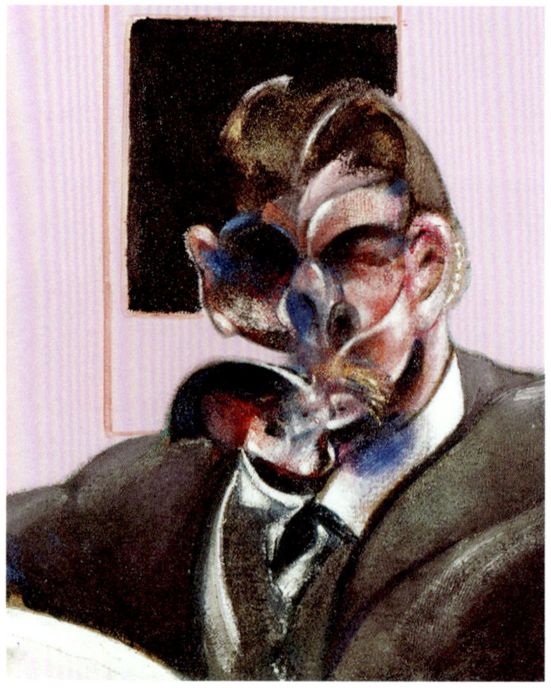

117. *Study for Portrait*, 1969 (detail)

Unusually for Bacon, he retained at least part of Ted's distinctive moustache.

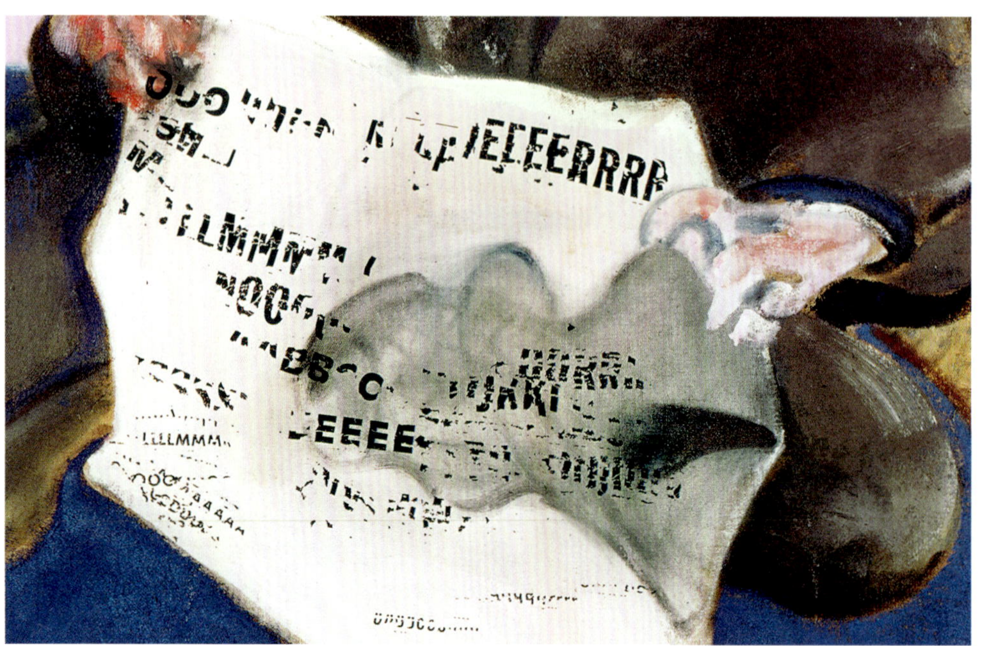

118. *Study for Portrait*, 1969 (detail)

This was the first painting on which Bacon applied dry-transfer lettering. The dark blue marks on Ted's hands relate to tattoos that he still has, including one running down a finger. The enigmatic 'head' at right angles on the newspaper was a device Bacon had introduced in the right panel of *Three Studies for a Crucifixion*, 1962.

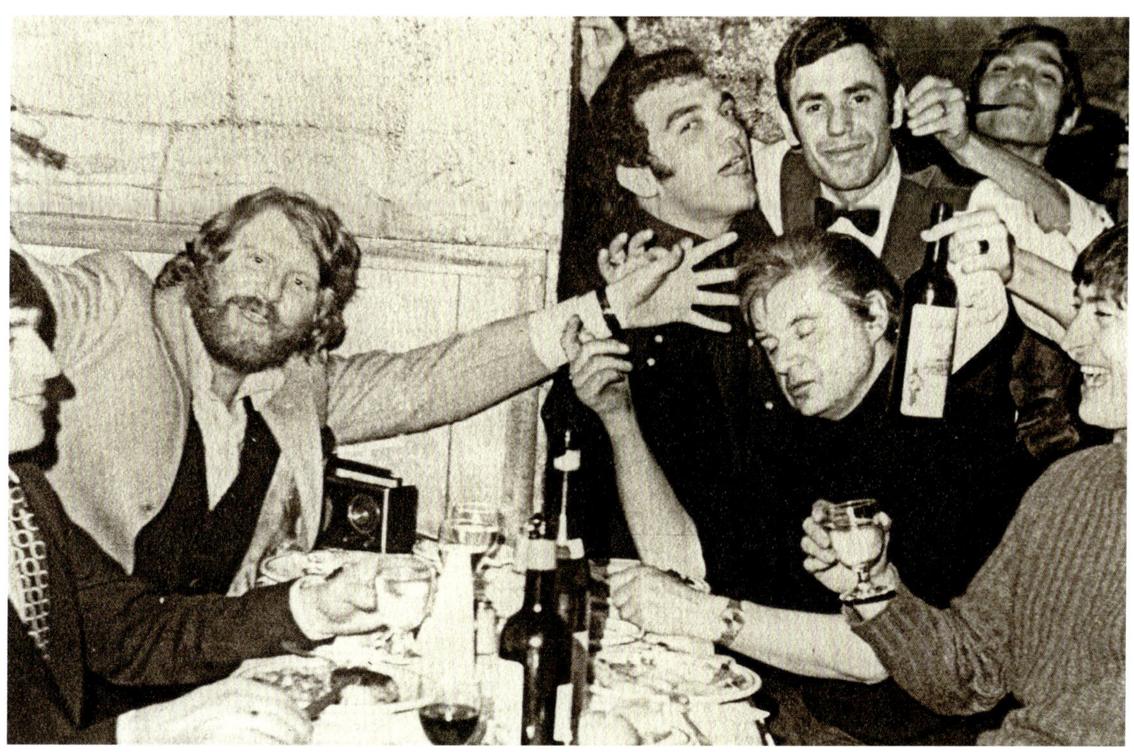

119. Ted Westfallen (left) and Bacon at a party, Bianchi Restaurant, Frith Street, Soho, 1969

In September 1969, Ted Westfallen (now Edward Onsloe), recently released from jail, was working at the Mazurka Club, a gambling den in Soho's Denman Street. Bacon visited the club with Denis Wirth Miller, when three men set on them as they were leaving; Ted ('I was handy with my fists') flew downstairs to defend the two artists and the miscreants soon fled. Bacon was impressed, and an hour-and-a-half later returned on his own and invited Ted to lunch the next day at Wheeler's. A friendship between Francis and Ted ensued, and the following month Bacon invited Ted to join him in Paris, where he was starting to plan his 1971 exhibition at the Grand Palais. They travelled on to Monte Carlo, and *Study for Portrait*, 1969, was painted shortly after Bacon returned to London in November 1969. One night, Ted and Francis arrived at 7 Reece Mews completely drunk. 'It was after midnight and Francis offered to sleep on the sofa'. But about 4 a.m. Ted was awoken by noises coming from the studio, 'and it was Francis, shouting repeatedly, "Oh you will, will you, have that, and take that"'. This account places Bacon's vaunted 'attack' on the canvas in a startling new dimension.

In explaining that literal portraits were made redundant by the invention of photography, Bacon told Ted: 'I paint the inside of the person'. When Ted's mother was suffering an interminable wait for the NHS to carry out a cataractomy, Bacon quietly arranged for his ophthalmologist, Patrick Trevor-Roper, to step in; he paid for everything, including a room full of flowers after the operation. Smitten, and attracted by his intelligence, Bacon offered Ted all of his paintings if he would live with him; Ted reminded him, 'I'm not that way', to which Bacon responded, 'I know'. Ted opted for a more regular family life, yet although the friendship could not continue in the same manner, he accompanied Bacon to the court case in June 1971 after George Dyer had planted marijuana in Bacon's studio.

(The Estate of Francis Bacon will film an interview with Mr Onsloe in 2025.)

Picture Credits

**Unless otherwise stated, all images
are © The Estate of Francis Bacon.**

9. Monkey regarding a mirror; detail of leaf in *The Isabella
Breviary*, 1480s/90s, British Library Collection, Add. 18851, f. 270

17. Wyndham Lewis, *Apes of God*, 1930, dust jacket
Courtesy Shapero Rare Books, London. Photo, Shapero Rare
Books Ltd

27. Martin Bloch, *Dream of the Dragon*, 1941,
oil on canvas, 45.7× 50.8 cm © The Martin Bloch Trust;
photograph Peter Nemmin

34. William Blake, from Illustrations to *Dante's Divine Comedy;
The Wood of the Self-Murderers: The Harpies and the Suicides*,
1824–27 Graphite, ink and watercolour on paper, 37.2 × 52.7 cm
London, Tate. N03356. Photo, Tate

40. Salvator Rosa, *The Torture of Prometheus*, 1646–48, oil on
canvas, 224 × 179 cm, Gallerie Nazionali di Arte Antica, Palazzo
Barberini, Galleria Corsini

74. Claude Monet, *La Barque*, 1877, oil on canvas, 146 × 133 cm,
Paris, musée Marmottan Monet, Inv. 5082. © musée Marmottan
Monet

76. Claude Monet, *Les Dindons*, 1877, oil on canvas, 174 × 172 cm
Paris, Orsay Museum, Inv. RF1944–18
© GrandPalaisRmn (musée d'Orsay) / Hervé Lewandowski

82. Rembrandt Harmenszoon van Rijn, *Portrait of Margaretha de
Geer, Wife of Jacob Trip*, 1661, Oil on canvas, 75.3 × 63.8 cm
Inv. NG5282: London, The National Gallery

83. Rembrandt Harmenszoon van Rijn,
Portrait of Margaretha de Geer, Wife of Jacob Trip, c. 1661
Oil on canvas, 130.5 × 97.5 cm
Inv. NG1675: London, The National Gallery

85. Georges Seurat, *Bathers at Asnières*, 1884
Oil on canvas, 201 × 300 cm
Inv. NG3908: London, The National Gallery

86. Paul Cézanne, *Bathers (Les Grandes Baigneuses)*, c. 1894–1905,
Oil on canvas, 127.2 × 196.1 cm
Inv. NG6359: London, The National Gallery

93. Flying Green Scarab Beetle, Image ID: CXHN5C
Photo, Zoonar GmbH / Alamy Stock Photo

Special thanks to:

Flaminia Allvin
Rachel Billinge
Jennifer Blatchford
Aviva Burnstock
Sir Brian Clarke
Nathan Daly
Charlotte Grant
Birkin Haward
Brian McLaughlin
Carolina Olcese
Martha Parsey
Ellis Woodman

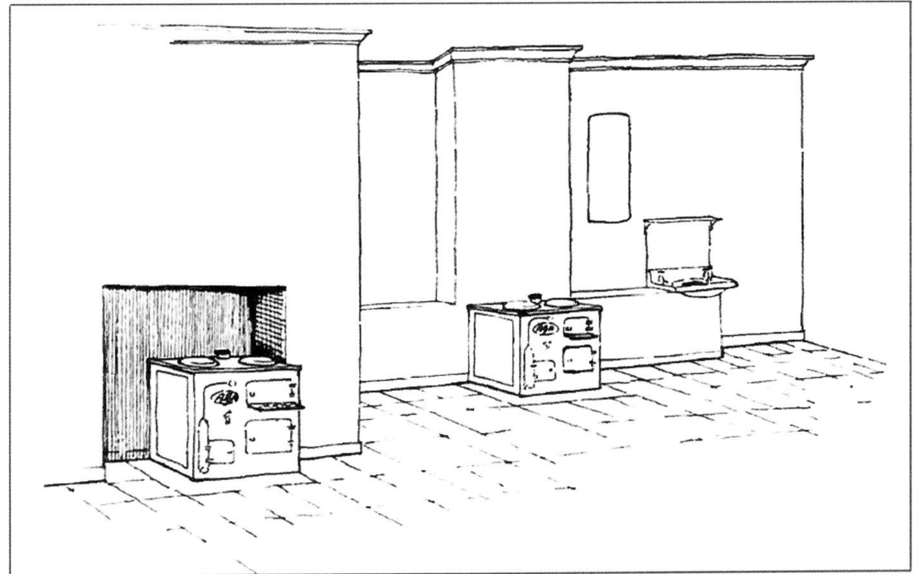

Bell's Heat Appliances, Ltd. (Row T, No. 304.) Designed by Francis Bacon. The stand is dependent for its effect on its simple treatment with plain surfaces, and has a striking colour scheme of a carefully chosen blue and rich buff which sets off the firm's Aga cookers of beige and chromium.

120. This intriguing item was brought to our attention by an architect friend, Birkin Haward, who relayed a discovery made by Ellis Woodman. The small illustration was part of a feature on the product stands at the 1932 Building Exhibition, held at Olympia, London. It is unlikely that Bacon drew the sketch, but it is possible he was more than merely 'colour consultant'. It is interesting to see Bacon, his painting career barely under way, still reliant on interior design commissions.

First published in the United Kingdom in 2025 by
EFB Publishing and Thames & Hudson Ltd,
6–24 Britannia Street, London WC1X 9JD

First published in the United States of America in 2025 by
EFB Publishing and Thames & Hudson Inc., 500 Fifth Avenue,
New York, New York 10110

British Library Cataloguing-in-Publication Data
A catalogue record for this book is available from the
British Library

Library of Congress Control Number: 2025933127

ISBN: 978-0-500-96627-3

Printed by Geof Neal, London
Bound in the UK by Diamond Print Services

Design and production: Brett Harrison
Picture researcher: Sophie Pretorius
Copy editor: Liane Jones
Proofreaders: Ben Harrison and Liane Jones
Print consultant: Danny Kirk

Francis Bacon Studies Series:

I:

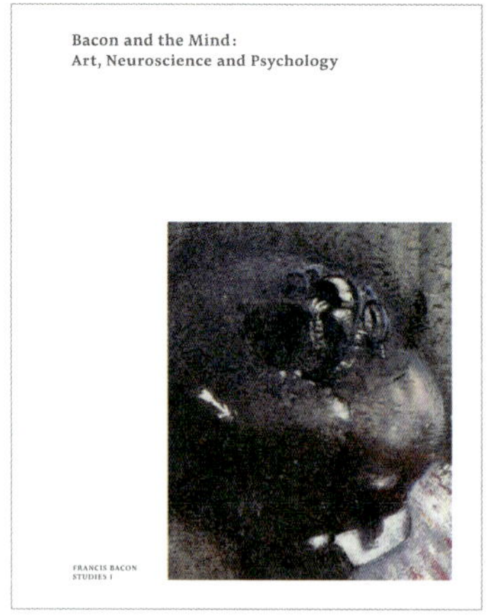

**Bacon and the Mind:
Art, Neuroscience and Psychology**

(Published 9 May 2019)

II:

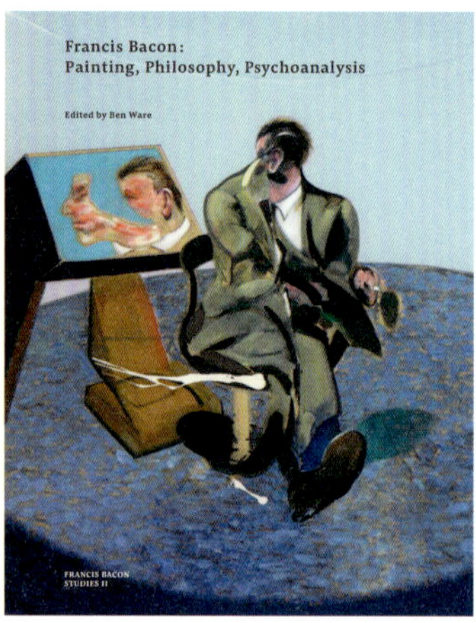

**Francis Bacon:
Painting, Philosophy, Psychoanalysis**

(Published 17 October 2019)

III:

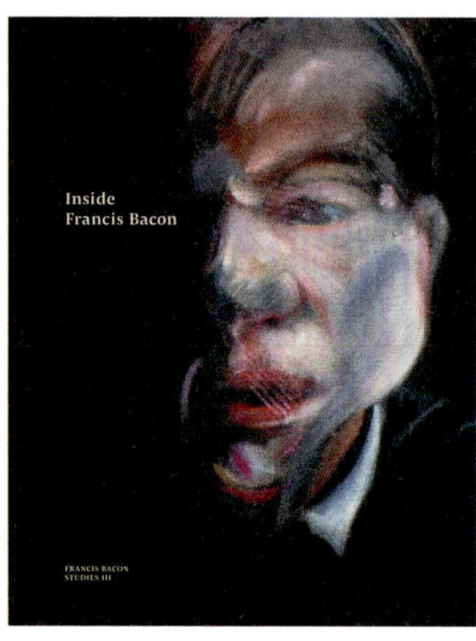

Inside Francis Bacon

(Published 6 August 2020)

IV:
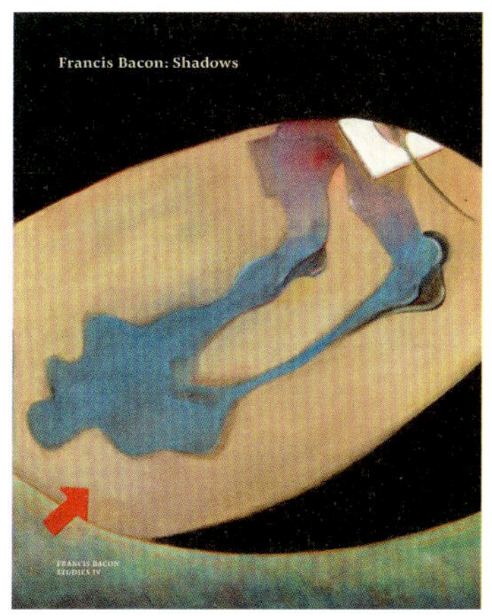

Francis Bacon: Shadows

(Published 24 June 2021)

Also published:

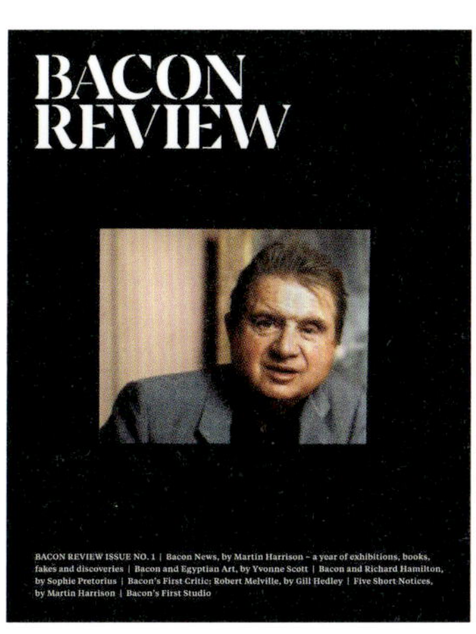

Bacon Review

(Published 6 June 2023)

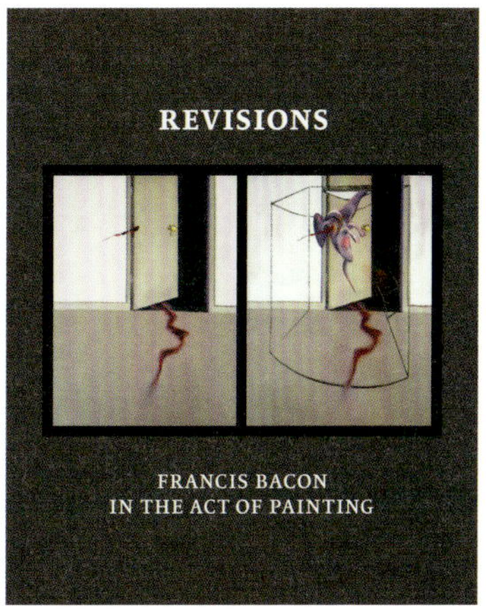

Revisions:
Francis Bacon in the Act of Painting

(Published 24 November 2024)